SLICED

BILL REYNOLDS
Editor in Chief, *FLEX*

and NEGRITA JAYDE
Canadian Overall National Champion

CONTEMPORARY
BOOKS

CHICAGO

Library of Congress Cataloging-in-Publication Data

Reynolds, Bill.
    Sliced : state-of-the-art nutrition for building lean body mass /
Bill Reynolds and Negrita Jayde.
       p.   cm.
    Includes index.
    ISBN 0-8092-4116-1
    1. Bodybuilders—Nutrition.   I. Jayde, Negrita.   II. Title.
TX361.B64R48   1991
613.2′0247964—dc20   90-49391
                                       CIP

Photo credits:
All uncredited photos by Mike Neveux
Published by Contemporary Books, Inc.
180 North Michigan Avenue, Chicago, Illinois 60601
Manufactured in the United States of America
International Standard Book Number: 0-8092-4116-1

To Jaan, whose love and support made everything possible.

N.J

To my coauthor. Long may she pump iron!

B.R.

CONTENTS

The first family of international bodybuilding: Seven-time Mr. Olympia Lee Haney with his wife, Shirley, and son, Josh, on the occasion of his sixth Olympia win in 1989.

FOREWORD

Five years ago, Bill Reynolds asked me to write a foreword to his book, *Supercut*, which included a variety of recipes backed up by state-of-the-art nutritional information. I was happy to do so, and my wife, Shirley, ended up using some of the recipes in the book to feed me before my last few Mr. Olympia victories.

Now Bill has asked me to write the foreword, this time to *Sliced*, a sequel to the original book. But after reading a draft of the contents of *Sliced*, I discovered that it is much more than a mere sequel to *Supercut*. It is, in fact, superior to the first book in every way. The nutritional information, written jointly by Bill Reynolds (Editor-in-Chief of *Flex* magazine) and Negrita Jayde (a former Canadian Over-all National Champion who is currently competing successfully in the pro ranks), is well chosen and tremendously detailed and authoritative. And the recipes in *Sliced* have been taken from Negrita's voluminous files and have all been used by her in her own dietary preparations for competition.

The section on nutritional information is mind-boggling. It starts off with a chapter on the psychology of peak condition that is guaranteed to get you on the right diet and keep you on it until you end up, well, sliced. Chapter 2 is unique in that it presents precise guidelines for a range of seven degrees of muscularity, from basic off-season shape up to Shredded. And Chapter 3 reprises the off-season dietary and training guidelines Bill included in his first book.

Chapter 4 presents another vitally important topic that has heretofore never been covered in a nutrition book: the role of nutrition in hyping up the immune system and improving between-workouts recovery. Chapter 5 is another gem, an extensive discussion of the various nutritional ergogens currently available for bodybuilders who wish to train naturally. With Mr. Olympia being drug tested for the first time in 1990, that includes me, Lee Haney, so I read this chapter with interest and zeal.

Chapters 6 through 8 discuss metabolic optimizer drinks, carbohydrates and their role in bodybuilding nutrition, and amino acids. Chapter 9 gives plenty of practical tips for improving a bodybuilder's basal metabolic rate, so he or she can burn off excess body fat more quickly. Chapter 10 outlines various food supplements that will improve your look, and Chapter 11 tells you how to use nutritional techniques to optimize your energy levels during workouts.

I'm sure Shirley can't wait to get at the recipe chapters, which include recipes for chicken, fish, beef, rice, yams, bananas, and supplements. None of these recipes are repeated from *Supercut*, so you're getting all new material.

The book concludes with a variety of meal plans and instructions for using them to get ripped up for your next competition. The second of those two chapters is one of the book's real gems: Negrita Jayde's personal program for peak muscularity. Since she gets as cut as any woman who's ever stepped onstage to compete for a bodybuilding title, you *know* this chapter will be interesting.

Sliced has a couple of great authors, and they have done an exhaustive job of researching and writing. As a result, *Sliced* has my highest recommendation!

Lee Haney
Seven times IFBB Mr. Olympia (1984–1990)

Only an accumulation of thousands of total sets of exercise for each body part and a nearly flawless diet will build the type of physique that wins seven Mr. Olympia titles. Here Lee Haney does one-armed dumbbell triceps extensions.

FOREWORD

No athletes have taken the study and practical application of nutrition to the heights that we bodybuilders have. All champions in our sport realize that training and nutrition are approximately a 50-50 proposition during an off-season mass-building cycle, and that nutrition rises to as much as 90 percent of the formula for success during the last few weeks before competing. Over the final two or three days before a show, training means nothing, and nutrition is virtually 100 percent of the battle. It's little wonder that bodybuilders—from beginners through seasoned professionals—constantly study nutrition books and magazine articles.

With drug testing universally applied in competitive bodybuilding, nutrition has become even more vitally important than it was during the era of anabolic drug usage. As a lifetime natural competitive bodybuilder who has never taken a drug stronger than aspirin, I've probably been more consistently and completely interested in studying nutrition during my eight years of competition than any woman athlete with similar competitive credentials.

When Bill Reynolds told me a few months ago that he was working on a sequel to his successful book *Supercut*, I was very interested in obtaining a copy as soon as it became available. Bill has vast credentials in our sport as both a competitor and journalist. For nine years, he was Editor-in-Chief of *Muscle & Fitness* magazine, and for the past four Editor-in-Chief of the hard-core bodybuilding bible, *Flex*. He's trained and communed with all the champions over the years,

Germany's vivacious and highly muscular Anja Langer possesses many of the qualities of a winning woman bodybuilder—a good degree of muscle mass, aesthetic symmetry, well-balanced physical proportions, sharp muscularity, and a fantastic posing routine.

which has resulted in over 40 published books and over 2,000 magazine articles.

Bill's coauthor is Negrita Jayde, a former overall Canadian Champion as an amateur, and currently a very hot IFBB pro bodybuilder. She has written a host of insightful articles for *Flex*, and was chosen as coauthor both for her writing and for her culinary abilities. (Negrita prepared all of the recipes included in *Sliced*, most of which have found their way into her precontest dietary regimen over the years.)

After reading the manuscript of *Sliced*, I was tremendously enthusiastic. In addition to more than 130 practical recipes, many meal plans, and Negrita's personal precontest training-dietary program, chapters have been included on the psychology of peak condition; degrees of muscular definition; off-season diet and training; nutrition, the immune system, and recovery; ergogenics; metabolic optimizers; carbohydrates; free-form amino acids; hyping the metabolic rate; cosmetic appearance; and how to peak out workout energy.

As a natural competitor, I read the gigantic chapter on ergogenic aids with zeal. I learned a lot from it in terms of achieving an anabolic effect through nutritional means rather than drug use. This chapter itself is worth more than the price of the book.

I'm sure you'll enjoy and profit from reading *Sliced*. I almost wish I had the only copy available, because it would give me a definite edge on my competitors at the next Ms. Olympia competition!

Anja Langer
IFBB European Champion
Junior World Champion
2nd/Ms. Olympia (1988)

PART I
THE POWER OF PROPER NUTRITION AND TRAINING

The psychology of peak condition: confidence and mental focus.

1

PSYCHOLOGY OF PEAK CONDITION

We like your attitude. The fact that you are reading this book sets you apart from millions of other people, both physically and mentally. By choosing bodybuilding as your lifestyle, you've made a deliberate choice to improve yourself. That makes you a doer and not a watcher.

If you are truly ready to begin dieting, we must tell you something very important: You are going to war! A psychological war. It will be against your toughest opponent—yourself.

It is a war that has littered the field of physical culture with many casualties. You could receive serious injuries to your self-esteem. Or you might have your self-discipline shot apart. You may even have your enthusiasm killed.

Once you start to diet, you'll encounter all kinds of traps, traitors, and temptations along the way. Only a handful of dieters will remain unscathed. Those who make it through will be heavily rewarded. They will be called heroes.

In truth, it's simple to become sliced. Armed with the advice in upcoming chapters, you can take your physique to the exact condition you want, and we do mean *exact*. However, we didn't say it was easy. As a matter of fact, it's very tough. Many bodybuilders lose the battle. And the toughest part of the battle—the one that determines whether you win or lose—occurs right in your mind.

At a recent national competition, three bodybuilders from various weight classes dropped out before the show. One of them did so because he feared a certain competitor would be there. Another one bailed out because he was burned out from training. (He had only two weeks left to go.) The third bodybuilder had blown her diet, largely because of personal problems.

After an entire year of strict dieting, gut-wrenching workouts, and huge personal sacrifices—not to mention financial output for supplements—they defeated themselves before they even got to the contest site. These are psychological casualties.

Of those who did grace the stage, many showed up way off their mark. No doubt head games were responsible for this as well. And while the faces and places may change, and so may the level of competition, the story remains the same.

All of these bodybuilders could have avoided their disappointments. That's the main purpose of this chapter. We don't want to lose a single bodybuilder in the battle for physical excellence. You should reach your intended physical condition every time out of the chute.

And you will! We take you on a trip down the hallways of your mind and show you where the enemy hides out. The covert operations of the enemy will be fully exposed for you to see. Once you know their plan of attack, you can maneuver your mind accordingly to smash their offensive. This way, you'll always know which direction you're going.

A well-known psychologist once said it best: "If you don't know where you want to go, you will probably end up somewhere else." Carefully consider and apply what this chapter offers, and success will be yours.

THE POWER OF PASSION

During a seminar Arnold Schwarzenegger was giving, a skinny teenage boy stood up and asked, "Arnold, I want to become a professional bodybuilder. What must I know to make it happen?"

Arnold looked at the boy with a knowing glance and said, "Unless you go to bed with a burning desire to turn pro, and wake up with a burning desire to turn pro, you might as well forget it, because that determines everything!"

The boy replied. "What if I don't feel that way?"

Arnold responded, "Well, you look kind of tall. Maybe you should play basketball!"

As complex as human behavior may seem, when you are dealing with the *desire* to get cut, you are actually dealing with an emotion. Somewhere in your past, something happened to you to give you a powerful urge to change your body. Whatever did happen, the logical part of your brain joins in and starts supplying you with reasons why you should continue that urge. The more moving the experience was, or the higher the degree of arousal at the time it occurred, the

"You don't know what mental commitment is until you have a bar-bending weight across your shoulders and six more reps to do in your set," says Mike Quinn, U.S. Champion and successful IFBB pro bodybuilder.

stronger the emotion and also the rationalization behind that drive. When the emotion becomes intense, it turns into a passion.

Once passion is put into action, you become unstoppable. It makes you relentless. When this emotion takes over, a huge reservoir of mental and physical energy comes pouring into your life. Suddenly your body needs less sleep. Any barrier that lies in your path seems to be a minor inconvenience. Passion is the driving force behind the shakers and the movers in this world.

Donald Trump became a multimillionaire because of passion. Arnold's numerous bodybuilding and acting successes are due to passion. Frank Sinatra still sings even though he's over 70, and George Burns did films in his eighties. You see, it doesn't matter what area of life you're in, if you love what you're doing, you keep forging ahead. Clearly, it is passion that fuels the famous.

You need this emotion. Passion makes you train harder, prevents you from cheating, and gives you energy when scientific knowledge says you shouldn't have any. Of course, you can get into shape without this powerful emotion, but it will become very difficult and wearisome. With passion, you turn into a fighter! Your efforts carry much more oomph behind them. Remember, superior rewards go to superior efforts.

Don't worry if you currently lack passion. You may have entered bodybuilding ever so quietly and casually, and never had a significant emotional experience to spark your interest. That's fine. The following list of points is designed to increase the enthusiasm behind your drive:

- *Never consider failure.* Once you make a decision, put everything you have into it. Do not think for a moment that you'll fall short of your desires. Otherwise, fear will creep in and weaken your passion severely. Fear is the greatest enemy of human potential. On the other hand, a bodybuilder filled with passion is a fearless competitor. That person believes in all of his or her actions and consequently progresses much faster than bodybuilders of little faith. Have courage in every effort you make. Fix your thoughts on success.
- *Seize every moment.* At every given moment, try to do the most productive thing possible to improve your bodybuilding. When you analyze the dieting methods of successful and unsuccessful bodybuilders, you find they basically use the same procedures to get sliced. The difference in their physiques comes from the fact that the winners do *more* every moment while they are dieting. They weigh all foods, keep accurate calorie counts, check their bodies more often under various lighting conditions, and so forth. These things have a way of adding up to make a critical difference. Make every moment count, and you'll be amazed at your progress. Your passion will grow as a result.

"Mental concentration is of paramount importance during a workout," reveals Mr. America Gary Leonard. "Training a muscle group one arm at a time automatically strengthens mental focus, because it needn't be split between both limbs."

- *Forget the past.* Live in the here and now. It does not matter whether your upbringing was ideal or unpleasant. You are the master of your destiny, and the present is all you have to act on. Few things are more depressing than listening to a bodybuilder tell you how he "used to look" or what might have really happened to his physique had he known "back then" what he knows now. Give us a break. Every bodybuilder who whines about the past is also full of apathy. His passion left him when gas was 32 cents a gallon. There will never be a better time than now, so give it everything you have—today.
- *Speak the language of winners.* Never start off any of your sentences with these phrases: "I can't," "We'll see," "I'll try," "If only I had . . . ," "I'd better not," "It probably won't," or "I never will." We could list many more of these confidence-destroying

comments, but these make the point. Simply put, when our self-instructions are negative, our actions will also be negative. We can only do what our programs tell us to do. Therefore, speak like a winner. Say things like "I always," "I will," "We can," "You will," "Of course," and "Yes." You'd be amazed at how often winners answer a question with a resounding yes, while losers give all kinds of vague and wishy-washy affirmatives. When your speech is passionate, your emotions are highly charged with energy and positivity. Speak in the absolute.

- *Avoid negative people.* Their constant barrage of gloom and doom carries a message into your subconscious. Of course, it doesn't happen overnight; the process is slow and insidious. But don't underestimate its effect on your emotions. We've seen normally "up" bodybuilders change into complacent toads once they hooked up with a negative training partner. And don't think of trying to convert such a person to your line of thought. You see, negative people don't know they're negative. They think they're being realistic and everyone else is screwed up.

- *Believe in yourself.* Set no limits whatsoever on your bodybuilding potential. Forget the notion that you can only bench or squat with so much weight. Without even meeting you, we know that you haven't even begun to tap your potential. That's not hype, it's the truth!

  Fill your mind with the belief that your physique is far more amazing than you now believe it to be. Remember, when it comes to bodybuilding, your major barriers are your own self-limitations.

  If you totally expect to bring up a lagging body part, everything aligns itself consciously and subconsciously to make that desire come true. When Arnold Schwarzenegger came to America in the late sixties, he fully expected to dominate the bodybuilding world, and he went on to do just that. The more you believe in yourself, the more passion you attach to all of your actions.

- *Develop a sense of urgency.* When people are full of passion, they can't wait to get things done. You can spot such people easily. They have a purpose in their walk, a certain look in their eyes, and you notice them as soon as they enter a room. You can get this kind of essence yourself.

  First, start going to bed earlier and getting up earlier. This is a trademark of successful people. It gives you more time in the morning to organize your day, and this helps to psyche up your mind. After all, we warm up our muscles before we work them, so why not set aside time to warm up that mind?

  Once the head is fully psyched up, it's ready for action. And just as inertia causes an object in motion to remain in motion, the psychological "inertia" from your early start will keep you moving. Your workouts will run exactly on time, meals will be planned perfectly, and you'll eliminate any feelings of confusion.

THE GREATNESS OF GOALS

Before you spend the next several months dieting, you should spend a few minutes defining what you want. In most cases that we have encountered, you'd be surprised how many bodybuilders have vaguely defined goals. Sure, they'd like to get more cut, or get bigger, but that's not concrete enough. These desires are far too general. You need to get specific. The mind loves to focus on all kinds of little details. Just *how* sliced do you want to become? *How* much bigger do you need to be?

Start out by breaking down your ultimate goal and setting yourself some short-term, easily obtainable goals. You could decide to lose four pounds in two weeks, or one inch off your waistline in 20 days. The more precise you are, the better. Taken over a period of time, these little goals have a big way of adding up to dramatic results. Goals give your workouts a sense of meaning and purpose. That mental keenness in wanting to reach your goal lightens the actual physical load of weight you're lifting. Remember this simple equation:

$$U \text{ (Understanding)} + E \text{ (Effort)} = R \text{ (Results)}$$

The more you know what you want, and the more effort you put into it, the more clearly defined the result. Once, a week away from a big show, a bodybuilder asked me (Negrita) to take a look at him. Seeing he was way off, I asked him, "Did you want to look like this a week away from your show?" He replied in a disappointed tone, "I didn't know what I wanted, but I didn't want to look like *this!*"

Talk about a waste of effort! Even though he had dieted for weeks and trained hard, a poorly defined goal gave him a poor physical result.

This is a very powerful concept, and it must not be taken lightly. Goals are extremely important for success. They direct all of that passion.

To help you in your bodybuilding progress, here are a few points you should know about goals:

Burn Goals into Your Subconscious

Your goals must be burned into your subconscious mind. There are several ways to do this. Begin each day by writing down what you want to accomplish that day. This makes every day an exciting contest with yourself. People thrive on challenges, especially when they know what they're up against.

When you write your goals down, they become easier to stick to and harder to neglect. In addition, this practice persuades you to make important decisions right away instead of leaving them until later. This helps to eliminate a potential conflict before it even develops; it brings to your attention what should be done.

Do not skim over this point about writing down your goals. Studies show that when we write our own signatures, the message comes from the subconscious. That's why a graphologist can find out about a person's character through his or her handwriting. The expert taps straight into that person's subconscious.

When you write your bodybuilding goals down every single day, you are *directly* reinforcing your subconscious. You are burning that goal in there. Once it enters your subconscious, it enters your *master control center*. Automatically, everything you do will be programmed to obtain that goal.

This is heavy stuff! But wait, there's more. We don't just stop there, we continue to feed the subconscious with the *spoken* word. Do this by quietly repeating to yourself several times throughout the day exactly what your goal is. Four times a day for 30 seconds at a time is the required amount. This continues to reinforce your subconscious.

Rising from the ashes in Venice, California, from time to time, bodybuilding's own phoenix, Robby Robinson, obscures the chances of most pros for placing in the top three at an IFBB Pro Grand Prix event. He's been a superstar for more than 15 years!

To complete the process of implanting the inner mind with your goal, end the day with *visual programming*. Do this while lying in bed at night. Take a few minutes to clear the mind and become totally relaxed. Then begin to imagine what you *want* to look like. At first, the picture of yourself will be swirls of half-baked features and briefly flashing images. However, within a few days, you will see exactly what you want to become. The detail and clarity of your mind's image will appear so real it's almost scary. (Hmm, reminds us of a commercial for television sets.) By using these tools that are available to you, you will attain your goal! The subconscious will make sure of that.

Make Goals Realistic

Whenever you choose a goal, make sure it is totally believable to you. It would be nice to win the Mr. or Ms. Olympia contest after two years of training, but it's not very realistic. Interestingly enough, your subconscious knows when a goal is realistically obtainable. Your subconscious will back you up 100 percent if the goal is realistic. If it is too far out, and yet you still plan to achieve it, you are simply acting under a delusion. Time itself will reveal this to you.

Keep in mind that it doesn't matter who else believes in your goals. Take our advice, don't even bother to tell others. It is totally unimportant for your success. You are the one behind the driver's wheel, and they aren't even in your backseat!

The key point is this: when the goal is realistic and believable to you, it will happen. If *you* don't really believe it can be done, but you're hoping it might, it will *never* happen. There are no gray areas at all.

Update Goals Constantly

It's amazing how many bodybuilders drift away from their goal-setting techniques once they acquire some good results. And yet, real success in bodybuilding is not merely a place where you arrive and then sit down for years. It is an ongoing process. The key word in bodybuilding is *building*. Look at how many bodybuilders continue to improve year after year, literally adding muscle at will, while others look absolutely identical year after year.

Of course, the ones who don't improve have all of the answers. They blame it on genetics, or the fact that they haven't used growth hormone or some other exotic drug. Nothing could be further from the truth.

Successful bodybuilders keep improving simply because they refuse to be satisfied with attaining just one goal. They constantly create new goals. An excellent example of this can be seen in the pro

Lee Haney (left) and Rich Gaspari placed one-two in three consecutive Mr. Olympia shows, 1986–88.

ranks. A few years ago, cross-striated glutes were a rare sight to see. Now it's standard issue for the Mr. Olympia finalists. That's because the pros are always updating their goals. They see someone with deep grooves in their behind, and they think, "I want to get those, too!" Bingo, they've just updated their goal. Then they go ahead and make the necessary changes in their diet and training, and pretty soon they've got that venetian blind behind as well. That's the real secret to bodybuilding success.

Updating your goals carries another advantage as well—it prevents the trauma of success. Shortly after you reach any big goal, there is an emotional letdown. It's because the challenge, which gave meaning and excitement to your life, is no longer there. You have achieved your goal. Unless you pick up another goal soon, you'll become depressed and bored, and all of the finer qualities of your character will start sliding downhill. That explains why some athletes who achieve incredible success in their chosen field are never heard from again once they retire.

Has anyone heard anything about Mark Spitz *after* he won those seven gold medals at the 1972 Olympics? Granted, he was a truly amazing swimmer, but had he channeled all that energy into a new field, you definitely would have heard of him by now. Conversely, has anyone heard of Arnold Schwarzenegger *after* he left competitive bodybuilding? Just the whole world. Update your goals for continuous success.

Define Goals Clearly

As discussed earlier, goals must be specific to set everything into motion. But we *really* mean specific. Let's put it this way: we've come across thousands of bodybuilders with vaguely defined goals, but never, ever, have we met a single bodybuilder with overdefined goals.

Why are we harping on this point? Because many people will read this and then create a very general goal, and that wrecks the whole process. A general goal is really an idea, and an idea is simply a starting place for creating a goal. Worse yet, a weakly formed goal is actually a wish, and a wish is a goal with no energy behind it.

Does that sound like a bunch of word games to you? At a recent amateur bodybuilding contest, we questioned several competitors before the show regarding their dieting methods. We paid careful attention to *what* they were saying and *how* they said it. The result? When speaking about their precontest planning, three finalists used the word *goal,* and two who placed poorly used the word *idea.* Just words maybe, but there's more. All of the finalists spoke with much more feeling and conviction compared to those who did poorly. Clearly, there was a correlation between the clarity of the goal and the final result. It has everything to do with your success. Make your goals very clear.

Do It Now

Strange as it may seem, many bodybuilders know exactly what their physique needs, but they won't go ahead and get it. They are putting it off until they're *ready.* To them, doing it right now is just too soon. Everything has to be perfect, and then they'll go ahead.

"What needs to be perfect?" you may ask. First, they have to get their head together from a relationship they just ended. You know how rocky that can sometimes be. Then they have to quit working that night shift. That makes it harder to arrange your meals, you know. Of course, there's that vacation they planned. No point to train toward a goal *before* a vacation; after all, you're supposed to relax while you're away. Plus, they have to wait for the constellation of the Bear to appear on the second full moon past the first equinox of the year. When that happens, they can really feel their strength soar and their manhood calling them. Sure, buddy.

As you can see, someone who wants to procrastinate can think of any excuse. And when a person does it often enough, the rationalization for the delay simply becomes an everyday exercise. Truth is, you never get every single detail in your life totally perfect. There is always some form of inconvenience or stress. Superior people function in spite of this. So pick a goal and start it now. The more time you waste, the more you delay your reward. It's already rightfully yours; you just have to invest the time in order to take it.

The main reason some people don't invest the time is that they're scared of the work. To them, it's too much effort to change the way things are. They have entered the Comfort Zone! Simply put, the Comfort Zone is the place where people have grown so comfortable and complacent that they do not wish to alter their lives greatly, when doing so would markedly increase their bodybuilding progress. Make no mistake about it, the Comfort Zone is a deep rut! And pardon us for being blunt, but the only difference between being in a rut and being in a grave is death!

The Comfort Zone has ruined millions of people who had great potential. It kind of sneaks up on you until all of your efforts are feeble ones at best. Then you become one of the dreaded "nothings." The Comfort Zone in bodybuilding can be quickly spotted in any gym, any night of the week. A typical remark will sound like this: "See that guy over there. I'd look as good as him if I trained that hard and ate that much food."

Excuses, excuses. The person making that comment simply doesn't want to make the necessary changes in his diet or training. That's because these changes would require a greater effort on his part. Because he's not pleased with his own physical image, that great physique serves as a reminder that he's done *nothing* to make himself improve. It tells him he's inferior; he's had a chance to make the move, and he's not acting on it.

Look at all the psychological trouble you put yourself through simply by delaying the fulfillment of a goal that you truly want. This should *never* happen to you. Get out of the Comfort Zone! There's really no point for you to be frightened of that extra effort, because in reality it's *less* than you imagine it to be! That's right: less.

According to the Momentum Theory of Success, it takes 10 units of energy to start a strong drive toward a goal, yet once you have started, it requires only 1 unit of energy to keep it going. (The units of energy are a relative form of measurement designed for purposes of this example.)

A rocket ship works on the same principle. It uses an enormous amount of fuel to get off the ground and only a minimal amount to maintain its trajectory. What we're getting at is this: All of that fear that's causing you to delay the fulfillment of your goal is completely unfounded. Your goal requires nowhere near as much work as you thought. Once you make that commitment and work hard to get it off the ground, it actually will become *easier* as it goes along.

Drives have inertia behind them, so they stay in motion once

In less than one year, Franco Santoriello transformed himself from a 170-pound fatty to a 195-pound National Champion by eating 7,000 calories a day and pumping heavy iron an average of more than 30 hours a week.

they're started. Translated into everyday living, it means that dieting will at first appear difficult and bothersome to you, and you'll have to remember all these little details throughout your day. It will bug you a lot. Within a few days, however, the whole thing becomes an unconscious process that seems second nature to you. You'll actually feel foolish for not starting sooner than you did.

The Momentum Theory of Success also says that if you stop your drive completely, it'll take another 10 units to start up another goal-oriented effort. Thus, we strongly advocate that you update your goals constantly. There really is nothing to hold you back anymore, because there's nothing to fear.

You have also learned something about fear itself. Move away from what you fear, and pretty soon it'll dominate your life. Move toward your fear, and it gets smaller. That's the difference between cowardice and courage. Become full of courage! Start those goals *now*.

DISCIPLINE YOUR SELF-DISCIPLINE

The greatest bodybuilding genes in the world are useless if they are not backed by self-discipline. The body is inherited at birth; self-discipline is something you acquire. To develop self-discipline, you have to take possession of your mind. Sounds a bit weird, doesn't it? Take possession of something you already own by using it to possess itself. But it's not weird at all when you look at it closely.

In effect, self-discipline is about control—the ability to control your mind with such strength that your emotions and desires are regulated and managed in any direction you want. In a way, self-discipline is a kind of mental and moral training session. You can develop it, or you can lose it, just like your physical condition. But self-discipline is a lot trickier to maintain, because it involves the *need* for a harmonious arrangement of the parts. You must balance the emotions of your heart with the reasonings of the mind, and that's always a tough thing to do. An old saying sums it up well: "The man who controls his mind has more power than the man who controls a city."

In today's entertainment-oriented, excitement-loving, don't-work-too-hard population, self-discipline is something of a rarity. Most people do not want to be disciplined. They'd rather please the first emotion or desire that pops into their head. After years of this kind of behavior, it's little wonder that the majority of the public is overweight, is out of shape, and eats incorrectly. People have trained themselves to have zippo self-discipline, and the effects are plain to see.

Bodybuilders are an entirely different breed. Even the average bodybuilder is an absolute expert at weight control when compared to the masses. But that's not saying much. The purpose of this section is to take the self-discipline that you already have and make it into a steel trap.

We want you to become a very powerful human being—something akin to a superhero. This can happen when you increase your self-discipline. To do that, carefully consider the following points about this valuable bodybuilding feature:

Learn from the Leaders

Throughout the ages, all great leaders seem to have one thing in common: they consciously fight against the human tendency toward comfort. Leaders are keenly aware that people follow the weakest part of their human nature, allowing this to dominate their actions. Leaders dominate their own human nature. They resist the urge to become comfortable. They stay hungry. They are constantly challenging themselves rather than succumbing to the easy way. There's a very important but subtle point here.

The key word is *easy*. Leaders *never* take it easy. This makes them very special human beings. While all the others are choosing the fastest and easiest way to get what they want now, with no thought for secondary consequences, leaders apply their willpower and rise above this weak tendency of humanity.

This natural quality of leaders tells you something you should know about bodybuilding. Every time you put forth an effort in some particular direction, a part of your mind will offer you an easier route. Not more effective, just easier. *Watch* for it! When it happens, fight it and destroy it.

When you start watching out for this seductive mental offer, you strengthen your mind. It may occur while you're dieting. Say nobody's looking around to monitor you, so you go ahead and have that tiny piece of pastry. Your mind says to you, "It's OK. You'll need the extra carbs for your workout, and you won't notice it on your physique, so go ahead!" *There's the offer*. Resist it!

Even if that piece of pastry may not seem to make a cosmetic difference, it is making a serious difference in your mind. By giving in to the urge, you lower your self-respect, you set yourself up for an easier mark the next time the Monty Hall in your mind wants to play "Let's Make a Deal."

If you give in again to another mental "offer," your self-respect will continue to spiral downward, and your self-discipline will weaken also. Refuse the offer instead! Do what you should do when you *should* do it, whether you like it or not. *Never* give in to a passing fancy, whim, or impulse. By resisting, you'll raise your self-respect, and your self-discipline will increase as well. That's exactly why people who have great self-respect also have great self-discipline.

Ever sit in a diner and watch overweight people put down all kinds

At the 1988 Ms. Olympia, Tonya Knight (left) outmuscled Marjo Selin to make it into the top 5 on her first try at the competition. Selin finished in the top 10. She's been in every Olympia since 1982.

of food? You are seeing poor self-respect in action. It's not a very inspiring thing to see.

Keep in mind that temptations come in a wide variety of formats and in subtle degrees. In the gym, for example, we have seen many bodybuilders give up during a set long before they should have, simply because it was easier to quit at that point. To the untrained observer, they still look like they're working out. But they are succumbing to the weaker part of their mind. Monty appears again and says, "Come on, you've done enough already, plus you're going to miss that television program at nine o'clock unless you hurry up!"

Conversely, we have also seen many bodybuilders set personal records in a lift when they *did not know* that extra weight was slipped on the bar before their set. That's because the Monty in their minds didn't know either; otherwise he would have surely struck up another "deal" to make certain the bodybuilder took it easy. Get the quality of leaders—*never* take it easy. Be on the lookout for Monty Hall and his enticing "offers." Turn them down when they show up, and your self-discipline will grow.

Delay Gratification

Having great self-discipline doesn't mean that you deprive yourself of pleasures or that you can't have fun. It simply means that you delay the fun whenever necessary. For example, let's say you've just finished watching a movie with some friends, and they suggest going out to a restaurant. Knowing you have a leg workout the next morning, you decline because it'll take two hours out of your sleep time. If it were a day off for you, then you'd accept the offer. Sounds simple enough, but it's surprising how many bodybuilders try to get the best of both worlds, only to end up losing.

Furthering the example, you decide to go to the restaurant, and within minutes you're having a great time. Although your original intentions were to go for only half an hour, a quick glance at your watch reveals you've just blown two hours! You rush home to get to sleep, but the next day your leg workout suffers anyway. You had to go light because your strength just wasn't there. As you can see, those were a very critical two hours. But you weren't thinking about them when you were laughing and joking in the restaurant.

Never make the mistake of serving two masters. You'll only end up serving one, at the cost of the other. Delaying gratification is an all-or-nothing proposition, not a halfway measure.

Bodybuilders who are unable to delay gratification will experience lots of trouble when dieting. It can be a costly habit.

Also, don't fall into the trap of believing you're missing out on all of the fun. We have two things to tell you about that ridiculous notion. First of all, where is all this fun? In a bar? If you think so, then go to one. You'll encounter loads of out-of-shape, overweight people who smoke and drink and talk a lot but say things of little substance. That's a bar. They typically are depressing environments crammed full of people who wouldn't even think for a moment to delay gratification. They want it all *now*. They've got it, all right. But they don't have great bodies, healthy lungs, or good nutrition flowing through them. What they have is not much in the way of bodybuilding. If they did have, you wouldn't catch them in a bar.

Second, do you think the fun is whatever your friends happen to be doing while you're not there? Phone them from where you are, and you'll see that not really all that much is going on. We're not trying to throw a big downer on the whole process of socializing. Of course, it's necessary, and it should be done.

The main point is that you're not missing out on *all that fun*. Those people in the bar would *love* to look like you. They think *you* look like fun. The whole idea of missing out on all this action is a big myth. There is plenty of time for you to do anything you want. You just have to know when to delay gratification. Believe us, the fun will all be yours in the end.

Follow Through

Discipline yourself to persist. It builds character. Character is the ability to follow through after the enthusiasm and emotion that started your resolution have passed.

Regardless of how much passion you have—and we are advocating that you should have a lot—there will be times when everything seems to get you down. This is normal. The only kind of people who are "up" 100 percent of the time are brainwashed people who belong to cults. They are up all of the time because their brains have checked out for a long time.

It is to be expected now and then that somehow all your efforts are feeble and your actions inconsequential. However, it's also true that these states are transitory. They last briefly, and they're gone. Ever notice how the next day has a way of making yesterday's concerns seem nonexistent?

We are emotional creatures, and as such we will waver now and then. Don't be too hard on yourself when you hit a temporary low spot. The main point is to remember to keep on going. Follow through with your original intentions, and soon those clouds over your mind will clear up and give way to sunshine. These little back-slides won't stop you; they just put a few extra hours between you and your goals.

When you've made a mistake of some kind, move aggressively to limit the damage. Don't dwell on it. Keep following through, and you'll soon forget about it.

Sometimes we need mistakes. They put us back on track and inform us how we can improve for the next time. A famous philosopher once said, "That which does not kill me only serves to make me stronger!" Follow through on your efforts; it pays off in the end.

Be Responsible

We are all self-employed. Our job is to look after ourselves. *You* are in charge of the research and development, production, and marketing of the product known as "you." In effect, you *own* the place known as yourself. As such, you have a responsibility to yourself.

Since you are the primary creative force in your own life, you should always look after your best interests. You are the architect of your own destiny, so design a good foundation for yourself. Be a responsible person. When you finally realize that no one is coming to your rescue, that you are the one who determines everything in your life, you have to go ahead and *take charge!*

Those who rule must also learn to obey. Obey the orders that you yourself have set into motion. If you are dieting for a certain look, follow through by being responsible to yourself and your goal. That means you should make that special meal for yourself even though you don't feel like it. That means you should do that extra calf work even though you feel tired.

When you set out to do something, you must follow through. Make that commitment to yourself and to your goals. *Lock in* that goal, and burn your bridges. Don't turn back from your journey. Forge ahead like a juggernaut. Remember, you are 100 percent responsible for what you become. You own the blueprints to yourself.

If you control yourself through self-discipline, you can never be controlled by other people. You call the shots. Whatever you ask of yourself, go ahead and do it with everything you have. You're counting on it. Don't let yourself down. Be a responsible bodybuilder, and run that physique of yours into peak condition.

Those are the psychological principles that will guarantee your success as a bodybuilder. You need that special flame called passion to give you the desire, you need goals to direct the flame, and you need self-discipline to keep the fire going. When you put them all together, you'll forge yourself a beautiful body.

2

DEGREES OF MUSCULAR DEFINITION

Did you know that the Eskimos have 39 different words to describe snow? It sounds unnecessary at first glance, but it makes sense. Given their harsh and demanding environment, verbal preciseness about snow would be crucial when dealing with sled mobility, hunting conditions, or even igloo building. In fact, those primitive Eskimos are far ahead of bodybuilders when it comes to word clarity.

Given the harsh and demanding criteria by which physiques are judged today, it's clear that a deeper vocabulary is needed to describe the cosmetic properties of a muscle. Sure, you can call this guy "tight" or that girl "cut," or say to a bodybuilder that he looks "ready," but what does that actually mean? At best, these are vague and ephemeral terms. Everyone's interpretation is going to be different. Furthermore, there is no official book for you to consult in order to find these things out. Not until now, that is.

We feel strongly about the need for semantic clarification with regard to the topic of getting cut. One reason why so many bodybuilders fail to achieve their best shape is that they don't have a definitive list of terms to judge themselves by. When someone is preparing for a competition and his buddy tells him, "Wow, you look ripped," it is highly unlikely that the bodybuilder and his buddy are on the same page. After all, what are they using as a reference point?

Now the guesswork is removed. Whether you are getting ready for a contest or simply want to get into shape, you never have to play hit and miss again. This chapter, for the first time, thoroughly discusses

The tremendous chest-waist differential of Tony Pearson is visible both in the off-season and prior to a competition, because he doesn't allow his off-season body weight to get out of control. He's cut all year, sliced at contest time.

the various levels of muscularity. You get to know exactly where your physique is now, where you would like to take it, or where you need to go, should you decide to achieve the ultimate degree of muscularity. This way, you can accurately monitor your progress, because you always know which category to strive for. As complicated as many would have you believe that bodybuilding has become, which is easier—to pick out 39 different types of snow or 7 states of muscularity?

STATES OF MUSCULARITY

The basis for our rating system is quite simple. Everything is based on the word *cut*, and there are seven total states or gradations of muscularity. The first two categories are totally absent of recognizable cuts. The third state is Cut itself, and the next four are increasing degrees of being cut. Listed in ascending order of severity, they are:

1. Full House
2. Hard
3. Cut
4. Defined
5. Ripped
6. Sliced
7. Shredded

This type of rating system removes the use of adverbs and provides an exact and clear format to follow. For example, instead of saying "really Cut" or "extremely Cut"—and who knows what either gradation means?—you simply add more cuts if you want to move from one category to the next. Therefore, if you are Defined, you need to add more cuts to your physique in order to become Ripped. Adding more cuts to a Ripped condition will make you Sliced. Cutting up even further at the Sliced level will get you Shredded, the highest degree of muscularity attainable.

Remember this golden rule! It takes a great deal of time and effort to move up through the seven stages of muscularity, but it takes no time to drop down. For instance, two months of dieting can make you go from Hard to Ripped, yet just two or three poorly chosen meals can plummet you to Cut within 24 hours! So believe us—don't give in to any impulses when dieting, because you will pay dearly for it.

Another item to keep in mind is the Law of Exponential Effort. Simply stated, the effort required to move up to another state of muscularity increases exponentially as you proceed higher up the ladder. Most bodybuilders can easily muster up the willpower needed to change from Hard to Cut. However, to move from Cut to Defined requires not just a little more discipline, but a lot more. And each stage after that becomes hairier still. At the highest level of achievement, the degree of physical exertion and discipline needed to become Shredded is truly awesome. That is why so few bodybuilders have ever achieved this state.

MIRROR TRICKERY

Before we precisely define each of the seven states of muscularity, we should discuss the use of mirrors and various types of lighting when assessing your physical condition. You would be positively shocked to note how many champion bodybuilders see something totally different in the mirror than anyone else sees.

We must admit we have a thing about mirrors. While we don't go around trashing them as a bodybuilding tool, we view them with caution. Lots of caution. And you should also. That's what this section is all about. We're going to cover some areas that have never before been dealt with in any other bodybuilding publication. That information will change the way you look *at* mirrors, and it'll change the way you look *in* them. As a bodybuilder, you'll benefit from that change.

Playing Favorites

A highly common practice among bodybuilders goes virtually unnoticed. Here's how it happens. You've just finished your arm workout,

Analyzing available light source in a mirror.

and those pipes are pumped like crazy. So you go ahead and check out that pump in the mirror. However, you don't check it just anywhere in the mirror. Instead, you go over to your "favorite" location, the one that makes you look especially good. And you don't just stand in front of the mirror. Rather, you stand at a specific, predetermined distance that gives you your best look.

What's wrong with that? Lots.

In truth, you are not getting an accurate picture of your physical development. You have deliberately maximized your look under the best lighting conditions in the gym. Such a practice is great for doing photos or showing your friends how freaky you look, but it is not accurate.

Is an accurate look all that important? Well, would you like to prepare for a contest under the influence of a mind-altering drug?

"I won't settle for anything but sliced at my next competition," says gigantic Brian Buchanan as he forces out a final, painful two reps on flat-bench dumbbell flyes for his chest.

Obviously not. In essence, however, that's what you are doing: you're "altering" your look. It's not a bad practice; it's just not accurate.

Keeping things in perspective, we have to remember that we are people first, then bodybuilders. Everyone, not just bodybuilders, has a natural tendency to want to exaggerate. An artist's rendering of a particular house for sale makes it appear bigger than when it is actually viewed. Car commercials use carefully selected camera angles and light enhancement to make the vehicles look out of this world. And those beer commercials—wow, don't those parties look like fun? The trouble is, we've never been to a party like that. Enlargement is a product of human nature and has been present in society since the very first "I caught a fish this big" story.

As a bodybuilder, you must make an effort to resist this tendency. Check yourself in various kinds of lighting situations, not just favorable ones. Believe us, scores of bodybuilders have lost contests simply because they entered with a false confidence that a "favorite" mirror location gave them.

Let There Be Light

Imagine it's the night before your contest. You just took a look at your muscles and thought they looked flat. So you decide to take in more carbs. The next morning, you check yourself again and still look flat. In response, you continue to carb up. By the time you step on stage, you're spilling over like a champagne bottle on New Year's Eve. What happened?

Just as certain lighting conditions can make you look better than reality, some lights can also make you look worse. We've seen many bodybuilders who were perfectly on schedule look smooth, small, and flat in the wrong light. The key is to follow the guiding light. Know which light provides which effect.

When you check yourself in the mirror, you're totally dependent upon the available light source in that particular area. However, all light is *not* the same. The method of light creation can vastly affect its intensity, and this in turn can radically alter your total appearance. To shed some light on the subject, we've broken it down into three main groups.

SUNLIGHT AS MAIN SOURCE If you have gazed through the classic book *Pumping Iron*, you'll probably recall the outstanding black-and-white photos that Art Zeller took of Arnold Schwarzenegger in his prime, as well as the other greats of that era. Many of those shots were taken at the original Gold's Gym (on Pacific Avenue in Venice, California) and used the afternoon sunlight as the main form of light. Sunlight is the most "precise" light. It has an even balance of the color wavelengths, is not overly harsh except at noon, and, depending on the time, its low angle of occurrence is perfect for high-lighting muscular detail.

Morning light has a slight blue overtone, and it tends to make you appear very hard-looking when you view your physique in the mirror. Checking progress in this light is reliable for nutritional assessments or monitoring body fat and water level. Keep that slight hardness-enhancement property in mind, however. If you think you're very hard when sunlight bounces off a mirror, you should be looking like a freaked-out bundle of crushed rocks under flesh.

INCANDESCENT BULB AS MAIN SOURCE Light from incandescent bulbs is a wild-card kind of light. Smaller community gyms usually use this light, and hotels have it in their rooms as well. Remember, a lot of monitoring goes on in hotel rooms, because many of the big contests are held in far-off metropolitan locations.

Generally speaking, incandescent bulb light is much less intense than pure sunlight. It's also much less reliable. I (Negrita) have seen myself look like the "Thing" from Marvel Comics or, on the other hand, like a girl who needs to join a gym.

To help you avoid the potential extremes, stand in the mirror so that this kind of light causes a shadow beneath your chin. This shadow should fall only to your collarbone. If it falls lower, you'll darken yourself and flatten out. You'll also look very sinister. If you back up, you won't have enough relief to your muscles, so you'll flatten out without enough light.

Bulb light in hotels can make you appear more cut than you actually are. Solution? Try posing in the washroom (especially in Holiday Inns), because there's usually better light there than in the rooms. If you don't look shredded in those mirrors, you probably shouldn't compete.

In summary, bulb light is the trickiest. Exercise caution when making any physical assessment in this light.

FLUORESCENT LIGHT AS MAIN SOURCE Whoever invented fluorescent light was obviously not a bodybuilder. This light is garbage. It's too weak to show detail and too diffuse to allow shadowing, and that's probably why you seldom see bodybuilders working in offices. Also, as if that's not enough, fluorescent light emphasizes the yellow and green wavelengths. This makes you look sick and pale. About the only assessment you can make using this kind of light in a mirror is that you shouldn't make any assessment at all.

The following table tells the story. As you can see, fluorescent light isn't much better than a candle. Oh sure, some fluorescent lights can be quite bright, and the principle behind them is impressive, but for checking out your body in the mirror, you may as well use a flashlight. Fluorescent light just doesn't show detail.

LIGHT INTENSITIES

Source	Intensity in Lumens
Morning sun	125,000
Incandescent bulb	500
Fluorescent tube	2
Candle	1

From Gym to Stage

We don't know why most bodybuilders don't know this, because it seems so obvious, but *you* should know about it. Implant this sentence into your mind: whatever you look like in the gym, expect to look slightly less like that onstage. Your tan will be about 40 percent less, your definition will be 20 percent less, your density will be about 30 percent less.

Regardless of the light sources in a gym, they are *never* as bright as they are onstage (unless, of course, someone is shooting a movie in your gym). The difference isn't even close. Stage lights are super harsh, cutting through your skin color like nothing, and show the judges everything. What you saw in the mirror on Friday suffers a serious meltdown on Saturday. Those mild gym lights treat your body better in the mirror than those harsh stage lights do during the prejudging.

This discovery first came to me (Negrita) during the Women's Pro World Championships a few years ago in Toronto. Backstage I asked one of the competitors to show her thighs. She hit them, and they were feathered on both sides of her leg. However, when that competitor got onstage, under those harsh lights, you could barely see those feathered markings when she flexed.

To get around this, in order to look the best onstage, you must appear completely shredded, dense, full, and have muscle separation beyond belief! You must look truly amazing. This will help to ward off that wild-to-mild, gym-to-stage metamorphosis. Knowing this fact, you can use a mirror much more effectively than ever before.

See Reflections Accurately

It's been said that if we could see ourselves as others see us, few mirrors would be sold. Apply that to bodybuilding, and it seems certain that many of us wouldn't enter contests. Some people just aren't good at seeing themselves accurately. Or are we all a bit like that?

Psychologists conducted a study wherein the subjects were placed in front of a grossly distorted mirror and then asked to correct the image until it resembled them most closely. They were shown how to

Light-heavyweight/Overall NOC National Champion Vince Taylor is definitely in the sliced category, if not higher. He has such a fast metabolism that he diets for only 6 weeks (compared to the usual 12 or more) prior to a major competition.

manipulate two controls so that the mirror could change its shape. They were given as much time as was necessary to change the mirror's shape and therefore master the task. Keep in mind that none of these people were mentally deficient.

The result? The subjects tended to choose a reflection that represented more of a mental picture than a realistic one. They enhanced their looks, for example, by pulling receding jaws forward or pushing protruding ones backward. In short, they "corrected" themselves.

As a whole, bodybuilders are a bit more critical than the average citizen. This has to be the situation if improvement is to occur. However, it seems quite clear that, regardless of the lighting, time of day, or the shape some bodybuilders are in, they'll only see what they want to. If you suspect that you may be one of those types, don't worry. Ask someone with a reputation for telling it like it is for a critique, and you'll probably start winning contests.

Solo Symmetry

Assuming everything is ideal, you can still look into the mirror and fall prey to a common mistake. It's so common, in fact, that you can't really call it a mistake. It happens when you look into the mirror and simply assess yourself without comparison to someone beside you. This is likely to occur if you're the only one in your gym getting ready for a show. As soon as someone who's out of shape attempts to stand beside you, you'll blow that person away. Consequently, you'll appear extra freaky. In essence, you are standing alone when you look in that mirror, and you are doing a solo assessment. This can be dangerous because you have nothing substantive to compare yourself with.

When you enter that show, you may suddenly feel that you need more size, or better symmetry, or even deeper cuts, simply because you now have someone to compare yourself with. Worse yet, many bodybuilders cannot see how they look standing in a lineup, so even though they may be contest-ready but don't place well because of some structural flaw, they start blaming the judges. After all, they flash back to how they looked in the gym mirror and how often everyone said, "You're gonna win." Assessing your physique from a solo standpoint requires a strong piece of advice: make sure you know what you're doing, and that means *how* you stack up as well.

We've reflected on many valuable points, so consider them well for future successes. And remember, when you spot a competitor at a show who's huge, cut, full, separated, dense, and deeply tanned, you can confidently tell yourself, "It's all done with mirrors!"

OBJECTIFYING STATES OF MUSCULARITY

Now it's time to get down to brass tacks and objectively describe each of the seven states of muscularity. Then you can accurately assess your relative condition and determine what it will take to achieve the next highest level.

Full House

The Full House state is characterized by a liberal deposit of interstitial and subcutaneous water and fat that has the cosmetic effect of blending all the muscle groups together into a uniform smooth appearance. This is the official "off-season" look. If you were in Full House condition and gained any additional water and fat, you would become big and fat. Unless you were born with deep facial dimples, you have no cuts anywhere on a Full House physique. Other points of note:

- Waistline is slightly distended, yet firm to the touch and capable of shrinking to a smaller state once the abs are tensed.
- Although muscular girths measure the biggest, they appear the least impressive visually of all the states.
- This is your physically strongest state because the additional water provides your joints with extra leverage.
- The face is typically puffy: vascularity is almost entirely absent. A male would weigh more than 30 pounds over the Sliced state, and a female bodybuilder more than 20 pounds over.
- People may mistake you for a football player or wrestler in this state, as your muscle clarity and overall shape would not directly indicate that you are a bodybuilder.
- You should still be able to see obscured muscle lines or blurry portions of muscle separation in your abdominal region.
- Although you appear massive in clothing, you look much better with your clothes on than with them off.
- When you strike a double-biceps pose, there is no striking visual transformation in your physique. Remember, you can't flex fat.
- When you start dieting, your body changes overnight.
- More and more bodybuilders are staying away from the Full House look and are opting instead for a tighter off-season appearance. This should be your goal as well, and the state to shoot for is referred to as Hard.

Hard

The Hard state is typified by a moderate amount of interstitial and subcutaneous water and fat around the body that has the cosmetic effect of gently rounding out the muscle groups into a shapely, powerful look. This is the true off-season look you should aspire to. If you gain additional water and fat when you are Hard, you become Full House. Although there are no cuts on the Hard physique, the lower percentage of body fat creates a visually perceptible difference in the outward contour of the muscle groups. This makes them more pleasantly shaped and enhances the overall symmetry as well. Here are additional points that are unique to the Hard condition:

- Even though you weigh less than Full House, you actually appear bigger because of the improved muscle shape.
- The state of being Hard is a wide condition. Unlike Full House, a several-pound loss produces varying degrees of the same look.
- The waist is the first region to change dramatically. Males typically lose about 2 inches from their waistlines, and females 1–1½ inches, when they become Hard.
- Although muscle separation still appears as obscured lines, the number of prominent lines rises sharply from Full House to Hard.
- When you strike a double-biceps pose, the arms appear to have more height, the upper torso has a better V-taper, and there is greater detail to the lower rib cage when compared to Full House.
- When viewed outdoors from a distance of 30 feet, the Hard body looks big and shapely. When it is viewed from 6 feet away, there is a large drop in visual impressiveness.
- More facial contours start to appear, and vascularity starts to hint more prominently near the surface of the forearms.
- A male would weigh between 24 and 30 pounds over the Sliced condition, plus or minus 2 pounds. A female would weigh between 16 and 21 pounds over Sliced, plus or minus 2 pounds.

Cut

The Cut physique is the first state where genetically predisposed areas of the body start to display groovelike formations of muscle fibers. These are the first signs of being Cut. For some bodybuilders, this may occur in the deltoid region, for others in the abdominals, but all weight-trained bodies have a particular muscle group that shows cuts first. This also means that the remaining regions of the physique will be less cut as a result of greater amounts of interstitial and subcutaneous water and fat stored there. From an overall standpoint, muscle roundness becomes considerably more pronounced in this state. Cut carries these features as well:

- Although you appear weight-trained in clothes, you look slightly better with your clothes off than with them on.
- The face becomes more etched, vascularity is clearer in the forearm region, and most people immediately recognize you as a bodybuilder.
- A male weighs between 14 and 24 pounds over the Sliced state. A female weighs 12 to 16 pounds over Sliced. This is the widest state because it takes a steady weight decrease in order for cuts to appear in new locations.
- When viewed from 30 feet away, the Cut person looks big and

symmetrical outdoors. When he or she is seen from 6 feet, the viewer's eyes tend to be drawn toward the less impressive regions, as visual contrasts now exist on the body of a Cut bodybuilder.

- When you are posing the double-biceps shot, your legs show the general outlines of some of the muscle heads.
- You lose about 1–1½ inches from your waistline when you become Cut.
- With a good workout pump, this is the first state where you begin to look impressive in the gym mirror, especially in morning light.
- When improving from Hard to Cut, you lose slightly more size in the thighs than you do in the arms.

Defined

This condition carries a minimal amount of interstitial and subcutaneous water and fat, which has the visual property of defining the outlines of each muscle group. Simply stated, when you add more cuts to the Cut stage, eventually you carve out and separate each muscle group from an adjacent one. The morphology of the muscles becomes visually defined, and you in turn achieve the Defined state. If even one area shows no detail to the muscle area, you are still Cut, not Defined. In addition, a good rule of thumb to remember is that once your naturally cut area starts to melt into the rest of your physique, it is quite likely you are Defined. Here are more pointers to Defined:

- You will experience your first real power drop during the Defined stage.
- Cheekbones start to push outward, hints of vascularity start to appear on the thighs, and veins on the arms raise higher from the skin's surface.
- When you hit the compulsory double-biceps pose, muscle lines occur everywhere. The biceps and triceps are cleanly separated, you can see where the lats insert, the waist forms an indentation underneath the rib cage, and the thighs show more distinctness in each muscle group.
- When viewed outdoors from 30 feet away, the Defined bodybuilder looks impressive. When he or she is seen from 6 feet away, the viewer observes a greater uniformity to the bodily definition but is still drawn to areas that need more surface detailing.
- Although you appear athletic in clothing, you look definitely better with your clothes off than with them on.
- You lose another 1–1¼ inches from your waistline.

One factor making up muscle density is mass, and England's Bertil Fox, a four-time Mr. Universe winner, personifies the quality. That upper body was developed with bench presses over 500 pounds every chest workout and alternate dumbbell curls with a pair of 120s.

- While certain lighting conditions make you look very good, when you stand under fluorescent light, most of your lines become less pronounced. The Defined cuts are still not deep enough to resist the washout effect.
- The weak points on your physique become clearly noticeable when Defined. It is an excellent time to start specialization work.
- A man would weigh between 8 and 14 pounds over the Sliced condition, a woman between 6 and 12 pounds from the state of being Sliced.

Ripped

The Ripped physique is characterized by less than minimal degrees of water and body fat, which tends to highlight the striations and

"I train with pretty much the same routine year-round," says Mike Christian, Pro U.S. Champion, "but the intensity goes up close to a show. It's sort of a panic factor. I don't want to look bad, so I train and diet that much more intensely."

surface irregularities of various muscle groups. Anatomically speaking, as you add more cuts to the Defined stage, your skin starts to fold over and fall into numerous angles that are unique to a specific muscle. This creates the presence of striations and sets up the multi-angled look to each muscle group. Over 70 percent of all bodybuilding contests are won in the Ripped state. With two stages left, this tells you how difficult it is for most bodybuilders to surpass Ripped. Here is how you know whether you are Ripped:

- The cheekbones are quite prominent, vascularity is scattered over the entire body, hints of cross-striations occur in the thighs, triceps, and possibly the abdominal regions. A clean pectoral line is still evident, even when you put your arms above your head.
- When you strike the double-biceps pose, the forearms should appear knotted and hard, the biceps will have surface markings on the peak, and the middle head of the thighs will be clearly visible and separated from the inner and outer thighs.
- When viewed from 30 feet away, you look quite impressive in the outdoor light. When seen from six feet away, you still appear impressive, although less so.
- You appear somewhat average in your clothes, but when you take them off, the transformation is striking.
- A bystander who sees a Ripped bodybuilder will stare intently.
- The state of being Ripped is a narrow condition. That is because, at this point, the addition of cuts will produce a radical cosmetic difference in your physique.
- Guys who are Ripped will weigh three to seven pounds over the Sliced level. Women will weigh two to five pounds away from Sliced.
- As you graduate from Defined to Ripped, your thigh measurement will further decrease, up to one inch less from one stage to the next.
- Although you won't look your best in fluorescent light, the Ripped physique will not suffer the same degree of washout that Defined did.
- Members of the opposite sex will notice you much more in the Ripped state. Even if they see only your face, the deeper contours will draw stares of curiosity and perhaps even an unexpected date after the show. Hmmm.

Sliced

The Sliced bodybuilder carries trace levels of water and body fat, which creates the dramatic visual effect of adding new cross-striations to certain muscles, as well as deepening the already existent cross-striations. Achieving the Sliced stage accounts for 29 percent

Bev Francis, Pro World Champion, shows the chest and shoulder muscles that have bench pressed more than 330 pounds. A five-time World Champion in power lifting prior to turning to competitive bodybuilding, she owns a gym on Long Island.

of the victories in all bodybuilding shows. This is also the stage where everyone calls the winner Shredded, but in truth he or she is not really Shredded. Incidentally, the Sliced state increases the apparent density of the physique as well (more on this later). Here's how you know if you have become Sliced:

- An amateur magician has just accidentally sawed your body into three sections (just kidding!).
- When viewed outdoors from 30 feet away, the Sliced body looks fantastic. When seen from 6 feet away, it still appears truly impressive.
- The cheekbones are very prominent, and the veins are raised prominently away from the skin's surface, no matter where they are located.
- It is extremely easy to flex a muscle group and cause it to jump out at you visually.
- Men who are Sliced have about three pounds to play with in this state; once they go over that, they immediately drop to Ripped. Women have a two-pound leeway to float with. As you can see, a two- or three-pound weight gain is all it takes to slide you back to Ripped. Conversely, those two or three pounds removed can almost assure you of a victory. With Sliced, we are dealing with a subtle state.
- When you do the double-biceps shot, the transition from relaxed to flexed is phenomenal. The skin has a translucent quality and appears to be wrapped tightly around the muscle bellies like freezer plastic wrap. Every muscle group stands out in bold relief.
- Unless you compete as a heavyweight, you will look small in clothes. Once you remove the clothes, however, it is not uncommon to hear shrieks of amazement from a crowd of onlookers. Even your dog will stare at you.
- The glutes have striations running across them. The triceps and thighs are heavily feathered, although a certain amount of this is genetic as well.
- Moving from Ripped to Sliced will further decrease the waistline by about a half-inch.
- You can see your cross-striations even in fluorescent light, and in the gym light you appear to be bordering on the freaky.

To go from Sliced to Shredded, you need to drop an extra three to four pounds. Obviously, it won't be coming from fat loss much, so the majority of this change will be in the amount of subcutaneous water.

Shredded

The highest condition of muscularity you can attain is Shredded. Less than 1 percent of all bodybuilders ever achieve the Shredded state. It is characterized by an absolute zero appearance of water and fat, which makes the possessor of this state look as though he or she has no skin covering the muscles. This state is the zenith of cosmetic levels and is truly freaky to behold. Cross-striations show up in strange and unheard-of locations when one is Shredded.

I (Negrita) can vividly recall a competitors' meeting at the 1986 Canadian Nationals, when a woman named Donna Flamont was seated beside me. Donna was chewing gum, and her jaw muscles were deeply cross-striated and dancing wildy like rows of piano keys. Every square inch of her was like that. Even her middle thigh, the rectus femoris, was radically cross-striated. Donna literally did not have to flex her muscles in order to show those hundred thousand striations across every muscle fiber. (By the way, Donna Flamont won so convincingly that it was actually hilarious when other women stood next to her onstage.)

No pro bodybuilder carries more sliced muscle mass per square inch of skeletal structure than Night of the Champions victor Phil Hill. Hill's life goal is a bit unique: he'd like to become mayor of Trenton, New Jersey, his hometown.

Here's what to expect if you want the ultimate degree of muscular definition:

- When viewed from 30 feet away in the outdoor sunlight, the Shredded physique will *not* look much different from a Sliced one. However, when seen from 6 feet away, it will absolutely stun you visually! Your eyes will keep darting all over the body because it is so totally mesmerizing to look at. Seriously, it will appear freaky from 6 feet away. For some people, such a body will be too much to like right away; others will be visually G-forced but completely appreciate it anyway. Believe us, being Shredded creates strong reactions from the bodybuilding population. As for the general public, they may lose their breakfasts. It is simply beyond their wildest imagination.
- The state of being Shredded can only be held for hours at a time. Since so many biochemical processes have to be maximized to create this effect, it is very easy for the body to start changing one thing, and then the whole picture reverts to Sliced. Bodybuilders who are Sliced can be photographed the next day and still hold that condition. Shredded types should be photographed immediately.
- Shredded bodybuilders look like rakes in clothes. When they take their clothes off at a weigh-in, however, all the other bodybuilders get the immediate urge to go home.
- If a Shredded bodybuilder stands beside a Cut one, the Cut person will look like a Full House. The state of being Shredded is the instant eliminator of anyone wishing to stand beside a Shredded bodybuilder. It is the ultimate giant-killer state.
- When a Shredded bodybuilder makes the slightest physical movement, everything flexes and striates. Even eating an apple seems to take on an out-of-this-world look of importance and purpose.
- The Shredded state gives its possessor a unique advantage. It is excellent for hiding the structural faults of the development. Because the observer's eyes are kept so busy, it is much harder to view the symmetry objectively.
- Each muscle group appears as though it is sitting right off the bone for you to grab.
- You can usually see the insertion points of the lower jaw mandible, the veins are hanging out big-time, and even the muscles of the feet are clearly prominent and separated.
- Fluorescent light does nothing to weaken the visual picture of a Shredded physique.
- Members of the opposite sex will probably wonder whether they should feed you. If they do, you will instantly drop to a Sliced condition, and then you can give the situation a more interesting ending.

- The muscular measurements of a Shredded bodybuilder will be much smaller than what you imagine. However, once that person stands under the bright lights on stage, he or she will appear enormous.

LEAN BODY MASS TESTING?

The foregoing descriptions of various states of muscularity made no mention of grading by body fat content. There are several reasons for this. First, none of those methods—and there are several extremely accurate ones—tell *what you look like*. Of course, they are excellent for measuring changes in one's body composition, which can prove helpful to a dieting bodybuilder. But they are not always readily available when you are assessing your physique.

The purpose of this chapter is to provide you with enough information so you can decide on your own where you are and where you would like to go with your physical condition. And you can do it without the aid of expensive and sophisticated equipment. After all, bodybuilding is a highly visual sport, so it should be monitored according to the appearance of your physique in order to land your contest prep right on time.

There are many variables that contribute heavily to the look of a muscle. These do not show up in the water-immersion test or potassium radiation method. For example, some bodybuilders have striated triceps even during their Full House state. Others have *never* been striated except for their pectorals or deltoids. This difference depends entirely on genetics. Still other bodybuilders have incredible body symmetry that catapults them past many others who may be even more cut but lack that gift of symmetry.

Then there is the problem of holding water. Some bodybuilders who do not make the top five could actually be Shredded, but a microthin layer of subcutaneous water is obscuring their fantastic muscle detail. We have seen this occur many times.

Add to all this the property of muscle density. Many bodybuilders seem to get extremely dense, while others find this feature very elusive. As you can see, it is not simply a question of guessing your percentage of body fat.

DENSITY VS. CUTS

To further complicate matters, many bodybuilders blend the meanings of density and cuts. Simply explained, a cut in a muscle is a division that occurs on the surface of the muscle. More cuts to a muscle bring greater clarity to its structure. Density is entirely different. It is composed of several parts which add up to create the effect of density. If one part is lacking, the density also will be.

To be specific, density is composed of seven conditions. When all of them are met, you get serious density on the appearance of a physique. Here they are:

1. *Thickness*—You can't make an effective carving unless you have a substantial amount of raw material to work with. In this case, the material is muscle. The more raw material you have, the more pronounced the final effect will be. Massive muscle thickness buffers the effect of losing size while dieting. This explains why the majority of contest booing comes from the back rows. Those spectators are too far back to see muscle quality, so they base their judgments on size. This is a valuable muscle property.

2. *Definition*—Of course, you can't display muscle density unless you have a low enough level of body fat. That sounds straightforward, but there's a subtle point here. The more you become defined, the greater your potential of having muscle density. Definition is not a property of density, but rather a necessary condition to see whether density is there.

3. *Hardness*—Anything you do that makes you feel harder to the touch also increases your density. It's no surprise that the hardest-feeling bodybuilders are also the densest. You can read more about this quality in Chapter 10.

4. *Separation*—The deeper the muscle separation, the greater the difference between the high and low points of a muscle. This enhanced elevation causes superior shadowing effects when a muscle is exposed to good lighting conditions. This in turn causes the muscle to project outward more prominently and to appear more three-dimensional.

5. *Striations*—Although you can't train for striations, as they are purely genetic once you have achieved low body fat levels, you can maximize their potential by monitoring your fluid intake. Holding even the slightest bit of water under your skin can make a dramatic difference in appearance.

6. *Fullness*—To maximize all of the cosmetic qualities of a muscle, you must also maximize your ionic gradients inside and outside the muscle cells. (This technique is explained in detail in Chapter 10.) This means that enough potassium must be inside the muscle to attract water to the cell, and sodium must be removed from under the skin to prevent water retention. This creates the shrink-wrapped effect of muscle fullness, which in turn heightens the physical features of a muscle.

7. *Vascularity*—While some bodybuilders have inherited veins that are closer to the skin, everyone can make his or her vascularity more prominent. There's a correlation between volume training a muscle and enhancing vascularity. Also, an adequate supply of carbohydrates, sunlight, a dark tan, niacin, and holding your

Bob Paris won the Heavyweight and Overall Nationals and Heavyweight Championships in a single year as an amateur but has rarely tasted pro success. His classic physique has put him among the top 10 Mr. Olympia competitors twice, but he has never won a pro show.

breath all help to accentuate your vascularity. The visual effect of freaky veins can actually make a bodybuilder place higher than he should in a competition. The veins can draw attention away from areas that should be scrutinized more closely. Great vascularity puts the crowning glory on the look of muscle density.

These seven conditions of ultimate muscle density and the various degrees of muscularity will help you blueprint your progress clearly. Study the information closely, and then decide how far you want to take your physique toward ultimate muscularity.

3

OFF-SEASON NUTRITION AND TRAINING

Quickly, name one physical quality all bodybuilders would do virtually anything to achieve. Obviously, the answer would be *huge muscle mass*, and plenty of it! Even the puniest pencil-neck geek in the gym has dreams of one day looking as hugely muscled, proportionately balanced, and sliced to the bone as Lee Haney, Arnold Schwarzenegger, Richie Gaspari, and the host of bodybuilding superstars who appear regularly on the pages of *Flex* and other muscle mags. The problem for the young, undermuscled fellows is that they have little idea of how to go about achieving the incredible physiques of the stars.

Even many well-developed men and women covet the superstars' development, and a lot of them know little more than the pencil-necks about how to go about packing on quality muscle mass. They act more like a French Foreign Legion foot soldier lost in a sandstorm than a bodybuilder well based in science using the tools of his sport with élan.

If you know what you're doing with your training, diet, and mental approach—as we will teach you in this chapter—it is relatively easy to put on muscle mass. But the process is seldom, if ever, very fast. It may start out quickly when you begin bodybuilding training, but there is a state of diminishing returns. The longer you train, the more slowly you make good quality gains in added muscle mass.

Each time you reach a plateau (a point at which you are no longer improving, regardless of how hard you train), you can usually soon

43

Training legs during the off-season.

discover a more intense workout program that will help you smash past that plateau and allow you to make good gains for a few more months. But long-term bodybuilding training is studded with these progress plateaus, and it becomes more and more difficult to smash past them.

At the upper end of the sport, male bodybuilders are happy to gain three or four pounds of muscle mass per year, and women are overjoyed with one or two pounds of shapely new muscle mass. Thus, it takes time to build a great physique, the same as it takes time to construct a record high-rise building or large city.

Therefore, you have to be patient and doggedly fanatic at the same time in building up your muscle mass. When someone says to be patient, it's easy for some individuals just to give up the fight then and there. The real champions *never* abandon their quest, but rather leave no stone unturned in building superhuman muscle mass.

THE CYCLE TRAINING PRINCIPLE

Of the ten thousand athletes who competed in the 1988 Olympics, perhaps 10 percent of them fell into a physical category that could be called heavily developed—shot-putters, discus throwers, hammer throwers, some wrestlers, some boxers, and some weight lifters. The other nine thousand athletes—although highly developed and well conditioned—were mere lightweights with smallish muscles through-out their physiques.

All genetic factors aside, it doesn't take much imagination to realize that a different type of training is needed to develop a large, powerful physique than to produce a lean, mean fighting machine capable of running and/or swimming literally hours at a time. Certainly, you can imagine the difference between 260-pound shot put Gold Medalist Ulf Timmermann and 90-pound multiple swim Gold Medalist Janet Evans.

A similar situation occurs in bodybuilding, where a specific type of training and nutritional program builds up gargantuan muscle mass in men and women, while an entirely different training and nutrition cycle is undertaken to shape the muscles, peel off all superfluous stored body fat to reveal optimum muscularity, and in toto to ready a bodybuilder for competition.

Except for rare individuals—those with incredibly high basal metabolic rates (BMRs)—it is virtually impossible to build up and rip up simultaneously. Therefore, an experienced athlete alternates off-season building cycles with precontest defining phases—intelligently scheduling short transitional periods between the longer off-season and precontest modes—in an effort to first build up mass, then rip up that new muscle tissue for a competition. When the show has been completed, such athletes are right back into the off-season mass-building cycle, placing most of their emphasis on bringing up a lagging body part until it is balanced with the rest of the physique, before the athletes have initiated another peaking cycle.

This entire process has been dubbed the Cycle Training Principle, and it works wonders for most bodybuilders. This chapter concentrates on the off-season phase of cycle training, while the precontest cycle will be discussed later in this book in the context of IFBB pro bodybuilder Negrita Jayde's personal peaking program.

TRANSITIONAL CYCLES

Before we discuss off-season mass building, we should explain why transitional cycles between major phases are necessary. The human body rebels at abrupt changes, because they shock the body and often lead to minor infectious diseases. Abrupt change is particularly hard on the pituitary and hypothalamus glands, which have a direct bearing on muscle growth.

Since there is a considerable distance between off-season and precontest training and dietary cycles, knowledgeable bodybuilders schedule transitional cycles between the main building and defining cycles. This practice goes back at least to Arnold Schwarzenegger when he was first winning his series of seven IFBB Mr. Olympia titles, starting in 1970.

When most of Arnold's contemporaries couldn't wait to reach a supine position on the nearest bed or couch, he scheduled a two- or three-week period of active rest after each competition. "That's when I went to the beach regularly, went swimming, worked on my archery, rode my motorcycle, took time to snorkle and scuba dive, rode my bicycle up and down the beach, and generally stayed physically active," the Great One says. "This was also a period of high recreation for me.

"Then when I began to feel an overwhelming urge to get back into the gym, I knew my bodybuilding layoff was over and it was time to get back and pump some iron. My mind and body were simply demanding that I go back into the gym and go to work. After all, bodybuilding at that time was my business."

Any type of physical activity can be indulged in to wind down from the rigors of peaking-style training. A few suggestions include hiking, mountain biking, disco dancing, canoeing, and spending time with loved ones who might have gotten short shrift while you were preparing for your show.

The equal rigors of precontest dieting have frequently resulted in postcontest foraging sessions that would have made Sherman's march through Georgia during the Civil War look like a picnic—and do about as much damage to the human body. The 1982 Mr. Olympia victor Chris Dickerson once confessed that he endured hiccups

"It's appropriate to do forced reps on the last set or two of each movement in your mass-building routine," says seven-time Mr. Olympia Lee Haney. "But be sure to use strict form when performing forced reps in order to avoid injuries."

for 48 hours straight after a postcontest food binge! Other only slightly less amazing stories have come to light, like Rod Koontz gaining 40 pounds in one week following his Mr. USA win in 1977.

Obviously, pigging out like this *cannot* be good for the digestive system. It would be far easier on the system to gradually increase food consumption following a competition, perhaps with an occasional small serving of a treat you might have been craving over the course of your peaking diet. Within two or three weeks, you should be back on a true off-season nutrition program with no pain and no strain on your system.

"Research shows that optimum muscle hypertrophy occurs when you do four to six reps with a weight which extends you close to your physical limit," notes Rich Gaspari, three times runner-up in the Mr. Olympia competition.

After two or three weeks out of the gym following a competition—much of that time spent attempting to determine the weak areas of your physique that might have caused you to place lower than you'd expected—you will want to get back into the Hall of Iron and start building up new muscle mass. But again, you should take it easy, or you'll suffer muscle soreness and shock your central nervous system.

With each routine you plan to follow during your off-season building phase, start back at only about 50 percent intensity, doing only half of the total sets you might have originally scheduled. Then with each succeeding workout—during a period that should take three or four weeks to complete—you should be up to your full-intensity off-season program, which you might follow for six months to a year before deciding to peak for another bodybuilding championship.

The point at which champion bodybuilders begin to specifically diet and train for a show varies from about 16 weeks out from the competition down to 6 weeks. Regardless of the length of peaking cycle, you should include training and nutrition transitional cycles between off-season and precontest phases.

Generally speaking, the transitional cycles from off-season to precontest phases will be somewhat longer (perhaps 50 percent longer) than those between precontest and off-season. Nutritionally, the occasional junk food treats are eliminated first, then high-fat foods, sugars, oils, baked goods, and so forth, until you begin to zero in on your exact precontest diet—low-cal, low-carb, or whatever.

In terms of training, you gradually switch over from heavy, low-rep workouts primarily featuring basic exercises to lighter sessions, higher reps, shorter rest intervals between sets, and a much higher percentage of isolation exercises than basic movements. There is also a gradual switch from a minimum level of aerobic training in the off-season to considerable aerobics when in a peaking mode.

Follow these cycles from one competition to another, and your body will get into progressively better shape with less strain than would be the case if you jumped abruptly from off-season to precontest cycles and back again to an off-season phase. *And* you'll get into much better shape in the long run if you pay attention to your transitional cycles between major preparatory and competitive phases.

MASS-BUILDING TRAINING

According to hypermassive Mike Quinn (who has been a Mr. Olympia finalist several times and as an amateur won the Heavyweight and Overall U.S. Championships), "When adding mass to your frame, most of your program should be centered around basic exercises on which you can use big weights for relatively low repetitions. Basic exercises work the larger muscle groups of the body synergistically with other large and/or small body parts. Good examples of basic exercises are bench presses, squats, bent-over barbell rows, standing barbell presses, and machine or barbell shoulder shrugs." A comprehensive list of the best basic movements for each muscle group appears in Table 3-1.

TABLE 3–1 THE BEST BASIC EXERCISES FOR EACH BODY PART

Body Part	Exercises
Legs	Squats (full, partial), leg presses (angled, seated, vertical), stiff-legged deadlifts, Russian hyperextensions
Back	Barbell/dumbbell shrugs, barbell bent-over rows, T-bar rows, seated pulley rows, various types of chins, various types of lat machine pull-downs, Nautilus pull-overs, deadlifts
Chest	Barbell/dumbbell/machine bench presses, incline presses, decline presses, parallel bar dips
Shoulders	Barbell/dumbbell/machine overhead presses, cable/barbell upright rows
Triceps	Close-grip bench presses, parallel bar dips (torso held erect), all types of overhead and bench presses
Biceps	Standing barbell curls, barbell preacher curls, all types of rowing, chinning, and pull-down movements
Forearms	Barbell reverse curls, barbell wrist curls, standing behind-back barbell wrist curls
Calves	Seated calf raises, standing calf raises, donkey calf raises, calf presses (on leg press machine)
Abdominals	Hanging leg raises, incline sit-ups

According to Rich Gaspari (IFBB World Pro Grand Prix Champion), "It's best to perform relatively low repetitions when attempting to add muscle mass. Research shows that optimum muscle hypertrophy occurs when you do four to six reps with a weight which extends you close to your physical limit. However, no bodybuilder in his right mind would jump right up to a heavy set of four to six reps without a warm-up, due to the greatly enhanced injury potential brought on by such circumstances.

"My solution to using heavy weights for low reps is to gradually warm up for them using a half-pyramid system in which the weight is increased and reps decreased each succeeding set. If you follow this pyramid system on all heavy basic exercises, you should never have a problem with the usual training injuries." An example of Rich Gaspari's weight-rep pyramid for a series of sets of squats appears in Table 3-2 on page 53.

"It's appropriate to do forced reps on the last set or two of each movement in your mass-building routine," instructs Lee Haney (seven times Mr. Olympia). "But be sure to use strict form when performing forced reps, in order to avoid injuries. It's possible to use

"There's a direct relationship between the amount of weight you use for reps in an exercise and the size of the muscles which move that weight," notes IFBB pro Vince Comerford. "You have to lift big to look big."

cheating reps to extend a set past failure, as well, but there's often too much risk of injury when you abandon good biomechanics while using heavy poundages."

A suggested mass-building routine, contributed by Berry de Mey (IFBB World Games Champion and a third-place finisher in Mr. Olympia), appears in Table 3-3 on page 53.

It would be nearly impossible to find a woman who epitomizes the sliced appearance better than Diana Dennis, the Earth Mother of our sport. Involved since the early 1980s, she has won National Amateur, Pro World, and numerous Pro-Am Mixed Pairs titles. She may still be competing in the year 2000.

TABLE 3–2 RICH GASPARI'S WEIGHT-REP PYRAMID

Set Number	Weight (lbs.)[a]	Reps
1	135	15
2	165	12
3	185	10
4	205	8
5	225	6
6	245	5
7	265	4
8	165	15–20[b]

[a]Weights are chosen arbitrarily, for the sake of illustration.
[b]Set number 8 is a pump set in which the weight is greatly reduced and a maximum number of reps are performed with it just for a finishing pump.

TABLE 3–3 SUGGESTED MASS-BUILDING ROUTINE

Monday–Thursday

Exercise	Sets	Reps
Hanging leg raises	2–3	10–15
Leg extensions (warm-up)	2–3	10–15
Squats	7	15–5*
Stiff-legged deadlifts	5	12–8*
Seated pulley rows	7	12–5*
Barbell shugs	5	15–8*
Standing barbell curls	5	12–5*
Seated calf raises	5	15–8*

Tuesday–Friday

Exercise	Sets	Reps
Incline sit-ups	2–3	20–25
Barbell incline presses	7	12–5*
Parallel bar dips	5	12–6*
Seated machine overhead presses	5	10–5*
Barbell upright rows	5	12–6*
Close-grip bench presses	5	10–5*
Barbell wrist curls	5	15–8*
Standing calf raises	5	15–8*

*Pyramid all exercises marked with an asterisk, increasing the weight and decreasing the poundage with each succeeding set.

RECOVERY FACTORS

"The most fundamental and important aspect of gaining muscle mass is complete understanding of the recovery cycle," says Lee Haney. "It should be noted that very few young bodybuilders give recovery a moment's thought, thus failing to make good gains simply because they neglect between-workouts rest and recuperation.

"It's axiomatic that muscles increase in mass and power *following* a workout, during the period when the body is allowed to rest. Muscles may be temporarily pumped up during a training session, but growth doesn't occur during the course of a workout. Rather, muscle growth takes place during the two- to four-day break between workouts for a particular body part.

"Overtraining is the biggest enemy a young bodybuilder can face, because it negates his efforts in the gym. Muscle growth will not and cannot occur when an athlete is in an overtrained state. In extreme cases of overtraining, a bodybuilder can actually lose muscle mass, tone, and strength. Finally, in all cases of overtraining, a bodybuilder is more prone to injury and open to infectious diseases.

"Overtraining occurs as a result of two factors: overly frequent training sessions and excessively long workouts. For most bodybuilders, I suggest a four-day split routine—twice per week for each muscle group—when in a mass-building phase. That's the type of program I personally followed until the last three months before I won the heavyweight and overall NPC National Championships in New York City and the heavyweight World Championship in Brugge, Belgium, in 1982. For the very advanced bodybuilder, good gains in muscle mass as a result of optimum recovery can occur when following a three-on/two-off split routine.

"In both of the foregoing splits, emphasis is placed on taking very few workouts each week. Few bodybuilders can make any gains in mass when training six days per week. Long experience—both personally and through the young men I coach—has demonstrated conclusively that a four-day-per-week split yields the optimum number of weekly workouts when shooting for mass.

"Yet another way to avoid the overtraining syndrome calls for keeping under control the total number of sets performed for each muscle group in a workout. I've always done significantly fewer total sets per body part than most comparable bodybuilders, a primary reason why I have been so successful in building muscle mass beyond the ordinary. I perform no more than about 15 total sets (after warm-ups) for large muscle groups and fewer than 10 for smaller ones when in a mass-building cycle. This contrasts dramatically with the 20 to 30 sets per body part many top men do.

"If *I* do 10 to 15 total sets per muscle group, then a relatively less experienced bodybuilder should perform even fewer if he wishes to avoid the overtraining syndrome. For most bodybuilders I recommend 10 to 12 total sets for large and more complex muscle groups such as legs, back, chest, and shoulders, and six to eight for smaller and less complex body parts. Beginners should do even fewer sets—generally speaking no more than three to five sets per muscle group.

A relative newcomer to the sport, Germany's Anja Langer has rocketed from obscurity to superstardom in record time. At 20 she was European Champion, and at 22 she placed second in Ms. Olympia. Her dorsal muscularity is unforgettable!

The Flying Dutchman, Berry de Mey, won the European Championships at the tender age of 19 and has been shooting toward the top ever since. His best professional placing has been third in Mr. Olympia.

"There are exceptions to the preceding parameters. Perhaps 5 percent or 10 percent of all bodybuilders would fall into the category called 'hard-gainer.' They find it easy to overtrain, yet difficult to gain mass. Hard-gainers should *never* work out more than four days per week, while reducing the recommended number of sets for each muscle group by about 25 percent.

"Anyone can pack on muscle mass if he pays strict attention to recovery factors. Interestingly, no one ever gains muscle weight as quickly as he would like. Simply put, it's a slow process, slow enough that most advanced and contest-level bodybuilders are overjoyed to make any gains at all!"

REST AND SLEEP

"Sleep and rest are essential elements of between-workouts recuperation and recovery," adds Berry de Mey. "Recovery won't take place unless you obtain sufficient rest and sleep each day.

"By rest, I mean maintaining a low-energy-loss approach to each day. Avoid doing much aerobic training when in a weight-gaining phase, and try to keep emotional energy leaks to a minimum. Stay calm and collected all day, train hard, and then get a good night's sleep.

"The amount of sleep time each night is highly individualized, varying from 6 hours in some cases to as many as 12 per night. Whatever the length, the object is to sleep long enough each night to feel completely rested the following day. You can arrive at an appropriate amount of sleep for yourself through experimentation. Once you have discovered the correct amount of sleep for your individual mind and body, you should stick to it. If you don't sleep soundly or long enough one night, make it up the next night.

"Also, most of the best bodybuilders in the world take naps during the day to recharge their energy batteries. Twenty to thirty minutes of sleep during the afternoon works wonders in encouraging optimum training sessions."

RECOVERY FOR OLDER BODYBUILDERS

In general, between-workouts recovery tends to slow down with age. Andreas Cahling (IFBB Pro Mr. International) and I (Bill) recently hit upon a type of low-frequency training program that allowed a maximum amount of recovery time (seven days) between workouts for each body part. The program worked sensationally well for both of us, with Andreas placing fourth in his pro comeback at the 1990 Pro Gold's Classic after six years out of competition, and me totally reshaping my physique.

The entire idea was based upon the fact that Andreas was 37 and

I was 44 years of age when we began the experimental program. The program itself consisted of six training days per week but only one workout per body part each week. Here's the split routine that we were using for the year leading up to Andreas reentering pro competition:

Monday	Back
Tuesday	Shoulders, abs
Wednesday	Legs, calves
Thursday	Upper arms, forearms
Friday	Chest
Saturday	Lower back, glutes, hamstrings
Sunday	Rest

"We highly recommend this type of program for any bodybuilder over the age of 35, as well as for anyone who might be a hard-gainer, regardless of age," explains Cahling. "By training a muscle group once per week, we were able to do quite a large number of sets for it and still be completely recovered a week later. For example, our back routine was a minimum of 40 total sets, about 20 of those sets chins. And my back width and overall development have never been better!

"The only other key Bill and I found important was to avoid completely going to glycogen depletion in our training sessions, because that invariably resulted in a subpar training session the following day. Going to about 80 percent of depletion was just sufficient to allow us to recover our energy supplies prior to the next day's workout. That way we could go all out every time we went into the gym."

MASS-BUILDING NUTRITION

"There's no question about it—protein is essential if you intend to increase muscle mass," says this book's cover man Gary Strydom (winner of many IFBB World Pro Grand Prix titles, the overall National Championship, and the heavyweight U.S. Championship as an amateur). "Your object when attempting to gain muscular body weight, then, should be to ingest sufficient amounts of high-quality protein, along with enough carbohydrates to fuel heavy workouts.

"Animal-source proteins—meat, fish, poultry, milk, eggs—are the best for most bodybuilders. Several vegetarian bodybuilders have become high-level competitors, although even they have relied heavily on eggs and milk products for protein. To a significant extent, your diet should also include supplemental sources of protein in the form of concentrated protein powders and both free-form and branched-chain amino acids."

Adds Robby Robinson (winner of the first two Night of the Champions shows, plus many other IFBB pro events), "I personally don't consume much red meat during the off-season or precontest

Possessor of one of the mightiest sets of arms in history, Robby Robinson has been an active pro bodybuilder since 1977. He won the first two Night of the Champions events and a host of other IFBB pro titles. Huge, lean, and hard as marble, Robby's every lump and bump spells s-l-i-c-e-d.

Pro World Champ Ron Love (here spotted by Powerhouse Gym impresario Will Dabish) forces out a few extra reps of incline presses for his upper pecs and anterior deltoids. Most bodybuilders benefit from using forced reps to push a muscle past its normal failure point and thus induce greater hypertrophy.

phases—perhaps only once or twice per month in the off-season. I find red meats high in fat and too difficult to digest. I also don't rely too heavily on milk products, although many other bodybuilders who can tolerate milk make it a staple in their mass-building diet. My chief sources of protein are chicken, turkey, fish, egg whites, and amino acids.

"Classic weight-gaining nutritional practice always involves eating more than three meals per day, usually six to eight being the norm. The reason is simple: It's possible to force a lot more amino acids— the end product of protein digestion—into your bloodstream when eating more frequently. The human digestive system is capable of processing between 20 and 25 grams of protein from any given meal, so it's obvious that six meals per day will allow you to digest twice as much protein as three meals.

"Each of your six to eight meals should be spaced about two hours apart and include animal-source protein—at least 20 grams of it per meal—as well as sufficient carbohydrates to blast through every workout. My own preference is starchy complex carbs from potatoes, rice, grains, yams, and pasta, because they yield a more sustained type of energy flow. Simple sugars from fruit and any type of junk food tend to give everyone an energy peak, followed immediately by a low-energy valley, something that is not conducive to successful bodybuilding.

"As a final note on off-season eating, be sure to supplement your diet each meal with digestive enzymes, which you can purchase in any health food store. Alternatively, you can eat high-enzyme foods each meal, such as papayas, pineapple, and kiwis, with your protein and complex carbs. The enzymes you consume will digest and make assimilable a greater amount of protein than is possible under normal circumstances."

Robby contributed the weight-gain meal plan listed in Table 3-4.

TABLE 3–4 ROBBY ROBINSON'S SUGGESTED OFF-SEASON MEAL PLANS

Meal 1	Eggs (throw out half of the yolks), oatmeal with nonfat milk, one kiwi, aminos, vitamin-mineral supplements
Meal 2	Protein drink: 1–2 heaping tablespoons of milk and egg protein powder, fruit to taste (peaches, berries, etc.), all blended to a smooth consistency; add shaved ice if you like it particularly cold
Meal 3	Broiled fish, baked potato, green salad, slice of pineapple, iced tea, vitamin-mineral supplements
Meal 4	Tuna salad, cup of pasta, slice of papaya, ice water
Meal 5	Broiled chicken (no skin), rice, green vegetable, slice of pineapple, herbal tea, vitamin-mineral supplements
Meal 6	Omelet (reduced yolks in eggs, with cheese, onions, green peppers, etc.), baked potato, one kiwi, ice water

"Food supplements are vitally important when attempting to gain muscle mass in the off-season," notes Gary Strydom. "Because of my high metabolism, I have experienced difficulty in gaining mass over the years. Now I routinely consume 7,000 calories per day in the off-season, and I firmly believe that heavy use of supplements has helped me greatly in packing on the mass.

"Obviously, free-form amino acids and branched-chain aminos are essential. I will go through bottle after bottle of these supplements both in the off-season and prior to a show. They are relatively expensive, but so is a Porsche, and my philosophy is to always rely on the best supplements available. Amino acid capsules are almost directly assimilated into muscle tissue, requiring little or no digestion. They prevent unnecessary burden on the digestive system.

"I'm also careful to consume a couple of multipacks of vitamins

"When adding mass to your frame, most of your program should be centered around basic exercises on which you can use big weights for relatively low reps," says Mike Quinn, a top IFBB pro and winner of the overall U.S. Championships.

and minerals per day, always with meals. They provide nutritional insurance against any dietary deficiencies that might be holding me back from awesome gains in muscle mass. And I take additional amounts of the water-soluble vitamins—B-complex and C—which can't be stored in the body like oil-soluble vitamins. The water-solubles must therefore be ingested frequently throughout the day.

"B-complex vitamins are fundamental to weight gain, because several of them stimulate the appetite and help to increase muscle mass following a hard workout. I don't think it would be excessive to take one or two high-potency B-complex vitamin capsules every couple of hours throughout the day when in a mass-building cycle. By 'high-potency,' I mean 100 milligrams or more of each individual B vitamin in each capsule."

If you look ahead to Chapter 5, you will find a complete discussion of ergogenic agents, which you should also include as part of your diet. Some of these ergogens will actually mimic the effects of anabolic steroids and other so-called bodybuilding drugs. Still others will increase your training energy and result in a much faster than normal recovery between workouts, which can only result in faster muscle building. The ergogenics chapter is rather long and may require more than one reading, but you'll find plenty of wisdom—to say nothing of ergogenic aids—which will boost your progress as a natural bodybuilder much faster than you might have ever thought would be possible!

Proper nutrition gives me a healthy-looking and vibrant presence.

4

NUTRITION AND THE IMMUNE SYSTEM

Missed workouts can sabotage any bodybuilder's progress in developing muscle mass. You can miss workouts due to injury or illness. Careful attention to preworkout warm-ups and strict exercise form will keep you relatively injury free. And attention to maintaining a healthy immune system—through a program that revolves around careful attention to proper nutritional practices—will keep you free from infectious illnesses that would cause you to miss regularly scheduled gym sessions.

What *is* your body's immune system, and how does it work? For a moment, imagine your body as a country. To maintain and protect your country's working order, you'd have a national defense system, a local and regional police force, an army, a navy, elite fighting divisions, secret agents, and customs officials. That's also how the immune system operates.

Your body's immune system is a highly organized network of microscopic armies and tiny troopers that patrol your body, protect it from foreign invaders, and control domestic disputes should the need arise. Incidentally, the need arises every day.

Regardless of where we live, our environment is swarming with bacteria, viruses, and microbes that are geared up to penetrate our natural lines of defense. They float in the water and even live in the knurls of an Olympic bar. Remember that shower you took today? By the time you put on your clothes, millions of new bacteria were born on the surface of your skin. Now they're lurking around in even greater numbers, trying to get in.

Ready to combat these invading bacteria, or antigens, are white blood cells called leukocytes. They form the major part of the body's protective mechanism against invasion by foreign microbes. However, within the motley crew of potential invaders exist certain bacteria that are highly sophisticated. These antigens have developed unique chemical defenses that render the general army of leukocytes completely useless. To complicate the war even further, viruses are also resistant to any defense maneuvers the leukocytes may launch.

Enter the lymphocytes. These are your defense system "specialists." Lymphocytes break down into two types: T and B cells. T cells have been chemically conditioned by the thymus gland to identify and destroy a specific antigen invader. T cells subdivide into suppressor and helper cells, which communicate closely to switch immune reactions on or off, as the situation demands. B cells are produced in the marrow of our bones, and it's their duty to produce antibodies, like neutrophils and macrophages.

Neutrophils are streamlined cells that like to move exceptionally fast and hurl themselves at invading bacteria, sort of like kamikaze pilots. The larger and slower macrophages are the "neat freaks" of the immune system. They cruise to "war zones" to clean up various debris, as well as bind bacteria with their long tentacles to make them susceptible to attack by immune cells.

As a rule, every lymphocyte packs a deadly poison that has been deliberately engineered to eliminate specific invaders. There are about a trillion of these lymphocytes in your body, protecting you 24 hours a day. A reassuring thought for sure. However, just when you thought those lymphocytes had been staying right on top of all of the latest developments in high-tech bacteria weaponry or vicious viruses, the plot twists.

Sure, lymphocytes are uncanny at recognizing familiar invaders, but when a strain of unfamiliar invaders enters your body, they'll go unnoticed. This means a new virus can go right ahead and multiply like wildfire, leaving you as sick as a dog. It happens for an obvious reason. To develop specific immunities against every antigen in existence, you'd have to live to be over 2,000 years old. Even Albert Beckles—who is an active pro bodybuilder at age 60—still has a long way to go to reach that mark.

Then there's the process called antigenic drift. This refers to the structural mutations that microbes constantly undergo during the course of their development. The wicked cold you had last winter could return to flatten you again if the culprit virus underwent antigenic drift. The slightest alteration in the original structure of the antigen will completely baffle the lymphocytes. In the tradition of a true military soldier, the lymphocyte simply refuses to deviate from its initial course of action. As you can see, there's a downside to

Now over 40 years old and still going strong as an IFBB pro, Ron Love is a former Detroit police officer. An on-the-job gunshot wound led him into the weight room, and the rest is history.

specialization. Of course, these new breeds of invaders don't trash you indefinitely. All a T cell needs to do is contact the surface of an antigen, and then it can produce a specific poison to combat it. Creating that poison takes a little time, and it's usually at the expense of your health. The question is, as a bodybuilder, how much time do you have to waste?

By way of a simple example, consider how a cold or flu takes out twice the number of days you might have thought. We call it *zero growth times two*. Studies show that muscle growth does not occur continuously, but rather in spurts of relatively brief duration. Close examination of these growth spurts reveals that, for them to occur, many ideal conditions have to exist simultaneously. These conditions include a high calorie intake, a wide variety of nutrients, ideal work-outs, great rest periods, a peaceful state of mind, and so forth. Taken together, they form a synergistic effect—that is, one that appears greater than the sum of its parts. A greatly accelerated rate of muscle growth is the result of such a union of variables.

Now, imagine yourself to be right in the middle of these "ideal

"Until recently I hadn't given much thought to my immune system and keeping it in tune," confessed two-time Mr. Olympia runner-up Lee Labrada. "But it just stands to reason that eating right will keep the immune system in balance, you won't get ill as often, and you'll make better progress as a result."

growth" curves, and then all of a sudden, *crash!* You get sick. Experts say it'll take 7 to 12 days to get over it. During that time, your muscle growth will completely stop, and your strength levels will drop slightly. However, once you get better (and let's say it takes 12 days to do so), you can't expect to jump back instantly to that same position on the growth curve. No sirree. Your strength needs to kick back in, and you'll need a few days of good food and rest. Before you know it, 12 more days will have passed.

It typically takes double the amount of your sick days to get back into that serious mode again. Thus, any flu or cold will create a *zero growth times two* situation. That is, whatever the duration you were ill and experienced zero muscle growth, you'll need at least that same length of time to really cook again. In this particular case, it would be zero growth of 12 days times 2, equaling 24 total days of zero growth.

Studies indicate that the average person gets four colds a year. That statistic is too high for health-conscious bodybuilders, because they're certainly not average people. Three is probably a more accurate figure. Even at three colds per year, if we use the previous figure of 24 days of zero growth and multiply it by 3 to get a yearly figure, the result of 72 days is staggering. Almost 2½ months each year can potentially be spent in bodybuilding limbo.

Is something obvious starting to sink in? Are you getting the idea that your immune system is a valuable key to uninterrupted muscle growth as well as greater net gains? We knew we'd appeal to your powers of deductive reasoning.

Through an extensive sweep of pertinent literature, we've identified five important areas that directly or indirectly maximize the effectiveness of the immune system. They are growth hormone (GH) releasers, optimal duration training, nutrition, enzymes, and mind power. We can say, having monitored these areas for immune system enhancement, you just don't get sick if you pay strict attention to all five.

GH RELEASERS

Have you ever watched kids closely? They run at high speeds all over the place, grow at alarming rates, and overflow with a special vitality. They also have loads of growth hormone coursing through their little veins. No wonder they giggle all the time.

Growth hormone is the Hollywood of hormones. It's full of star-studded roles that benefit the body in many ways. Stored in the pituitary gland, this polypeptide of 191 amino acids helps to convert fat into energy, accelerates wound healing, improves protein synthesis, strengthens ligaments and tendons, and improves resistance to disease. Bingo, that's our number!

Growth hormone releasers are substances that stimulate the production of GH. Keep in mind, even though your GH release may elevate by the smallest of fractions, when you're dealing with the microscopic world, "small" *can* make a world of difference. To help make that big difference, we recommend taking the following combo before bed: two grams of L-arginine pyroglutamate and two grams of L-lysine. Keep in mind that high levels of serum fat and blood sugar greatly reduce the production of endogenous growth hormone. So take a pass on late-night burgers and ice cream.

OPTIMAL DURATION TRAINING

Throughout our travels across the bodybuilding world, we've discovered that overtraining seems to be the norm at most gyms. We mean it's rampant. Well, brothers and sisters, someone has to be blunt with you: marathon training sessions are for marathon runners, not bodybuilders!

It's a known fact that muscle stimulation is best achieved through a workout that is high in intensity and brief in duration. So, if you desire new muscle growth, train more intensely, not longer. When you overtrain, you tax your nervous system, weaken your immune system, and diminish your chances for muscle growth.

The optimal length of a training session is between 50 and 75 minutes. About the only thing long workouts are good for is meeting people in the gym. Gee, that's great, because if any of them have colds, you'll certainly be getting one. Overtraining will assure you of that. So remember, if you can't totally fry a muscle group within 50 to 75 minutes, you're not training with sufficient intensity.

NUTRITION

Of the nutrients available for human consumption, five stand out as being particularly important to the immune system. They are vitamins A, C, and E and the minerals zinc and selenium. An undersupply of these nutrients can lead to atrophy of the thymus gland (regulator of the immune system's activities) and to reduced bacteria-killing activity by T and B cells.

Vitamin A helps to strengthen and protect mucous membranes against invading bacteria, a little-known fact among vitamin buffs. If you live in an environment that has serious levels of air pollution, you will be more vulnerable to colds than someone in Montana.

Vitamin C is the Arnold Schwarzenegger of the vitamin kingdom. It would take pages to list all the amazing things it does. Trust us when we say this: vitamin C is absolutely crucial for enchancing your immune system!

"The less often you are ill, the better your overall rate of progress, all other factors being equal," says Rich Gaspari, who won an amateur World Championship at age 20. "The right diet will keep your immune system in tune, and you'll avoid needless time on the sick list."

Once a commercial artist, Janet Tech has been a full-time pro bodybuilder since winning her lightweight class at both the Nationals and the World Championships. She was in the top five of her class at the Nationals an incredible five times before finally winning.

Mischievous molecules called "free radicals" can run wild in your body and end up causing cancer. Vitamin E helps to neutralize these potentially serious troublemakers and render them harmless, among a lot of other good things.

Selenium works closely with vitamin E, and together they increase the fighting ability of the white blood cells. Zinc plays an important role in the improvement of T cell activity.

Suggested dosages for these five vital food elements are:

Vitamin A	20,000 IU per day
Vitamin C	3–7 grams per day
Vitamin E	100 IU per day
Selenium	trace amount
Zinc	50 milligrams

Additionally, the following supplements also have particular merit in terms of the immune system: evening primrose oil, coenzyme Q10, royal bee jelly and ginseng (marketed in health food stores in a combination format), raw honey, and blackstrap molasses.

ENZYMES

Basically, a human being is an ingenious assembly of portable plumbing. A wide variety of subtances passes through our bodies every day. The key is how well we break down and utilize our foods. In today's enzymeless, fast-food society, it's often not very well. What has this to do with our immune systems? Everything. The better we absorb food, the more nutrients our bodies receive. Anything that increases the effectiveness of nutrition will immediately strengthen our biological constitutions. That effectiveness can be made possible by enzymes.

The easiest way to increase your enzymatic intake is to consume foods in their raw state. This means including more raw fruits, vegetables, milk, honey, and nuts in your eating regimen. Heat destroys enzymes, as do pasteurization, canning, and processing.

Make a deliberate attempt to include kiwis, pineapples, mangoes, and papayas on a daily basis. They're loaded with valuable enzymes and should especially be eaten when you consume meat. When you plan to dine out, bring digestive enzyme tablets along with you. Often, restaurant food sits around a while and contains zero enzymes. Without them, that meal will sit in your stomach like an old rubber tire.

MIND POWER

High-stressed and emotionally depressed people tend to get sick a lot. That's because the quality of your thoughts can greatly determine your biochemical status. For example, the body sometimes produces more cortisol than normal. Extra cortisol will lower the efficiency of the thymus gland and thereby lower its lymphocyte output. When that happens, you can get sick very easily.

The solution is to rewire your thoughts into other directions. Whatever happens to be depressing or stressing you, flee from that cause both mentally and physically. Call up your friends, get out of the house, acquire new interests, and circulate in different circles. Set up new goals and aspirations for yourself, and you'll soon see there's *always* light at the end of the tunnel. Your immune system will thank you greatly for it.

CONCLUSION

That's your battle plan. Follow it, and you'll win the war against foreign invaders and spend a lot more time in positive muscle growth. Neglect it, and you'll become a sitting duck to the swarms of evil armies that want to turn your body into a disease-ridden cesspool of biological chaos, while you watch your muscles shrink to nothing.

Well, soldier, what's your decision?

"I like the movement toward testing pros for drug usage at contest time," says Mr. America Tony Pearson. "Not being forced to use drugs makes me a more intelligent bodybuilder, one who uses ergogenic aids to the max."

5

ERGOGENICS

Unless you've had your head buried in the sand in recent years, you know that the biggest issue in bodybuilding is drug usage. Men have been using anabolic steroids and androgenic drugs to increase muscle mass and quality since the middle 1950s.

The drug epidemic didn't stop at anabolic and androgenic usage alone, however. A highly lucrative black market for the sale of the gamut of bodybuilding drugs sprang up during the early 1980s and ground to a halt seven or eight years later only when the government stepped in to quash drug-selling rings. The situation had become so pervasive that preteenaged boys had begun to use anabolic agents merely to look good for the girls in their school classes. It's little wonder that many states enacted laws making possession and sale of anabolics a felony.

In addition to steroids and androgens, bodybuilders were taking narcotic pain medication to mask training injuries so they could continue to pump iron for upcoming shows. They were taking a wide variety of thyroid stimulants in order to more easily reduce body fat levels for competition, and amphetamines were self-administered both to dull the appetite and to blast through a crucial training session when bodybuilders were dead on their feet from the rigors of precontest dieting. To induce sleep after using amphetamines, barbiturates entered the picture; special European drugs were injected to thin out and tighten up the skin; estrogen blockers were used by women to maximize the benefit of anabolic use and by men to prevent unsightly gynecomastia; and there was even a drug to help bodybuilders tan more quickly and to a greater degree. As long as the foregoing list is, we have probably left a drug or two off of it!

The drug explosion was so out of control that pharmaceuticals from Europe and other parts of the world were illegally imported to take up the slack when North American sources couldn't produce enough of the drugs. Then, as more and more individuals got hooked on bodybuilding drugs, clandestine labs sprang up in Mexico and throughout the United States to produce bootleg drugs, with little or no attention to sanitation as the brews were cooking. It's little wonder that many athletes suffered both localized and systemic infections after injecting themselves with tainted drugs.

At the peak of black market drug production and sales, the United States government estimated the steroid market to be turning over $30 million per year. And that figure is probably much too low. Enough money was available from drug sales to attract the Mob, as well as many violent and unscrupulous individuals whose only motive was to make a fortune as quickly as possible.

During the late 1980s, the FBI began investigating steroid wholesalers, arrested the principal players in the game, and effectively shut down the supply of drugs to gym pushers. After approximately 100 arrests, the supply of black market bodybuilding drugs effectively dried up.

Concurrently, the U.S. Food and Drug administration moved to discipline physicians who had become steroid prescription mills, and punished unscrupulous pharmacists who were literally selling anabolic and androgenic drugs without the required prescriptions. Several physicians and pharmacists lost their licenses to practice, and many others were warned that they would lose *their* licenses if they ever wrote prescriptions or supplied drugs to people who didn't clinically require the drugs in question.

Combined with tough new state legislation fighting steroid traffic, the FBI and FDA actions put a stopper in the bottle that was supplying drugs to literally anyone who could pay for them. Now it is very difficult for even a high-level pro bodybuilder to locate and purchase sufficient drugs to allow him or her to achieve the type of condition once achieved by purchasing sports drugs in every gym. Sometimes the only way such a person obtains drugs now is to have a "friend" smuggle small quantities from Europe into North America in luggage. Customs officials are so hip to this operation, however, that anyone with a 16-inch upper arm is thoroughly searched; that "friend" would have to be a complete pencil-neck.

What all of this means is that bodybuilders are literally being forced to train and compete naturally, without the use of any drugs that might show up on a test at contest time. And without the use of drugs, most bodybuilders have turned to using a variety of food

Typical of the new breed of pro bodybuilder, Troy Zuccolotto won the overall Nationals on his third try to qualify as a pro. He uses every possible ergogen to keep a leg up on his competition.

elements that have anabolic powers, help an athlete train harder and longer, aid in between-workouts recovery, help thin out the skin, and cause the release of human growth hormone into the system, all legally and completely within the rules. These food elements are called ergogenic aids.

Like thousands of other English words, *ergogenesis* comes from Latin root words. "Ergo" means "to work." And "genesis" refers to a type of beginning (perhaps you will remember that the Old Testament of the Bible begins with the book of Genesis). In essence, then, ergogenesis means something that starts work. In our usage, ergogenic aids are those food elements and nutritional practices which produce work, or muscle growth.

This chapter will discuss approximately 20 ergogenic aids in common use by bodybuilders. Some of them are valuable additions to a bodybuilder's dietary program, while others are virtually worthless. Whenever possible, we will point out whether a particular ergogenic substance is good or bad for bodybuilders or, more precisely, whether or not you should spend your hard-earned bucks on it.

In general, you will probably find that combinations of various ergogens will work best for you in building new muscle mass. Noted power lifting and bodybuilding author Dr. Fred Hatfield, Ph.D., has written an excellent book, *Ergogenesis* (Canoga Park, CA: Fitness Systems, Inc., 1985), and he discusses the question in this manner: "The best approach to the use of ergogenic aids seems to be a combinational one. Apparently, there is no single technique or elixir capable of catapulting an athlete from the rank-and-file into super-stardom. But by carefully selecting from among those substances and techniques available, an athlete can achieve significant performance improvement." And a bodybuilder can make significant improvements in his physique.

Dr. Hatfield continues by noting, "Sometimes the performance differences with ergogens will be less, sometimes more . . . sometimes the differences are so small that research scientists overlook them because of their *statistical* insignificance. But they're horribly wrong for doing so! Any increase—however slight—is hard-won by athletes, and is in their eyes highly significant."

Indeed, so many nutritional variables confront a bodybuilder that a slight improvement in only a few of them will visibly improve a bodybuilder's physique. Think of molehills, not mountains, because enough molehills stacked up will eventually form a very high mountain!

Our bodybuilding philosophy is to leave no stone unturned in nutrition, training, or mental approach. You'll become a great bodybuilder only if you explore every possible avenue toward success, patiently marking your map where you've found each shortcut, and adding up all of the shortcuts until they resemble a superhighway to success.

FRAC

Ferulic acid (FRAC) shows considerable promise as a natural anabolic agent. The FRAC revolution began with an article in *Flex* magazine by Luke R. Bucci, Ph.D., entitled "A Natural Magic Bullet?" (April 1989 issue). Dr. Bucci outlined research performed at the Biotics Research Corporation in Texas, some of it performed on the Houston Gamblers of the now defunct World Football League. His arguments were so persuasive that FRAC was soon available on the shelves of most health food stores, either in individual tablets or capsules or as a component of various weight-gain drink formulas.

According to Dr. Bucci, "In the late 1970s, scientists at Biotics Research Corporation were experimenting with nutritional animal growth factors for potential use in poultry and cattle. They found that a substance named gamma oryzanol accelerated without harm the growth of young animals. These findings were replicated in chickens, and recognizing a demand by weightlifters for safe alternatives to anabolic steroids, a new nutritional supplement was born. Preliminary reports from athletes showed that gamma oryzanol helped increase strength and muscle mass while reducing body fat. For several years, gamma oryzanol was sold only to health care professionals. Lately, it has been marketed to the public."

Dr. Bucci continued:

Gamma oryzanol is a molecule with two separate parts. One half is ferulic acid, the other is a sterol, meaning gamma oryzanol is a modified sterol, or a ferulate ester of triterpenyl alcohol. . . .

When taken orally, absorption of gamma oryzanol is low (less than 10%) since it has a fat-soluble sterol. Other plant sterols are also poorly absorbed (less than 6%) . . .

FRAC was developed from rice bran and contains water-soluble, free transferulic acid in addition to free sterols. Thus the inefficiency of ferulic acid delivery from gamma oryzanol is bypassed, and a defined source of natural, free ferulic acid is produced. . . .

Free ferulic acid is a potent antioxident similar to vitamin E and has anticarcinogenic effects stronger than vitamins E and C as shown in animal studies. Of more concern to athletes is the structure. By coincidence, ferulic acid closely resembles the catecholamine and brain neurotransmitter norepinephrine.

From animal studies, it is now known that giving gamma oryzanol or ferulic acid can slightly increase levels of norepinephrine in neurons of the autonomic nervous system that just happen to control bodily responses to stress, especially anabolic hormone synthesis and release. Experimentally, slight increases of norepinephrine allow brain cells, which control growth hormone and endorphin synthesis, to maintain their function a little longer. This means that pituitary glands would have more growth hormone and endorphins than normal.

These hormones are released by intense exercise to help in repair and recovery of muscle tissue. If more growth hormone and endorphins are available at the right time and the right place (after exercise and during deep sleep), then more results from these hormones should occur. These hormones have anabolic properties and counter muscle fatigue and soreness. Under these circumstances, faster rates of body-fat reduction and muscle hypertrophy and strength development should happen. This is precisely what has been seen in studies on weightlifters using gamma oryzanol and FRAC.

In his article, Dr. Bucci presented a table summarizing the results of a multicenter, double-blind study with weight-training individuals taking either FRAC or a placebo (an inert substance) over an eight-week period. These results appear in Table 6-1.

TABLE 6–1 RESULTS OF A STUDY OF WEIGHT LIFTERS TAKING A PLACEBO OR FRAC FOR EIGHT WEEKS

Group	Placebo	FRAC
Number of subjects	4	6
Body weight change (kilograms)	−0.63	+1.9
Body fat change (percent)	−1.6	−0.17
Strength gains (one-rep max)	+13	+24
Leg press		
Bench press	+3.4	+6.8
Shoulder press	−0.3	+5.3
Limb girth (inches)	+0.06	+0.29
Biceps		
Chest	+0.41	+1.00
Thigh	+0.36	+0.47

As this table shows, lifters who took FRAC rather than the placebo gained considerably more weight while still reducing body fat percentage, gained significantly more strength, and significantly increased the girth of three selected parts of the body. This would lead one to conclude that FRAC does work in combination with a normal diet.

But how does it do when compared with anabolic steroids? According to Dr. Bucci:

Anabolic steroid abuse cannot be condoned. These potent analogs of hormones cause many well-known adverse side effects, especially psychological dependency. This mental 'high' probably accounts for continued abuse regardless of potential physical problems or illegality. However, as every bodybuilder knows, underground use of anabolic steroids continues. . . .

For anabolic abuse to decline, other, safe alternatives, such as dietary manipulations, must be shown to produce results desired by 'roidheads.' Unfortunately, we and many other investigators cannot directly compare results of supplements and steroids in head-to-head competition for the obvious ethical reasons. Fortunately, there is enough data from medical literature to enable valid comparisons to be made between supplements and steroids.

When recent literature reports on self-administration of large, stacking doses of anabolic steriods for four to 12 weeks are examined, bodyweight gains of two to four kilograms, bodyfat changes (+1 to −3.5%), strength gains (16 to 18%), and many adverse side effects were seen. Plus, subjects using anabolic steroids also received a placebo effect, since they knew they were using potent drugs.

Nevertheless, these results compare closely with studies on gamma oryzanol and FRAC. While bodyweight gains are less with supplements (one or two kilograms), bodyfat decreases are more consistent (−4%), strength gains are almost as large (5 to 15%), and even more important, no side effects were seen. Larger weight gains from steroid users are partly due to water retention, a well-known side effect of anabolic steroids.

Analysis of blood from FRAC users shows normal reproductive hormone levels and normal blood chemistries, quite unlike abnormal changes seen for anabolic steroid users. In fact, several human trials have found that gamma oryzanol and FRAC may have benefit for persons with elevated cholesterol. Futhermore, gamma oryzanol and FRAC break down into normal dietary metabolites always found in the urine, meaning they are not detectable by drug testing. . . . Other factors to consider when comparing supplements to anabolic steroids is that supplements are not illegal and usually cost less than a steroid stacking program.

To sum up, FRAC seems to work by supporting the body's own normal responses to stress. Exercise is one such stress that the body partly counters by releasing growth hormone and endorphins. Unlike certain amino acids, which may or may not cause a sudden release of growth hormone, FRAC may allow the pituitary to 'stock up' on growth hormones and endorphins, to be released when the body calls for and really needs these hormones. This means efficient use of anabolic hormones is made, hopefully optimizing results of resistance training.

AMINO ACIDS

The topic of amino acid supplementation has become so important to hard-training bodybuilders that we have included an entire chapter on the subject. For in-depth information on aminos, please refer to Chapter 8 as well.

A natural-training bodybuilder should be concerned with finding the best and fastest means of increasing muscle mass. One food supplement that does this job well is amino acids in both free-form and branched-chain configurations, the most commonly used forms of aminos. While amino acids are relatively expensive and are normally consumed in large quantities, they are a good buy in the sense that they definitely provide the effect and benefits promoters claim for them.

Please understand that we are talking about L-form (*L* is for "left") aminos in this section, rather than hydrolized proteins, which are frequently touted as "liquid amino acids." These foul-smelling and -tasting liquids are manufactured by bathing animal by-products (hides, tails, lips, and—well, you can guess at the rest of the ingre-

"The recent advent of Soviet ergogenic aids opens up a lot of unexplored avenues for serious bodybuilders," notes John Hnatyschak, National and World Middleweight Champion. "It *is* possible to achieve druglike results without taking drugs."

dients), with the resulting "aminos" drained off later on. Such hydrolized proteins are completely lacking in the amino acid tryptophan, and they are unbalanced in several other essential aminos that the body can't manufacture on its own. (As of 1990, tryptophan has been removed from the market due to high body toxicity levels resulting from use of large dosages of the amino acid.) Hydrolized proteins serve no purpose in the nutritional program of a serious bodybuilder.

All L-form aminos are currently produced in Japan by a single firm, which owns the patent for processing them. Barrels of individual L-form amino acids, of which there are 22 different ones in human muscle tissue, are then shipped throughout the world, including to North America. Food supplement distributors then blend individual aminos into their own personalized formulas, encapsulate or tablet the mixture, and sell it wholesale to health food outlets. Occasionally, they sell amino mixtures in powder form, and a range of individual amino acids in capsules is available to suit specific consumer needs.

Of the 22 amino acids in human muscle tissue, 9 cannot be manufactured within the body and are thus termed "essential amino acids." The other 13 *can* be manufactured in the human digestive system and are therefore termed "nonessential amino acids." Together, these 22 amino acids serve as the building blocks of muscle protein. They can also be combined in hundreds of configurations to form the endless number of enzymes that ensure proper body function throughout the day.

Looking closely at human muscle tissue, a very large proportion of it is made up from the three branched-chain amino acids, valine, leucine, and isoleucine. These are called "branched-chain" because of their more complicated molecular structure compared to the remaining 19 amino acids. These three branched-chain aminos are absolutely essential for proper muscle growth.

"Immediately after each workout," says Lee Labrada (victor at numerous IFBB Pro Grand Prix events), "I take my branched-chain aminos separately from any other amino acids. They can be purchased individually in health food stores, or sometimes with all three branched-chain aminos in the same capsule in proper ratio. Suggested dosages vary according to body weight. I weigh about 190 pounds in the off-season and take two or three grams each of leucine, isoleucine, and valine. At other times during the day—including 30 minutes prior to training—I take capsules with mixed free-form aminos in them."

Lee Haney (seven times Mr. Olympia through 1990, and counting) says, "It's essential to be taking vitamins and minerals when using aminos, because there is a synergistic action between aminos, vitamins, and minerals. You simply won't have an efficient amino acid uptake cycle without vitamins and minerals present. This is particularly true of vitamin B_6, of which I consume 300 to 400 milligrams per day. When advising me on my diet, Dr. Fred Hatfield also warned me not to exceed the AMDR for vitamin D when supplementing heavily with aminos, since D interferes with the uptake and assimilation of supplemental amino acids."

When should free-form amino acids be taken? Anja Langer (runner-up in the IFBB Ms. Olympia) suggests, "Take free-form amino acid capsules about 30 minutes prior to each meal, plus 30 minutes before every workout. Premeal consumption means taking aminos on an empty stomach, which gives you the best pattern of uptake of these supplements, while preworkout they help peak out your energy for an all-out, gut-wrenching training session on the iron."

How many capsules should you take each day? Legendary Casey Viator (the youngest Mr. America at age 19, and in his late thirties still a serious threat at any IFBB pro competition) says, "I personally take about 30 capsules per day in the off-season, five each before my four meals and five more prior to each of my two gym sessions. But as a competition approaches, I rapidly escalate my amino intake. At peak intensity, I go through a bottle of 500 capsules every three or four days.

"If you decide to emulate my personal usage of free-form aminos, please build up slowly. It's possible to suffer digestive disturbances—even diarrhea—if you try to go hog-wild on these supplements too abruptly. And bear in mind that I always cut back on all of my supplements, even amino acids, once I have competed."

What results can you expect? "Amino acids will never give you the same amount of muscle mass as can be achieved on a heavy steroid program," notes Mike Christian (IFBB Amateur and Pro World Champion), "but you will be able to make some solid gains in muscle mass if you also train hard, while feeling better and avoiding drug side effects in the bargain. It will take you longer to reach your goals using amino acids, but you won't lose the mass as you would when going off of a drug cycle. And you'll have the personal satisfaction of having a massive physique that *you* built, not something which is a product of chemical science!"

Amino Testing

Individual bodybuilders assimilate amino acids (which, incidentally do not require digestion if in free-form state) somewhat differently from everyone else. As a result, your system may be deficient in one or more individual amino acids, or you may be consuming an excessive amount of one or more of them. Such a situation indicates that you are not getting the most out of your amino acid supplementation program.

This picture is further clouded by the incredible array of individual amino acid formulations packed and sold by various supplement promoters and distributors. A casual glance at the labels on bottles of three or four amino acid products—which are required by law to reveal the product's content, as well as the number of milligrams of each individual element in the formula—will convince you that it would be difficult to find two identical formulas.

If you have settled on a multiple-amino-acid formula and have been taking it for at least 30 days, you might consider having yourself tested to see which individual aminos are in excess or deficient in supply. This can be done with a simple noninvasive urine test, or in rare cases with a blood test should the urinalysis prove to be inconclusive.

You'll receive a computerized graph of the amount of each amino and the normal amount that should be expected. High and low values will be flagged, so you can adjust your amino intake to bring your individual profile more into normal ranges. Simply cut back a bit on amino acids you consume to excess, and supplement with extra quantities of those aminos you are underconsuming. Subsequent tests should help you to zero in on the scientifically correct amount of each amino acid that your unique body requires.

For test availability and cost, call sports medicine clinics and registered nutritionists in your area.

Growth Hormone Releasers

Informed bodybuilders realize that human growth hormone (hGH) is released during hours of deep sleep, with the highest concentrations occurring approximately two hours after one is deeply asleep. In adults, hGH is responsible for developing greater muscle mass and burning stored body fat reserves at a faster than normal clip. In children, hGH is necessary for growth of long bones, which ultimately determines a young man's or woman's stature, and general physical maturation.

Back in the early 1980s, Durk Pearson and Sandy Shaw published their first book, *Life Extension*, which became a runaway bestseller. Among other revelations, Pearson and Shaw stated that hGH could be significantly stimulated by taking dosages of two grams (2,000 milligrams) or more of the amino acids arginine and ornithine each night at bedtime.

Much additional research has taken place on these two amino acids in subsequent years, and dosages of 2,000 milligrams or more have been found to actually upset the metabolism of amino acids. If you feel you need to produce extra hGH, current research suggests that you will achieve the best results from taking 1,000 to 1,500 milligrams of arginine and lysine on an empty stomach both in the morning and at night before retiring.

"My main ergogenic aid is plenty of free-form and branched-chain amino acids," says Paul Jean-Guillaume. "I take the free-form aminos 30 minutes prior to each meal and the branched-chain immediately after every workout."

A Final Note on Aminos

With all aspects of your diet, you will find that responses to newly introduced nutrients can come slowly and be quite subtle. Body chemistry is usually reluctant to change very quickly, and you might need to be Sherlock Holmes to spot the obscure clue that signals a positive change in your chemical response to a new food. But even the tiniest changes gradually add up to significant results.

Two conditions—a diet high in animal protein and an overtrained state—can further hurt the metabolism of amino acids. So try consuming a maximum of 25 percent of your calories from animal protein sources while cutting back on the length of each of your workouts in the gym, and you should notice the benefits of amino acid supplementation more quickly and much more dramatically. At that point, you'll know you're on your way to developing a contest-winning physique!

YOHIMBE BARK

A highly touted ergogen consists of powdered extract of the bark of yohimbe, a tropical tree, which is encapsulated and sold widely across North America. Yohimbe bark's reputation as an aphrodisiac is undeserved, so don't bother scarfing down these capsules if you merely want to juice up your sex life. However, yohimbe bark does contain nearly 14 percent of its weight in naturally occurring methyltestosterone, one of the few forms of testosterone that is biologically active when taken orally.

Approximately 60 percent of the testosterone contained in a 25-milligram capsule of yohimbe bark extract is active and can be utilized by the body after it has passed through the liver. Two or three capsules daily are the recommended dosage, with the individual capsules spread out evenly over the course of a day. One yohimbe bark distributor estimates this dosage over a seven-day period to be equal in anabolic-androgenic effect to a 200-milligram injection of pharmaceutical testosterone.

Medical literature reveals that excessive intake of methyltestosterone can be highly toxic. Methyltestosterone can also aromatize into estrogen in male bodybuilders, a primary cause of unsightly gynecomastia, and result in the oily skin often seen among heavy drug users in our sport.

There *is* another school of thought on yohimbe bark extract—that it's worthless to active adults, whose systems are unable to derive usable testosterone from the bark. We have seen no studies to support this position, however. So, this is one more case in bodybuilding where you will have to experiment with a product and determine for yourself its relative value to you.

SMILAX OFFICIANALIS

Smilax officianalis is another popular ergogenic aid supposedly capable of raising the body's own natural production of testosterone, which in turn increases muscle mass and density. You are probably familiar with smilax officianalis, even if you haven't heard of it before, because it's been used as a flavoring agent in root beer for nearly a century.

According to George S. Zangas, President of the Marathon Nutrition and Distributing Company, Inc., in Palos Verdes, California, "The active components of smilax [officianalis] are a group of sterols called smilogens. These sterols have the unique ability to coax the body into producing greater amounts of such anabolic hormones as testosterone, without upsetting the natural hormonal balance of your body." This means that the body does not decrease its own natural production of testosterone after smilax has done its work, as is the case when the body's negative feedback mechanism senses excess endogenous testosterone in the system.

Smilax officianalis is supplied in liquid form for use sublingually, 10 to 12 drops both morning and evening under the tongue. If you can't find smilax officianalis in a health food store or gym pro shop, you can contact George Zangas or a member of his staff for an order form by calling 1-800-321-5064 (1-800-231-4070 in California).

DIBENCOZIDE

Dibencozide (known scientifically as 5-6 dimethyl-bensimadazole coenzyme) is touted in advertising literature as a powerful nonsteroidal anabolic agent. If so, it is a valuable addition to your arsenal of ergogenic agents.

Most of the evidence supporting dibencozide is anecdotal, or subjective feedback from iron athletes who have tried the product. Many power lifters report such amazing gains that most intelligent consumers should be skeptical of false advertising claims. Any product that is touted to exceed the muscle- and strength-building benefits of anabolic steroids probably is being oversold.

Dibencozide is available in both tablets and a sublingual liquid formula. A good course to follow would be to make a trial purchase of each form of dibencozide, experiment with a wide range of dosages, then decide for yourself whether it causes an anabolic effect, and whether or not it has any side effects.

GINSENG

Ginseng has been revered in the Far East for more than six millenia for its curative powers. Soviet researchers also have developed enthusiasm for the root of this perennial herb. They believe that daily dosages of ginseng improve the operating efficiency of both the pituitary and adrenal glands, resulting in increased vitality, endurance, and training capacity. To Soviet scientists and coaches, ginseng is an "adaptogen" that also relieves stress.

Long-term heavy use of ginseng should be avoided, however. Dr. Ronald Siegal of the UCLA Neuropsychiatric Institute studied a large group of individuals who had habitually ingested three or more grams of ginseng daily for long periods of time. He discovered that the group as a whole suffered from what he termed "ginseng abuse syndrome," which was manifested by insomnia, hypertension, irritability, nervousness, diarrhea, skin rashes and swelling, and feelings of depression.

We suggest daily use of ginseng in combination with royal bee jelly and honey. This elixir is available in 10-bottle boxes at larger health food stores. It is imported from mainland China. Take two bottles per day, one in the morning and one before bedtime.

BEE POLLEN

Every time you have passed a flower bed abuzz with bees, you have unwittingly witnessed little farmers harvesting their crops. Bees gather pollen from flowers, transport it back to their hive, and feed upon it whenever they need sustenance. In the United States, bee pollen can be sold legally only as a food, rather than as the drug many athletes feel it is.

Bee pollen emphatically does *not* improve athletic performance or bodybuilding results. This was proved in a 1975 study undertaken by the National Association of Trainers. A large swim team was split into three groups for the course of a six-month study. The first group received 10 bee pollen tablets per day, the second 5 bee pollen tablets per day, and the third group was given 5 placebo tablets each day. The entire team trained the same way, and when tested at the end of six months, all three groups were statistically equal, indicating that bee pollen did nothing to improve their athletic ability.

Bee pollen does not promote health to any measurable degree, nor does it retard the aging process. It's a perfect food only for bees, not humans, and individuals prone to hay fever and other allergies can have serious allergic reactions to pollen.

Obviously, bee pollen is a complete bust as an ergogenic aid.

CHROMIUM PICOLINATE

In an informative and literate two-part article in *Natural Physique* magazine (see the November 1989 and April 1990 issues), Dr. Ritchi Morris, Ph.D., concluded that chromium picolinate in small daily doses does increase muscle mass while decreasing body fat stores. Dr. Morris points out, "There is no 'testosterone manna from heaven.' Insulin is the most important factor for the production of lean muscle mass and it needs chromium picolinate for its biological efficiency and efficacy."

Dr. Morris cited two studies performed at Bemidji State University of Minnesota, undertaken by Dr. Gary Evans, a researcher for the U.S. Department of Agriculture. The first experiment lasted 40 days and used as subjects average college students, all of whom trained on the same program three total hours per week. Skin fold tests and body dimension measurements were taken before and after the test period. Half of the group took 200 micrograms of chromium picolinate; the other half received a placebo. At the end of the study, the chromium picolinate group had gained an average of $3\frac{1}{2}$ pounds of body weight, virtually all of it in lean muscle tissue! The control group taking the placebo gained an average of only 2 ounces of muscle mass.

Dr. Evans's second study involved the college's football players. Except for the fact that this study lasted for 42 days, all conditions were identical to the first study, including administration of the smallish dosage of 200 micrograms of chromium picolinate to the experimental group. This time the experimental group gained an average of 5.69 pounds, while total body fat decreased by 22 percent! In the control group, weight gain was statistically insignificant, as was the gain in lean body mass. Fat diminished by only 1.06 percent.

From the results of these two studies, it would appear that chromium picolinate is a wonder ergogen. But Dr. Morris cautions that "high cellular levels of this substance can cause toxicity." Negative side effects stemming from excessive dosages of chromium picolinate include muscular weakness, dizziness, migraines and other types of headaches, short-term memory problems, premenstrual syndrome (PMS), interruption of the menstrual cycle, and glucose tolerance problems leading up to and including sugar diabetes.

Due to the health problems associated with excessively high dosages of chromium picolinate, Dr. Morris recommends a maximum daily dosage of 50 micrograms, rather than the dosages in excess of 2,000 micrograms per day that he has observed some bodybuilders taking. Chromium picolinate should be taken with meals, Dr. Morris continues, and, for synergistic effect, "it's imperative that selenium be taken in a 3:1 ratio with chromium picolinate. Also, the cell salts calcium sulfate and potassium sulfate in *trace amounts* need to be consumed along with chromium picolinate for the same reason."

(Dr. Ritchi Morris and other informed authors are regularly published in *Natural Physique* magazine, which concentrates—as you might suspect—on training and eating for bodybuilding competition without resorting to the use of anabolics or other drugs. Edited by Peter Neff, *Natural Physique* is available quarterly on newsstands, or you can write to Chelo Publications, Inc., Suite 8216, 350 Fifth Avenue, New York, NY 10118, for information on subscriptions and availability of back issues.)

BORON

Boron is one of the newest so-called ergogenic aids, and some bodybuilders use it religiously to increase muscle mass naturally. After an exhaustive search, we were able to discover no conclusive studies proving this effect from taking boron on any regular basis. For a discussion of two conflicting studies on boron, see Chapter 6.

CAFFEINE

Many health-conscious bodybuilders would scoff at the use of caffeine as an ergogenic aid, but it *does* have far-reaching ergogenic effects on all individuals. Among these are increased endurance, greater workout drive, improved uptake of fatty acids, accelerated loss of body fat, increased alertness, and decreased perception of fatigue. Even health-conscious bodybuilders would like to have these benefits of caffeine use.

"I'm proud to say that I've never taken a drug to improve my bodybuilding results," says Arnold Classic winner Michael Ashley. "The key for me is fanatic attention to detail and diet, plus plenty of ergogenic aids."

There is a downside to caffeine, however. Negative effects include a decrease of protein and carbohydrate metabolism, something all bodybuilders would prefer to avoid. Other negative side effects include nervousness, insomnia, increased frequency of urination, anxiety, withdrawal headaches, and cardiac arrhythmias. These negative side effects occur in approximately 20 percent of the general population. Athletes with ulcers should also avoid using caffeine because it may cause an increase in GI tract acid levels.

One top bodybuilder who is high on caffeine is Don Ross (a former Pro Mr. America and currently bodybuilding guru in residence at Gold's Gym in Venice, California). Don suggests taking 200 to 400 milligrams of caffeine in tablet form about 15 minutes before the start of a training session. Caffeine tablets can be purchased at any drugstore.

DMG

Dimethylglycine (DMG) is used clinically on cardiac patients. A liquid form of vitamin B_{15}, DMG has oxygenating properties, which are quite valuable to heart patients with restricted blood flow through the arteries that serve the cardiac muscles. As a result of this heart-oxygenating effect, a rapidly increasing number of physicians have come to rely on DMG, even though it requires no medical prescription for its purchase.

A vast majority of the research on DMG has been published in the U.S. and Canada. Athletes in the Soviet Union take an average dose of 60 milligrams per day of DMG sublingually to improve muscular endurance. Soviet sports researchers have determined that DMG has only a negligible effect on athletes in explosive anaerobic sports (which would include weight lifting and most bodybuilding training). But DMG does improve aerobic endurance by up to 25 percent when used regularly.

For bodybuilders who take long rest intervals between sets (for example, Cathey Palyo, former IFBB Pro Ms. International), DMG would have little positive effect. For bodybuilders working out with very short rest intervals—making the activity more aerobic in nature—DMG would provide markedly improved workout endurance. And maximum effect from DMG would be felt during long precontest aerobic training sessions, such as stair climbing and stationary cycling. Regardless of whether workouts are aerobic or anaerobic, DMG significantly speeds up the recovery cycle.

DMG is widely available in health food stores and via mail order through advertisements in various bodybuilding magazines. Considering its ergogenic benefit, it is reasonably priced.

RAW GLANDULARS

Although their popularity is rapidly fading, tablets made from desiccated raw glands of various animals (most frequently bovine or porcine in nature) have been touted as remarkable ergogenic agents. The theory, since widely debunked, was that eating tablets of cardiac muscle would increase cardiac output, consuming raw orchic (testicles) would have an anabolic effect similar to injecting straight testosterone, and so forth.

Actually, this notion is thousands of years old, because Greek athletes in the first Olympian Games nearly 800 years before Christ's birth consumed selected organs of sheep to increase running speed, throwing strength, and wrestling aggressiveness. Unfortunately, this practice was mere superstition, and it had no practical value. It doesn't work any better now than it did in Greece in 776 B.C.

BLOOD BUFFERS

"Go for the burn," your training partner exhorts. "Crash past the pain barrier!"

Sound familiar? Of course it does, because you hear it in every gym you might enter. And we're sure there are similar words in every language. Being able to endure the burn caused by lactic acid buildup toward the end of a tough set allows you to push that set further than usual, which in turn gives you more muscle-building benefit.

Wouldn't it be nice to be able to take an ergogenic agent that reduces the pain of lactic acid buildup, enabling even the smallest fellow in the gym to push hard at every set? One of the simplest ergogens that will buffer your blood and reduce lactic acid pain can be found in most kitchens across North America. It is common baking soda, or sodium bicarbonate. A dosage of 300 milligrams per kilogram of body weight is suggested. Simply stir the powder into a glass of water and drink it 10 to 15 minutes before a workout, and you'll notice a big difference toward the end of an all-out set.

Considerable research has shown that sodium phosphate is an even more effective blood buffer than sodium bicarbonate. Twin Laboratories, Inc. (known more commonly as Twinlab) has introduced a product called Phos Fuel (it comes in capsules), which contains both sodium phosphate and sodium bicarbonate, plus carnosine, another effective blood buffer. It's available in any health food store and is highly effective—so effective and immediately popular among serious bodybuilders that other supplement companies will have followed Twinlab's lead by the time you read this book. (For optimum effect, you'll need to take 5–6 times the dosage Twinlab recommends on the label.)

If you have a water retention problem—particularly close to a competition—you should avoid using products containing either sodium phosphate or sodium bicarbonate. But in the off-season, when you're building up your general muscle mass, you should use a blood buffer to help fight off lactic acid buildup in the working muscles.

ATP

Readers familiar with the Krebs cycle know that adenosine triphosphate (ATP) is broken down into adenosine diphosphate (ADP) in the body, leaving one phosphate radical to supply energy for muscle contractions and many other bodily functions. ATP is manufactured in the mitochondria, small components inside the cell. The more mitochondria in a muscle cell, the greater the amount of ATP manufactured, and the greater the cell's energy potential.

For some time it was thought technically possible to increase energy potential by supplementing the diet with straight ATP tablets, which can be manufactured in a lab. This technique was researched by a number of food supplement firms, particularly Tyson and Associates in Santa Monica, California, a firm well known by elite bodybuilders for marketing amino acid supplements of exceptional quality.

Experiments were also done on racehorses, which evinced an increase of up to five times normal cellular ATP levels when supplementary ATP was given for two weeks. So the supplementary form of ATP was thought to have enormous potential as an ergogenic agent for human athletes.

Unfortunately, it was eventually discovered that supplementary ATP cannot penetrate the human cell membrane, which means it can't enter the cell, where it does its work in producing energy. Sometimes you can find a supplement company or medical researcher with ATP tablets, but they don't work and would be nothing more than a waste of money if you tried them.

"SUPER JUICES"

If you peruse iron game magazines, you'll see ads for various "super juices," liquid supplements (or powders to which liquid is added) that combine several of the ergogens discussed in this chapter. One common type of super juice is the metabolic optimizer powders, which can be mixed with milk, juice, or water to provide a wide range of ergogens in one drink. An in-depth discussion of metabolic optimizer drinks can be found in Chapter 6.

As with other elixirs, you will have to shop by comparing label information with the data on ergogenic effectiveness presented in this chapter. Then make your own choice.

SOVIET ERGOGENS

Within the bodybuilding community, any Soviet drug or natural food substance seems to be worth almost its weight in gold. This is because the USSR Academy of Medical Sciences has long maintained a highly organized and extensive program of research to discover ergogenic means of improving the performance levels of Soviet athletes. In a propaganda sense, a country that produces the world's strongest and best athletes must also be the strongest nation on earth.

To give you an idea of how systematic the Soviets have been, they have established six main research groups in Moscow (directed by Dr. Nikolai Volkov), Leningrad (directed by Dr. Viktor Rogozkin), Kiev (directed by Dr. Mikhail Kilinski), Tartu (directed by Dr. Atko

Viru), Tbilisi (directed by Dr. Levan Mudyuri), and Vladivostok (directed by Dr. Israel Brekhmann). These centers are concentrated in the more highly populated western section of the country (except Vladivostok, on the Soviet east coast), but are otherwise geographically evenly distributed from west to east and north to south.

It would be easy to debate whether successful athletes actually *do* come from a politically and economically powerful nation, if we could ignore the way such a country's citizens are forced to live at or near the poverty level to maintain a massive standing army with all of its modern weaponry, to support an extensive space program, *and* to produce the highly successful sports teams. Undoubtedly, the Soviet people would be happy to trade some of their athletic successes for much-needed consumer goods and a little more freedom.

What can't be debated is the haphazard way in which North American scientists carry on similar research to develop ergogenic aids for their own athletes. Contrast the USSR and USA, and it should come as no surprise to learn that Soviet scientists have indeed developed highly ergogenic food products. All of these ergogens—plus new ones still unreleased—are available in North America, however, either as imported substances or products manufactured in the United States strictly according to Soviet formulas and processes.

For information on the seven ergogens currently available and discussed in this book, write to Atletika, 1023 Hook Avenue, Pleasant Hill, CA 94523. Atletika also sells a 200-page softcover book, *Soviet Training and Recovery Methods*, for $18.95 plus $2.00 shipping and handling (add 7.25 percent sales tax for orders sent to California addresses). This manual can be telephone ordered at 1-800-621-2692 if you have a Visa or MasterCard, but please accept that this toll-free number is for orders only, not for the type of detailed information some bodybuilders seem to like to hear over the phone!

At any rate, we know scores of serious bodybuilders who swear by the use of Soviet ergogenic food supplements, even to the point of using hospital-grade amino acid powders, inosine, and L-carnitine from the USSR, when the same substances—with very comparable levels of biological activity—are available domestically in virtually all health food stores.

Why are these food products considered to be so helpful to bodybuilders striving like borderline maniacs to add a half-ounce of extra muscle tissue here and there on their physiques? Let's find out.

Mumie

The most ethnic of Soviet ergogenic aids is called "mumie." It is mined exclusively in the southwest corner of the Soviet Union along submerged ridges in the Black Sea. Don't get the idea that this substance has anything to do with Boris Karloff dragging one leg across the desert while trailing moldering bandages in *The Return of the Mummy*. Rather, it is a substance used to treat a long list of medical maladies. Its benefits are said to include the following:

- Treats stomach ulcers
- Inhibits tumors
- Treats myocardial infarction
- Helps to detoxify the liver
- Protects from radiation poisoning
- Heals and regenerates bone
- Acts as a general body and organ tonic
- Acts as an antibacterial agent
- Corrects blood disorders
- Serves as a dehydrating agent
- Acts as an antidote to pesticide poisoning
- Protects against environmental toxins

Mumie sounds like a magic bullet, doesn't it? And science has discovered no ill effects from consuming the substance.

Where does mumie come from? The trees, plants, and other vegetation that make it up are paleozoic in origin. As masses of vegetation were covered with water when the earth changed its levels, the organic matter slowly decayed and was pressed in strata. The last component of a tree that decays and mineralizes is the sap, or pitch, and that dark-colored substance is what the Soviets scoop up and bring to the surface of the Black Sea. At a nearby lab, the raw material is subjected to electrophoresis, which causes the goop to stratify into several layers, one of which is pure mumie, which can be drawn off and placed into containers.

Mumie normally is widely available throughout the USSR, however, for a period following the unfortunate nuclear reactor disaster at Chernobyl, mumie was used almost exclusively by the Soviet medical community to treat radiation sickness. Three or four years later, mumie was again universally available, and there were sufficient supplies for export.

Raw mumie looks almost like thick black shoe polish, and the taste is odd enough that it would have to be camouflaged by milk and fruit or some other type of sweetener in a blender drink. Fortunately, it is also available in tablet form—black, of course—which can easily be swallowed with any liquid.

Most bodybuilders who have regularly taken mumie report greater workout drive and energy, faster between-workouts recovery, and a moderate anabolic effect. To date, no scientific studies have come to light that actually prove mumie can produce a measurable anabolic effect, with its attendant muscle growth and strength increases. However, for a natural bodybuilder, even a very small anabolic effect would make a great difference in his or her appearance.

Paul Jean-Guillaume, a former IFBB amateur World Champion, is one of the premier natural bodybuilders around. Unlike some men, who can test clean at a show while taking anabolic agents for much of the year, Paul has never taken any bodybuilding drugs.

Suggested dosages are three or four 500-milligram tablets (they retail for about 50 cents each, since they must be imported) spread throughout the day. The Soviets suggest staggering mumie use, going either one week on and one off, or two on and two off.

Inosine

While in Moscow studying at the Lenin Central Institute of Sport and Physical Conditioning in 1983, Drs. Fred Hatfield and Bill Reynolds spent more time using Bill's Russian language ability to befriend athletes than attending classes. Soviet citizens go out of their way to entertain the infrequent Americans who can actually speak their language, and our intrepid pair made the rounds of dinner engagements, outings, and informal discussions in gym settings every day they were in the country.

In the process, Bill and Fred exchanged T-shirts, Los Angeles Olympic pins, and other Western souvenirs for the gamut of available Soviet ergogenic aids, both pharmacological and food-oriented. After translating all of the labels and package insets for each product, they concluded that the USSR then had only one unique substance that wasn't widely available in the West—inosine, the initial bottle of which held a finely granulated white powder. The amber bottle had a rubber stopper on top, suggesting that the product was intended for intramuscular injection.

After the pair's return to the United States, word got out about inosine, and it became a fad. It was soon available in tablet form over the counter and was used by most iron athletes, particularly power lifters. Practical and empirical studies showed that inosine has the following beneficial properties:

- Increases and conserves ATP, a key chemical component in the Krebs cycle
- Activates liver function
- Aids in oxygen transfer to working muscle cells
- Takes part in synthesizing nucleotides, which assist in the metabolism of energy and synthesis of protein
- Works hard at metabolizing sugar
- Activates enzymes in the body that oxydize pyruvic acid, which in turn assures smooth respiration even in a low-oxygen environment
- Is beneficial in a wide variety of cardiac maladies, including arrhythmia, senile heart, myocarditis, myocardiosclerosis, and amelioration of either low or high dosages of digitalis

Bodybuilders should take inosine to improve endurance, due to its positive effect on ATP production and oxygen transfer. Scores of low- and high-level bodybuilders have reported a 10–20 percent increase in workout energy while they were regularly taking two to three grams of inosine 1–1½ hours before workouts morning and evening. Inosine delays the onset of early fatigue in a bombing and blitzing session, then keeps the fatigue wolf at bay throughout the rest of a workout lasting 1–1½ hours. Continued use of inosine in the suggested dosages will also help accelerate recovery between workouts. This makes inosine almost a wonder supplement for serious bodybuilders.

Inosine of varying biological quality is available throughout North America in health food stores. It is most commonly available in 500- and 1,000-milligram tablets. The Soviet inosine-F is of the highest biological quality. But if it's not available to you, good-quality inosine can be found in most health food stores. Just be sure you don't purchase inosinic acid, which isn't the same product and doesn't produce comparable results. Also, for best results, cycle inosine on for a week, then off for the next.

L-Carnitine

Carnitine is an amino acid, and a nonessential one at that. The *carni* segment of the word pays homage to the Latin root word *carnis,* or meat. In 1905, Russian scientists extracted carnitine from quantities of meat. The *L* in L-carnitine, of course, merely refers to this product being the left-configuration version. While R-carnitine exists—and is sometimes sold by unscrupulous supplement promoters —it is toxic to humans.

L-carnitine plays a solid role in improving workout endurance. Studies have shown that carnitine actually delays the onset of aerobic collapse. As such, carnitine adds significantly to your ability to keep training drive alive and kicking for 10–15 minutes longer than you might expect if you didn't take the supplement daily.

IFBB Pro Ms. International, Laura Creavalle, gives us another way L-carnitine can be used to help competitive bodybuilders reach peak muscular condition: "Carnitine helps assist in transporting fat from storage areas throughout the body and to the powerhouse of the cell, where it can be burned to fuel muscle contractions. If I am restricting my carbohydrate intake prior to a competition, I will take both carnitine and inosine. This way, my glycogen is depleted, and my body must call upon stored fats for energy, rather than blood glycogen stores.

"Additionally, carnitine acts in the metabolism of the amino acids leucine and valine, which are able to provide as much as 10 percent of the energy your body expends during extremely intense bodybuilding training. And as much as carnitine helps to metabolize fats, it also dampens such negative effects of strict dieting as ketosis."

Isolated L-carnitine in tablet or powder form is very expensive, so a sufficient dosage would be one or two 500-milligram tablets $1-1\frac{1}{2}$ hours before a workout. However, carnitine can be synthesized from supplies of the aforementioned lysine and methionine, which are much less expensive. And L-carnitine is available in natural form in such meats as beef, mutton, and lamb. Consume plenty of steak along with lysine and methionine capsules, and you should be taking in sufficient carnitine—without excessive cost—to give you the benefits already outlined in this section.

The current price of 50 500-milligram capsules of L-carnitine in either a health food store or via mail order from Atletika is in the neighborhood of $20. But be careful to understand that this is the price as we write this book; it could go up a bit with time. Either way, carnitine is a good buy at almost any price, if you can afford it, because it helps you really fry your muscles every time you step into the gym for a serious iron-pumping session, then helps foster the quick between-workouts recovery necessary before muscle hypertrophy can occur.

Vitamin B₁₅

Vitamin B_{15}, also known as pangamic acid, was one of the first food-related ergogenic aids used and publicized by the Soviets. The USSR

Franco Santoriello is new on the pro scene, having achieved his pro card with a light-heavyweight victory at the Nationals. He alternates residences at two-week intervals between Cincinnati and New Jersey.

Academy of Medical Sciences has sponsored numerous research projects into the values of pangamic acid and published a massive book, which was available in English translation at larger health food stores before 1980.

Among the host of medical uses of vitamin B_{15} are treatment of circulatory problems, actual cure of gangrene in the extremities, ease of breathing problems associated with emphysema, and supposedly the cure of various types of minor tumors.

Bodybuilders and other athletes take vitamin B_{15} as an endurance aid, in that it markedly assists in oxygen transfer from the lungs to the working muscles, prolonging an athlete's ability to keep contracting a muscle long after he or she would normally have to stop. Obviously, this adds up to longer and harder bodybuilding workouts when B_{15} is taken regularly.

The Soviet researchers also revealed that pangamic acid helped speed recovery from a workout at an unprecedented speed. This is undoubtedly true, because their elite Olympic-style weight lifters frequently do *three* very heavy workouts per day over the final six weeks leading up to an important competition, and they never overtrain.

Perhaps you have already concluded that you want to lay your hands on some B_{15} and start administering it to yourself with benchmark regularity. The most common, weakest, and least effective form of vitamin B_{15} tabs can be purchased at virtually all health and natural food stores. In some places, such as Europe and Mexico, however, an injectable form is available, and it is many times more effective than the oral version. We certainly do *not* suggest that you make a pincushion of your rump to improve your workouts, since the entire thrust of this book is natural bodybuilding, without the use of drugs and other extreme measures. We merely present this fact for informational purposes.

Liverguard

Physiologically speaking, every toxin you take into your body—whether it be deliberately or accidentally, such as when walking beneath a tree that has just been sprayed with a pesticide—ends up in some form in your liver. And it is not uncommon for the liver to become clogged up with toxic residue, which causes inflammations in this vitally important organ.

In rare cases (we know of four to date), liver cancer and other liver diseases can be caused by the toxins the organ must endure. One of the most painful of these diseases is called hepatitis peliosis, which consists of numerous blood-filled sacs within the liver mass. And even though a rare and invariably fatal cancer called Wilms' tumor occurs almost exclusively in children under the age of 10, four cases of mature bodybuilders falling prey to Wilms' tumor have been reported in the medical literature. Sadly, all of these formerly healthy and muscular men are no longer with us.

If chronic steroid usage has brought you to the point where you are facing the chance of disabling liver illness—perhaps even cancer—you surely want to reverse the degenerative process. And it *can* be done by religiously using a Soviet product called Liverguard. (At the time of writing, it was available by mail order only from Atletika in bottles of 100 300-milligram capsules for $20.)

The supplement has not to our knowledge been scientifically studied and tested by unbiased researchers in the West—and Soviet literature was not available at press time—but scores of empirical studies have indicated that Liverguard really works, cleansing the liver, which in turn results in increased energy levels and a better sense of well-being. If you feel better and are more generally healthy, you will train harder and build bigger muscles.

The Soviet athletes we've engaged in conversation have told us that Liverguard is used cyclically, one tablet per main meal for two or three weeks following cessation of a steriod cycle, then followed up with a system of one week of these three tabs daily alternated with one week off of the supplement during the year. Since Liverguard is formulated entirely from herbs and other food elements, it is safe to take, certainly safer than any chemically concocted medication might be. And it won't show up on any drug test.

Pantocrine

The newest Soviet nostrum used by their athletes is called pantocrine. It's a substance extracted from the base of antlers of either red deer or Altai (from the Altai Mountains) elk. A careful translation of the product's package insert reveals that it comes in three forms—a liquid elixir, tablets, and a suppository.

Medically speaking, pantocrine is used to treat a wide range of cardiovascular system maladies, including senile heart, arrhythmia, impaired circulation of coronary arteries, and coronary thrombosis. But to date we know of no bodybuilders using pantocrine, since it's so new on the scene and virtually unavailable outside eastern Europe. If you happen to hear that the red deer and Altai elk populations are being decimated soon, however, you can be sure that the guys at Gold's Gym or World Gym are thriving on it.

We *are* aware of several track and field athletes using pantocrine, most commonly as an intramuscular injection. One pole-vaulter we talked with revealed that pantocrine—taken two or three times per day in liquid form with an eyedropper—has given him more energy, improved his ratio of lean body mass, and provided him with an elevated sense of well-being and self-confidence. Each of these benefits would assist a bodybuilder in achieving the type of physique that causes comment wherever it is viewed, whether that be onstage, while window shopping, or when sunbathing at the beach.

We've reiterated this statement many times, but it bears repetition: any small anabolic effect you might achieve through biochemical means adds up. Even if pantocrine gives you only an ounce or two of added lean muscle mass, that amount of muscle can transform the appearance of any part of your body!

Biogain

The least known and understood of Soviet ergogens is Biogain, which is roughly equivalent to the metabolic optimizer drinks (see Chapter 6) taken before and after workouts by competing North American bodybuilders. The domestic drinks are intended to increase workout energy levels, then assist in speeding up the recovery process once an athlete is out of the gym.

Currently selling at $25 for approximately 2.8 pounds, Soviet Biogain contains an exclusive microelement/anabolic formula, plus a measure of 100 percent pure amino acids of high biological activity. Unlike many metabolic optimizer drinks, however, Biogain contains no protein solids. According to Atletika's promotional literature, Biogain "puts all (other) metabolic optimizer drinks to shame. Stop fooling around with pixie-dust products. Get the Soviet answer to maximum power and muscle building."

Obviously, it is unwise to purchase by mail any product you haven't already tried, merely because of promises the manufacturer/distributor makes. An advertisement can make a can of kitty chow sound like it's filet mignon. We suggest asking around the gym first to see who's used Biogain—or any other supplement, for that matter—and how well that product worked for the bodybuilder you questioned. If you can't find someone who's used Biogain, purchase only one container, use its entire contents, then decide how effective it is in your individual case. Perhaps you'll want to order several more cans of the stuff based on that evaluation.

Future Soviet Advances

With *glasnost* in full swing, Soviet ergogenic food products will become increasingly available in North America. The Soviet Bloc countries are usually desperate to sell their products and even their raw materials for hard currency, since their own money is virtually useless on the international business market.

It's also possible that heretofore unknown food supplements will surface and become available to athletes and bodybuilders in the Western Hemisphere. Hopefully, such new products will have even more dramatic ergogenic potential than the food products we've already seen come out of the Soviet Union.

To close this section on Soviet ergogenics, we'd like to give you a word of caution. Be aware of the trap many bodybuilders fall into when using ergogenic aids, or even more classic foods and food supplements. This trap is to rely on ergogenics—or perhaps even outright use of anabolic steroids—to the point where you tend to slack off in the gym. Unless you are ill, you should take every workout to 100 percent of your ability for that particular day. Anything less, and you won't have gotten the amount of muscle hypertrophy from the workout that you should have.

Bodybuilding success rests solidly on a table supported by four powerful legs—nutrition, ergogenesis, mental approach, *and* training. Weaken one leg through inattention and the table will collapse, throwing bodybuilding success into the mud below. You have our word on it!

6

WAR OF THE METABOLIC OPTIMIZERS

There's a war going on in bodybuilding, and the warriors go by names such as Opti Fuel II, Metabolol II, and Metaphase. This is the War of the Metabolic Optimizers, and so much money is at stake in this war that some of the individual battles have been fierce.

Metabolic optimizer (MO) drinks are broad-spectrum nutritional supplements that are widely advertised in all of the muscle mags. MOs are so aggressively advertised that some of the ads show a can of one new product falling from above and crushing the can of a competitor's older product in mock hand-to-hand combat. The only things missing in the advertisements are Kevlar helmets, flak jackets, and assault rifles.

MOs come in powder form and are mixed with milk, water, or some other type of solvent to make a potion touted as a nearly perfect food. MOs can be used as a preworkout energy drink, a postworkout recovery beverage, or a convenient full-meal replacement for busy bodybuilders in too big of a rush to actually eat food.

With millions of dollars per year being spent by enthusiastic bodybuilders on MOs, one might logically question the value of metabolic optimizer supplements. Do they really work? Do they "optimize" the metabolism? Do they help build muscle tissue? Do they provide energy for workouts? Do they assist in postworkout recovery?

Specifically, no reputable scientist has done any research on MOs themselves, but some research does exist to prove the value of many of the individual ingredients of these drinks. Thus, it would seem

"Metabolic optimizer drinks are the newest dietary fad in bodybuilding," says dynamic Marjo Selin, a frequent top-10 Ms. Olympia finisher. "But they're more than commercial hype, because they do the job they advertise that they can do."

"In order to peak out my energy levels for a workout, then recover as quickly as possible after, I take a metabolic optimizer drink both before and after the workout," notes Tony Pearson, Mr. World and Mr. Universe.

that MO supplements *do* have some positive value to hard-training bodybuilders.

If nothing else, MOs are the logical extension of multiple vitamin-mineral tablets and combined amino acid capsules. They are the ultimate "multiple" supplement containing amino acids used in protein metabolism and muscle tissue formation, high-performance carbohydrates for preworkout energy production and postworkout recovery, a full range of vitamins and minerals to ensure optimum health and muscle growth, and a wide spectrum of ergogens touted as natural alternatives to anabolic steroids and other pharmaceutical drugs.

Bodybuilders on a budget could easily make good gains in strength and muscle mass using an MO drink as their only food supplement. For $50 to $60 per month, an aspiring competitor can purchase enough MO powder to take a broad-spectrum nutritional drink before and after every workout.

To answer the questions posed a few paragraphs back, metabolic optimizer drinks *do* help build muscle, they *do* provide energy for a workout, and they *do* assist in postworkout recovery. As such, they *do* work well for bodybuilders. But do they actually help to optimize the metabolism? In reality, they probably don't, but MO drinks *do* provide ideal conditions nutritionally for optimum muscle growth and general bodybuilding progress.

To better understand the value of MO drinks, consider each of the individual ingredients usually found in such a supplement. This discussion will gloss lightly over the individual amino acids (which are discussed in detail in Chapter 8) and individual ergogenic aids (discussed in detail in Chapter 5). Refer to those two chapters for more detailed information on aminos and ergogens.

BRANCHED-CHAIN AMINO ACIDS

Leucine, isoleucine, and valine are the three branched-chain amino acids, so named because their structures are more complex than those of the more commonly used free-form aminos. Branched-chain aminos join to form the largest portion of muscle tissue of any other individual amino acids. The branched-chain aminos are metabolized for energy during a hard anaerobic workout. They are also vital for quick and complete muscle and body recovery between workouts.

The proper proportion of the branched-chain aminos is three parts of leucine to one part each of isoleucine and valine, so check out these ratios in any MO supplement you're considering purchasing. We recommend a minimum of three grams of leucine and one gram each of isoleucine and valine per serving of MO drink.

FREE-FORM AMINO ACIDS

MO supplements also contain a variety of L-configuration free-form amino acids necessary for general health, tissue repair, and muscle growth. Look particularly for arginine and lysine, the hGH-promoting growth factors, with a minimum level of one gram per serving for each of these two amino acids. Other individual free-form amino acids found in most MO drinks are alanine, aspartic acid, cysteine, glutamic acid, glycine, histidine, methionine, phenylalanine, proline, serine, and tyrosine.

PROTEIN CONCENTRATES

Some of the lower-quality MO supplements contain protein concentrates in addition to branched-chain and free-form amino acids. These concentrates are *not* predigested, as the aminos are, so they don't enter the bloodstream as rapidly. The best protein concentrates come first from egg sources (particularly the egg white) and second from milk (usually in the form of calcium or sodium caseinate).

Protein concentrates are quite a bit less expensive than various amino acids. As a result, you can often judge the quality of an MO supplement formula by how much protein concentrate is in it. The more concentrate and the less amino acids, the lesser the quality of the MO drink powder for a hard-training bodybuilder.

GLUCOSE POLYMERS

Glucose polymers are glucose chains partway in length between simple sugars (such as sucrose and fructose) and complex carbohydrates (such as potatoes and pinto beans). Glucose polymers are an interesting source of blood and muscle sugar. They help to provide a sustained release of energy by breaking down faster than complex carbs but slower than simple-carbohydrate foods.

If you consume a combination of complex carbs, glucose polymers, and simple carbohydrates at each meal, you will experience the closest thing to sustained release of workout energy possible to a serious bodybuilder. Indeed, this is the basis of the Multiple-Carbohydrate Leverage Loading technique outlined in Chapter 7.

Bodybuilders will also be happy to know that glucose polymers—like all carbohydrates—are protein-sparing. In the absence of sufficient carbohydrates, the body will burn protein to meet its energy requirements. To prevent protein from being metabolized for energy, MO supplements have glucose polymers to provide carbohydrates. Some MO drinks also have fructose, or some other simple sugar, as a carbohydrate component, but simple sugars are less desirable to bodybuilders than glucose polymers.

SUCCINATE

Succinate (usually from potassium succinate) is also included in MO supplements as a source of workout energy. However, research about the value of succinate for this purpose has not been conclusive, because it is based on animal studies involving either oxygen-depleted heart tissue or huge dosages of succinate before exercise testing.

If animal experiments can be generalized to humans, it would appear that large doses of succinate at least two hours before a workout would result in up to a 15 percent increase in workout energy. But it should be pointed out that most MO supplement distributors recommend taking their product 30 to 60 minutes before a training session, at which point succinate would not have kicked in to help provide workout energy.

BLOOD BUFFERS

To offset rapid buildup of lactic acid in the working muscles—which can terminate a set short of actual muscle failure—MO supplements contain blood buffers such as potassium phosphate, sodium bicarbonate, and carnosine. These blood buffers are discussed in detail in Chapter 5. To summarize, they *do* work noticeably in retarding muscle burn caused by the buildup of lactic acid during a hard set.

MEDIUM-CHAIN TRIGLYCERIDES

Medium-chain triglycerides (MCTs) constitute the fat content of most MO supplements, but MCTs act more like a carbohydrate than a fat in providing workout energy. MCTs do not contribute to the storage of body fat in most bodybuilders. MCTs are much more easily absorbed by the body than any other type of fat, and they help to metabolize body fat stores. For more detailed information on MCTs, please refer to Chapter 11 on sources of workout energy.

INOSINE

Inosine is an anaerobic energy-enhancing ergogen found in most MO supplements. The minimum recommended dosage is 500 milligrams per serving, well above the usual 50–100 milligrams contained in MO supplements. In most cases, you will be forced to take extra inosine supplements if you want the full effect of this potent ergogen. More detailed information on inosine can be found in Chapter 5.

CHROMIUM

Chromium (mainly from chromium picolinate) has been shown to have an anabolic effect when used in moderation. As a result, most MO supplements now contain plenty of elemental chromium. Again, see Chapter 5 for more detailed information on the use and values of chromium picolinate.

BORON

Boron is a fashionable steroid replacement, but no hard evidence exists to prove claims for its effectiveness. Boron's notoriety came from a recent study on postmenopausal women. The study showed that boron supplementation increased their serum testosterone, which increased even more when magnesium supplies were low in the system. Extra testosterone could help to offset calcium deficiencies and bone loss, which are common in postmenopausal women.

Immediately, it was assumed that boron would increase testosterone levels naturally in the system of a bodybuilder or other iron athlete. But read on. A study on male rats was performed, and boron had an adverse effect on gonadal tissue, lowering testosterone levels and destroying reproductive tissue. If generalized to human males, this could mean that boron actually *decreases* natural testosterone production in the body.

Therefore, boron is a shot-in-the-dark ergogen at best. It is simply thrown into MO supplements in case it happens to have some value to bodybuilders.

ELECTROLYTE MINERALS

For proper function of cardiac and skeletal muscles, the electrolyte minerals calcium, potassium, magnesium, and sodium are necessary (although MO supplements rarely include sodium, which is in ample supply in most bodybuilders' diets). Look for AMDR (American Daily Requirements) percentages for calcium, potassium, and magnesium in the range between 50 percent and 100 percent in MO supplements, and you'll be on the right track.

OTHER INDIVIDUAL ELEMENTS

Most MO drinks contain a full spectrum of water- and oil-soluble vitamins, as well as most of the minerals with AMDRs assigned to them. Each of these ingredients is included mainly for health maintenance, although all of them also indirectly affect the rate at which you build up muscle mass.

Look particularly for B-complex vitamins with at least 100 percent of the AMDR for each. Other vitamins and minerals with AMDRs assigned should range above 50 percent of the AMDR for each element.

HOW TO USE METABOLIC OPTIMIZER DRINKS

MO drinks are used only during an off-season mass-building cycle, because drinking nutrients during a peaking phase can seriously bloat tissues, a counterproductive situation at contest time. At a minimum, you should lay off of MO supplements at least twelve weeks out from a competition.

During an off-season cycle, MO drinks should be mixed according to the instructions on the product's can, and taken about 60 minutes before each workout, as well as immediately after a training session in the gym. If you are working out on a double-split routine, then you will take four of these drinks per day. Some bodybuilders even take MO drinks before and after each aerobic training session.

"I use a metabolic optimizer as a catch-all multiple-formula supplement which provides my body with virtually every nutrient it needs to pack on muscle mass," notes Mr. USA, Vince Comerford. "You can use an MO drink as your only food supplement if you can't afford a full spectrum."

If you take two of these drinks each workout day, you will take in approximately 40 grams of protein (mainly in the form of amino acids) and 200 grams of high-class carbohydrates. That adds nearly 1,000 calories per day to your nutritional intake, which puts you seriously into the mass-gaining sector.

As with all other food supplements, we suggest that you experiment with various brands and dosage patterns of MO drinks. Within a few weeks, you should be able to work out a program of metabolic optimizer supplementation that is tailored specifically to your unique physical needs. Then you're well on your way to building a championship physique!

"High-intensity workouts—which by nature are relatively short—are responsible for my muscle mass," says Phil Hill, Night of the Champions winner. "They're fueled by the carbs I consume, built by the protein."

7

CARBOHYDRATES FOR MASS AND CUTS

Over the past several years, bodybuilding publications have carried much information about the importance of carbohydrates as a main source of dietary energy. Today, everyone recognizes that foods like potatoes, rice, and pasta provide excellent nutrient density to hard-training bodybuilders and athletes.

While it is true that carbohydrates are the chief source of energy for all of our bodily functions, some little-known facts about this food group can greatly assist you in achieving that highly desired, sliced muscle appearance.

When used correctly, carbohydrates help to establish conditions for ultimate muscle growth and fat burning. The trick is knowing how to set up the necessary biochemical environments in your body in order to achieve those desired states. This chapter focuses directly on just that—the special aspects of carbohydrates that enable you to become bigger and more cut up than you previously thought possible.

MULTIPLE-CARBOHYDRATE LEVERAGE LOADING

To get really sliced, you first have to get big. This fact easily bears out. How many times have you come across a skinny yet defined person with cross-striations everywhere on his body? Almost never. This is because a muscle needs to be full and massively developed in order for those surface etchings to be visible.

Perhaps you have already tried cutting up and found out that your muscles were much smaller than you thought they would be once the slicing process was complete. Or perhaps you have put off getting ripped because you are not satisfied with your mass yet. Whatever the case might be, this is exactly where Multiple-Carbohydrate Leverage Loading (MCLL) is the ultimate diet for you to follow.

Simply put, MCLL is for those who desire to develop maximum muscle mass. By specifically arranging your carbohydrate intake, this dietary regimen causes each muscle group to grow rapidly. It accomplishes this by creating ideal growth conditions in your muscles. When combined with hard workouts, MCLL accelerates your solid body weight gains and thereby edges you closer to the genetic limit of your muscle size. Then, when you decide to slice up that mass of yours, the newly added size will assure you of deeper cuts and a much more dramatic appearance.

Take note that MCLL requires lots of discipline and persistence to follow correctly. It is also not a diet for those who are on a tight budget. MCLL has you eating a wide variety of deliberately chosen foods, and quite often. So it is definitely the kind of diet for a highly motivated bodybuilder. However, we can assure you that your efforts will pay off handsomely, as MCLL is an extremely effective method of eating.

The theoretical cornerstone of MCLL starts with the chemical structures of carbohydrates. Simple carbs, like fruits, for example, have primitive chemical structures that cause them to be easily digested to yield quick energy. Complex carbs, like oatmeal or corn, are more complicated in form and thus take longer to break down in the body. Regardless of which type of carbohydrate is ingested, the main point is this: *No* carb gives you sustained energy as well as immediate energy. Each has a specific duration of action.

This point can be proved quite easily. Fast for half a day, and then eat some rice. Nothing else, just rice. You don't have to be as wise as Solomon to feel the effect. There won't be an instantaneous energy surge, but about two hours after its consumption, you'll be relatively frisky and not hungry. A chocolate bar will clearly produce the opposite result—shortly after ingestion, you'll turn into a Mick Jagger for about 20 minutes, and then you'll crash, suddenly becoming Roseanne Barr.

What MCLL involves is simple: You arrange your carbo intake so that each meal consists of two complex and two simple carbs, plus a metabolic optimizer drink. In total, you ingest six meals per day. With MCLL at every meal, you'll have a *continual* release of various short-term carbs and long-burning carbs as well. The metabolic optimizer plays an equally important role. It contains an ingredient consisting of a shorter chain structure than that of a complex carb, yet longer than that of a simple carb; it's sort of a medium carb.

Here's a summary of what happens when you follow the MCLL system:

- You'll have much more energy during your training sessions than ever before.
- Your pumps will remind you of the movie *Scanners*—you know, where people's heads explode like pumpkins. They will be truly radical.
- Your muscles will measure larger in a completely cold state.
- You will gain solid body weight as never before.
- Recovery time following a hard workout will be shorter.
- You'll throw off serious body heat. (Carbohydrates increase the temperature of the body. When carbon combines with oxygen in the bloodstream, a process known as thermogenesis takes place.)
- Your metabolism will speed up noticeably.
- Your strength increases will push you through all present sticking points.

To expand on this last point, MCLL ensures that a constant influx of carbs keeps pouring into your bloodstream. That flow includes water. The carbs cause your tissues to load up on that additional water ever so slightly, but the cumulative effect of thousands of slightly "loaded" cells creates a profound leverage advantage. Your bench, squat, press, and curl will all register new poundage increases. And this upward curve in strength will continue over the next several months. That means new muscle growth.

Don't assume that the MCLL approach involves overeating. The total amount you eat per sitting doesn't increase much, only the actual number of carbohydrate calories themselves. To squeeze two complex and two simple carbs onto your plate, you need much smaller portions than the total of one carb source in a normal meal.

Additionally, when you eat often, you don't need as much carbohydrate to achieve a positive effect. In truth, your portions should look tiny. It's the synergistic effect of all those carbs that you want.

A sample daily MCLL menu appears in Table 7-1 on the following page. This kind of eating may be too much for some people; if so, drop the last meal, and reduce the food portions. Also, due to time or location constraints, you may not always be able to combine two complex and two simple carbs into one meal. To avoid this problem, plan ahead, and take food with you wherever you go.

Note that the meal plan following your workout contains no protein, because at that stage we don't wish to slow down carbohydrate absorption. Carbs are crucial before a workout, but they are also required afterward to restock the muscles' glycogen supply, which has been depleted, thereby speeding postworkout recovery.

TABLE 7–1 SAMPLE DAILY MCLL MENU

7:00 A.M.
- ½ banana
- ¼ cantaloupe
- Baked potato, medium
- 4 ounces oatmeal
- 4 ounces lean ground beef
- 8–12 ounces pineapple juice with metabolic optimizer

10:00 A.M.
- 1 kiwi
- 1 box raisins
- 1 all-natural muffin
- 1 ear corn
- 2 boiled eggs
- 8 ounces orange juice with metabolic optimizer

12:30 P.M.
- 6 ounces chicken breast
- 4 ounces rice
- 3 ounces peas
- 1 kiwi
- Fresh pineapple slice (not canned)
- 8 ounces mineral water with metabolic optimizer

3:45 P.M.
- 1 banana
- 3 dried apricots
- 5 ounces salmon
- Microwaved potato, medium
- 1 piece Wasa rye-crisp
- 10 ounces pineapple juice with metabolic optimizer (half of the juice is watered down with mineral water)

5:15 P.M.
- Workout

6:40 P.M.
- 6 ounces pasta
- Baked potato, small
- 4 ounces green beans
- 1 kiwi
- 1 pineapple slice, fresh
- 4 ounces pea soup
- 2 pieces rye-crisp
- 8 ounces mineral water with metabolic optimizer

9:00 P.M.
- 2 boiled eggs
- 5 ounces lean steak
- 1 kiwi
- 1 banana
- 3 ounces rice
- ½ muffin
- 8 ounces mineral water with metabolic optimizer

Notice also that you don't consume gobs of protein on this kind of diet. That's because carbohydrates have a protein-sparing action. In fact, research shows that athletes on very high protein diets are more likely to be protein-starved than those who train on moderate-protein diets. With MCLL, your muscles are kept in positive nitrogen balance all day, and your glucose levels stay high for extended periods. All of this means that you're in an ideal biochemical environment to pack on muscle mass.

To maximize the MCLL diet's effectiveness, take a digestive enzyme tablet with each meal, four to six grams of vitamin C daily, and a high-potency B-complex vitamin every day. Also, five free-form amino acid capsules before your workout and five afterward are important for cellular nourishment.

Follow this diet until you are satisfied with your general muscle mass. Then go ahead and get sliced!

STARCHY VS. FIBROUS CARBOHYDRATES

Many bodybuilders think that complex carbs are more or less all the same. The issue is a little more complex than that, however. Let the truth be known: *all complex carbohydrates are not created equal.* Starchy carbs are entirely different from fibrous carbs, which are completely different from the carbs underneath your car's hood. One of them you eat for size, the other one you eat for cuts (and the third one helps to start your car).

All complex carbohydrates are composed of carbon, hydrogen, and oxygen, but the size of the molecules and the ways in which the atoms are joined differ from one specific carbohydrate to another. That's why there's such a wide variety of carbs for us to eat.

Complex carbohydrates, or polysaccharides, are large sugar complexes that contain repeating sequences of simple sugars, or chains of monosaccharides. The most familiar of these is starch, a massively built carbohydrate that actually contains two components, amylose and amylopectin. These two components are distributed throughout the structure of plants in the form of granules, and that mixture is simply referred to as starch.

Fibrous carbohydrates, or cellulose, are also polysaccharides like starch. However, the distinct difference between cellulose and starch is in the way the glucose units are linked. This difference gives the two polysaccharides their unique characteristics. The linkage found in fibrous carbs is called a beta linkage, while the type found in starch carbs is an alpha linkage.

Starch is hydrolyzed in the mouth by an enzyme called amylase, which slips between the glucose bonds and disintegrates the starch into smaller units. However, since the glucose bonds of the fibrous carbs are linked at a slightly different angle, the amylase cannot fit between them to break down the glucose molecules. This means that we are unable to absorb the food energy that is locked inside the fibrous carbohydrates.

Ever notice how you can chew on a toothpick for an hour, and all it does is shred down in size, but the wood will not change? That's because the wood is cellulose. But stick a small potato in your mouth, and it will completely vanish within a few minutes because it's starch. Those fibrous carbohydrates can be hydrolyzed by a specific enzyme, but that enzyme is produced only by certain bacteria. It is precisely for this reason that you cannot group complex carbohydrates together—we can digest the starchy carbs, but not the fibrous ones.

Does this mean that cellulose is basically a useless food? The answer is yes and no. The fact that it's useless is very useful to us. Cellulose carbs—collectively known as dietary fiber—tend to collect water and lend bulk to the intestinal contents, thereby stimulating the peristaltic movements of the digestive tract. In other words, fiber helps food to plow through your plumbing. It also reduces the passage time through the bowel. For a constantly eating bodybuilder, that's very important.

Protein is a complex structure that takes a while to break down. When you pile down the steaks and the chicken, your body needs the protein, but you don't want them sticking around on your insides. That's where fibrous carbs enter the picture. Acting as nature's body brush, they keep the traffic moving along and thereby prevent that protein from putrefying. Therefore, fibrous carbs do make a significant impact on your insides, even though they do not actually provide nutrients to the body.

Fibrous carbs also make a significant impact *on* your body. Fibrous carbs are fantastic foods for getting you sliced! The reason is obvious: since we cannot digest the cellulose into smaller glucose units, the caloric density of fibrous carbs will be much lower than that of starchy carbs.

This difference between these complex carbs forms the basis of our blueprint for getting sliced. Here's what you do:

- Gradually replace your intake of starchy carbs with fibrous carbs. The complex-carbohydrate portions of your meals should be as follows: breakfast consists entirely of starchy carbs, lunch should have a 50-50 ratio of starchy to fibrous, and your last meal is completely fibrous.
- While you are reducing your dietary intake of starchy carbs, gradually increase your intake of high-quality protein. This protein increase should occur at every meal throughout the day.
- Cut back from six meals per day to four or five. Try five at first, and if you notice it does not seem to make an appreciable change in your physique, then cut down to four.
- Increase your level of aerobic activity. (For a detailed explanation of this, see Chapter 9.)
- Increase the use of various ergogenic aids during this period. By way of trial and error, find out what works for you in producing better stamina, strength, and recuperation. Choose from the many ergogenics listed in Chapter 5.

"Complex carbs power me up for a workout, giving me a consistent flow of energy to get a two-hour job done at maximum intensity," notes Mike Quinn. "My favorite complex-carb foods are potatoes, rice, and pasta."

Your goal is to lose a maximum of 1½–2 pounds per week. Follow these guidelines until you reach your desired weight or cosmetic appearance. If you reach a plateau where your body weight starts to stabilize, simply change any one or all of these three variables:

1. Increase the duration and/or frequency of aerobic training sessions.
2. Decrease further your intake of starchy carbs, and increase fibrous carbs accordingly.
3. Do not eat past a point five hours before bedtime, and decrease the portions in your last meal of the day.

At *no* point do we advise you to cut out carbohydrates completely. For fats to be used as a source of energy in the body, some carbs must be present. *Fat burns in the flame of carbohydrates.* That's a common maxim among competitive bodybuilders attempting to reduce body fat levels to an absolute minimum for an upcoming show.

If you attempt to go on zero carbs for a few days, ketones (an intermediate product of fat metabolism) start to pile up in your system. This produces a condition called ketosis or acidosis. When this occurs, you'll lose muscle mass at a heartbreaking rate, and your full-muscle belly will turn as flat as a pancake.

Even as little as 50 grams of carbohydrate per day prevent ketosis from occurring. This is where those cellulose carbs can have a muscle-sparing as well as antiketogenic effect that's truly valuable for a dieting bodybuilder. Also of note is the fact that if any energy deficiency exists in your body and carbs are absent, protein will be used as an energy source. Conversely, when the carbs are marching in like a conveyor belt, the body will always use those carbohydrates as the first source of energy, sparing protein from catabolism.

Fibrous carbohydrates have the additional advantage of imparting a full feeling after you ingest them. This is because of their natural tendency to pool water as they pass through your system. Feeling satisfied is certainly a welcome feature to anyone who has ever tried dieting before.

Last but not least, a big plus to fibrous carbs is their physical mass. You can munch away in pure delight on half a head of lettuce, or you

"My workouts are as long and heavy as anyone's in the sport," says multiple Mr. Universe winner Brian Buchanan. "To keep my energy levels up, I'll consume a carbohydrate drink throughout my workout. That way I can bomb and blitz virtually all day long."

can eat the carbohydrate equivalent in a couple of spoonfuls of rice. Which one would you choose if you were hungry?

Of course, there is a downside to fibrous carbs if you eat too much of them. They can cause your food mass to move so rapidly through the small intestine that there is not sufficient time for the nutrients to be absorbed. When this occurs, calcium and zinc are typically prevented from being taken into your system. It's a good idea to supplement both of these important minerals during any dietary regimen.

In case you are wondering which carb is a starchy one and which one is fibrous, a handy list is presented in Table 7-2. Check with your calorie tables, and you'll see dramatic differences between these two complex carbohydrates. For example, 200 grams of red beans contains a whopping 686 calories and 127 grams of carbohydrate. An equal weight of cucumbers has only 30 calories and 7 grams of carbs.

TABLE 7-2 FIBROUS AND STARCHY CARBOHYDRATES

Fibrous Carbs	Starchy Carbs
Asparagus	Barley
Green beans	Lima beans
Broccoli	Red beans
Brussels sprouts	Black-eyed peas
Cabbage	Corn
Carrots	Whole-meal flour
Cauliflower	Lentils
Celery	Oatmeal
Cucumbers	Pasta
Eggplant	Peas
Lettuce	Popcorn
Mushrooms	Potatoes
Green peppers	Rice
Red peppers	Sweet potatoes
Spinach	Tomatoes
Squash	Shredded wheat
Zucchini	Yams

As you can clearly see, a small difference in atomic linkage angle makes all of the difference in the food's absorption efficiency. That's why fibrous carbs are so effective at promoting a sliced appearance. When you make the switch from starchy to fibrous carbs, you can expect a noticeable change in your muscle definition within three days.

A sample daily menu plan for consuming both starchy and fibrous carbs appears in Table 7-3 on page 123. In keeping with our general guidelines, note in this daily menu that breakfast consists of starchy carbs, lunch has both starchy and fibrous, and the last meal is entirely fibrous. The midmorning and midafternoon mealtimes act

"Fruit is okay for a quick energy burst right before a workout," says long-term pro Marjo Selin. "Where I live on Maui, you can pick it and eat it. But for sustained energy during a long workout, you need starchy carbs like potatoes, yams, pasta, beans, peas, and rice."

TABLE 7-3 SAMPLE DAILY MENU FOR STARCHY AND FIBROUS CARBS

7:30 A.M.	4 ounces oatmeal cereal
	4 egg whites
	6 ounces orange juice
10:30 A.M.	4 ounces tuna (water-packed)
	1 boiled egg
	1 carrot
	1 glass mineral water
1:00 P.M.	6 ounces chicken breast
	5 ounces pasta
	5 ounces green beans
	1 glass mineral water
3:30 P.M.	7 ounces haddock
	1 small potato (baked)
	5 ounces asparagus
	1 glass mineral water
6:30 P.M.	5 ounces lean steak
	4 ounces broccoli
	6 ounces cauliflower
	1 glass mineral water

as a tuning dial for the diet. If weight is coming off too rapidly, eat more starchy carbs during these two meals. And if weight loss seems at a standstill, then eat just fibrous carbs at these two meals, and increase your aerobic output. You should only go to four meals per day as a last resort. It is far better to increase your aerobics first than it is to decrease calories.

Regardless of which carbohydrates you consume, however, keep in mind that they must be ingested regularly in order to meet the energy demands of our bodies. Never miss a scheduled carb in your meals. They are vitally important. You'll see why when you look at this breakdown of carbohydrate storage in the body of a 220-pound bodybuilder:

Liver glycogen	165 grams
Muscle glycogen	367 grams
Extracellular blood sugar	15 grams
Total	547 grams (2,190 calories)

As you can see, the amount of carbohydrate in the body is relatively small. Those 547 grams of glucose in a 220-pound body provide energy for only 20 hours of moderate physical activity. Even the brain contains no stored supply of glucose and is therefore totally dependent upon a minute-to-minute supply of glucose from the blood. That's why when you've missed a few meals you can actually feel yourself getting stupid in the head. However, the point is clear:

we need carbs all of the time. From hitting the most muscular pose to the blinking of an eyelid, everything runs on carbs.

Clearly, Multiple-Carbohydrate Leverage Loading is the ultimate diet to follow for maximum muscle mass. Once you are satisfied with your muscle thickness, switch from starchy to fibrous carbs to carve that muscle into sweeping shape and deep crevices that will stagger the minds of many an onlooker. That's why we say, "When you want to get sliced, start slicing up some fibrous carbs!"

8

AMINO ACIDS

Free-form and branched-chain amino acids became hugely popular among competitive bodybuilders and aspiring competitors during the late 1980s. Aminos had been available to bodybuilders since the early 1970s, but only to a few elite athletes due to high cost and marginal availability. It wasn't until Japanese industrialists developed and patented a high-quality, low-price method of biological fermentation of aminos during the middle 1980s that free-form and branched-chain aminos became widely available to the public.

Bodybuilders are quick to exploit any nutritional advance, and amino acid capsules and tablets were quickly embraced by a broad spectrum of serious bodybuilders worldwide. The champs were quick to identify a variety of benefits derived from using aminos:

- Optimum muscle hypertrophy
- Quick tissue repair
- Conservation of energy normally expended in digestion, due to partial or full predigestion of aminos
- Sparing of muscle tissue when depleting-loading carbohydrates at contest time
- Higher workout energy
- A better pump from workouts
- Greater mental alertness
- Fewer hunger pangs when dieting
- A greater sense of well-being

Used individually, various aminos in therapeutic dosages can supposedly treat such diverse ills as liver disease, certain types of tumors, brain and nervous system disorders, lack of physical stamina, immune system suppression, muscular dystrophy, hypoglycemia, hyperglycemia, mental illness, pituitary dysfunction, allergic diseases, cardiac insufficiency, broken bones, open wounds, drug addiction, alcoholism, cold sores, ammonia toxification, sore joints, epilepsy, irritability, stress, depression, insomnia, and hay fever. Throw in the fact that various amino acids can promote the release of human growth hormone in bodybuilders, and free-form and branched-chain aminos look like some sort of magic pill.

Are amino acids really that great of a food supplement? The answer is yes and no. Some of the benefits of aminos have been thoroughly researched, while others are more a result of mere theorization than comprehensive research. In other words, some of the "proof" of various benefits of free-form and branched-chain aminos is shaky at best. We'll attempt to stick to the scientifically established *facts* when we discuss individual amino acids later in this chapter.

TYPES OF AMINO ACIDS

Five types of amino acids are currently on the market. In ascending order of quality and usefulness to bodybuilders, they are:

1. Hydrolized amino acids
2. Peptide-bond amino acids
3. Free-form amino acids
4. Branched-chain amino acids
5. Free-form L-crystalline amino acids

Hydrolized amino acids—sometimes called "predigested protein"—have been available for more than 20 years, and they enjoyed a brief fad status as a fat-reducing dietary aid during the middle 1970s. Hydrolized aminos were used as a fasting aid to quickly shed excess body fat. Subjects gulped several ounces of this liquid each day, abstaining from other foods during the day. And the weight *did* come off.

Thousands of individuals fasted off hundreds of thousands of pounds of unsightly fat. Approximately 50 others died in the process, victims of heart arrhythmias induced by the severely unbalanced diet fasters consumed. Quickly, the Food and Drug Administration issued an alert and ended fad fasting on hydrolized amino acids. But this crude form of aminos has persisted through the years, and the concoction still is available on the shelves of health food stores to this day.

Hydrolized amino acids are manufactured by drenching animal

"I like to take a powdered amino acid drink rather than swallowing a lot of capsules," notes World Lightweight Champion Janet Tech. "It's quicker and easier to take and goes to work in the digestive system much sooner."

hides and other by-products in acid, then drawing off the resulting aminos. Unfortunately, this process results in an amino acid concoction of very low biological quality, with several essential amino acids either totally lacking or present in very low concentrations.

Essential amino acids comprise the nine that cannot be produced within the human body. (Thirteen other nonessential aminos can be manufactured from the food we normally consume.) The essential aminos must therefore be supplied in proper ratios in the food you eat each day, or the aminos can't be used to build up new muscle mass and maintain existing muscle tissue. Since hydrolized amino acids are unbalanced in levels of individual essential aminos, they don't build much muscle mass. To put it bluntly, hydrolized aminos

"Amino acids are the building blocks of muscle tissue," says Mr. Universe, Tom Platz. "Branched-chain aminos are the most important for muscle growth."

are a total waste of any serious bodybuilder's hard-earned bucks. You might more profitably use them to fertilize your houseplants!

It's also difficult to get around the raunchy taste of hydrolized amino acids, even if these preparations *are* fortified with a ton of cherry or lemon-lime flavoring. At best, you'll have to hold your nose to gag the goop down. At worst, it might come back up faster than it went down.

Peptide-bond amino acids are a big step up in quality, yet still not that good of a buy for a hard-training bodybuilder. The reason is that this type of amino acid preparation has to be digested before your body can begin to assimilate the aminos. It's those peptide bonds, which have to be digested in order to free up the aminos, that make this product less than desirable for bodybuilders. Peptide-bond aminos work less efficiently than higher-quality aminos, which literally pass directly into the bloodstream, bypassing the digestion process and the large amounts of energy expended in digestion.

Like free-form, branched-chain, and free-form L-crystalline aminos, peptide-bond amino acids can be formulated with varying amounts of individual aminos. That means you *must* read all amino acid product labels to determine how essential and nonessential amino acids are combined and balanced against each other.

With each of the top four types of aminos, there is an easy method of determining whether or not a particular formulation is inferior. The most expensive individual amino acids are lysine, arginine, ornithine, tryptophan, phenylalanine, and tyrosine. If a formulation has very low amounts of these aminos, chances are good that it's a cheap formulation. And if it's priced as high as a superior formula, the supplement distributor is just adding insult to injury.

Free-form amino acids are the best-known type and the variation most widely used by bodybuilders. Still, they are an inferior bodybuilding value when compared to branched-chain and free-form L-crystalline aminos. But free-form amino acids are *not* attached to any other molecules—like peptide-bond aminos—which means they can pass directly into the bloodstream without having to be digested.

Almost all of the free-form aminos currently being sold are L-configuration (the *L* is for "left") amino acids, because R-configuration ("right") can be toxic in larger quantities. Still, you might see R-configuration free-form aminos on sale, so be alert for that scam when you read labels to determine formulation quality. It has also been determined recently that L-tryptophan has been toxic enough in large quantities to cause several documented deaths. By mid-1990 (when this book was written), most products containing tryptophan had been ordered recalled by the government.

Branched-chain amino acids are of great value to bodybuilders, because they make up a major percentage of the aminos that form muscle tissue. The branched-chain aminos are valine, leucine, and isoleucine, and they are most appropriately taken after a hard work-out to speed recovery and increase muscle hypertrophy.

Free-form L-crystalline amino acids are the top of the line for bodybuilders. They are also the most expensive, but well worth their price, because they are used more efficiently than any other form of amino acids. This type of amino acid is administered via intravenous means to nourish debilitated hospital patients.

Free-form L-crystalline aminos can be most quickly absorbed into the bloodstream by holding the amino acid powder beneath your tongue, where it is rapidly passed through body membranes directly into the blood flowing through the large vein under the tongue. The powder tastes a bit like rotten eggs smell, but you'll get used to the taste once you've experienced the immediate energy rush resulting from sublingual consumption of this supplement powder.

TAKING AMINO ACIDS

It's best to take peptide-bond, free-form, branched-chain, and free-form L-crystalline amino acid supplements on an empty stomach, which facilitates the assimilation of nutrients. Bodybuilders are usually advised to take amino acid supplements 30 to 60 minutes before a meal for maximum utilization in building up new muscle mass.

You might also consider taking your amino acid supplements with a dilute carbohydrate-containing fluid, such as apple juice mixed 50-50 with pure water. You have to use some type of fluid to swallow the amino acid supplements anyway, and the diluted juice provides an internal source of calories, which facilitates absorption and assimilation.

Dosage levels for amino acids vary widely according to body weight, personal preference, and proximity to competition. Generally speaking, the greater your muscle mass, the more amino acid cap-sules you should consume each day. And the closer a competition, the more aminos you should normally take.

A minimum dosage of amino acids would be 10 to 15 capsules per day. But many top bodybuilders take literally hundreds of capsules of various types of aminos each day during a peaking cycle. That level of consumption can get *very* expensive, but bodybuilders swear by it and willingly spend hundreds of dollars per peaking cycle on amino acid supplements.

The type, brand, and amount of amino supplements you use can only be determined through systematic experimentation over an extended period of time. To novice bodybuilders, judging between one type or brand of aminos and another seems totally subjective; experienced bodybuilders have highly developed instincts for what works best for them. But even experienced competitors take a year or more to work out a personalized amino acid supplementation program. Don't rush into anything yourself.

GROWTH HORMONE RELEASERS

With the publication of Durk Pearson and Sandy Shaw's popular book, *Life Extension*, during the early 1980s, bodybuilders began to focus on the individual amino acids arginine, ornithine, and lysine. Pearson and Shaw stated that these three aminos would release human growth hormone (hGH), which in turn would promote muscle growth and increase fat metabolism.

Pearson and Shaw even published their own physique photos in their book as proof of their theories. By bodybuilding standards, the authors' physiques were pitiful. But their theory on growth hormone release was still quickly embraced by bodybuilders, who would take several grams of each of the three recommended aminos at bedtime, in an effort to promote hGH release and speed up muscle growth and fat metabolism.

A logical question, however, would be, "But do these three aminos actually promote sufficient hGH release to be of value to a serious bodybuilder?" Subsequent investigation seemed to support Pearson and Shaw, but only when arginine, ornithine, and lysine were taken in huge dosages, 30 to 50 times what Pearson and Shaw recommended.

The most recent research indicates that a combination of 1,000 to 1,500 milligrams each of L-arginine and L-lysine—taken on an empty stomach in the morning upon rising and at night before retiring—does promote sufficient hGH release to make a difference to a bodybuilder, particularly to one who is training naturally, without use of anabolic steroids and other growth-promoting drugs.

A word of caution: Diabetic and prediabetic bodybuilders should strictly avoid using hGH releasers. Human growth hormone markedly elevates blood sugar levels, which are already excessively high in diabetic patients. It would be dangerous to elevate them any more due to hGH release.

CHARACTERISTICS OF INDIVIDUAL AMINOS

This section will discuss the characteristics and properties of selected individual amino acids. In each case, we will attempt to stick solely with information that has been scientifically confirmed.

L-alanine is a glycogenic amino acid involved in the metabolism of sugars and organic acids. L-alanine has been used experimentally with branched-chain aminos to conserve nitrogen in the system. Thus, it could directly affect the building of larger and stronger muscles.

"Free-form amino acids are better than peptide-bond aminos," says European Champion Marjo Selin. "The bonds between aminos in peptide-bond types have to be digested before the real aminos can be used by the body to build muscle."

L-arginine is intimately involved in muscle metabolism, in that it acts as a vehicle for the transportation, storage, and excretion of nitrogen. L-arginine also stimulates the immune system, ensuring optimum health. And experiments done at the University of Illinois by John Milner and Lela Stepanovich have shown that arginine supplementation appears to retard tumor growth.

Arginine is synthesized in the human body, and is thus considered to be a nonessential amino acid. However, the rate of arginine synthesis in adults is too slow to meet the requirements of most adult bodies. So, for all intents and purposes, arginine is actually an essential amino acid, which bodybuilders should always attempt to include in their diets in supplemental form.

As mentioned in the previous section, arginine and lysine in combination appear to increase the natural release of hGH, and thus have a direct bearing on bodybuilding.

L-aspartic acid is one of the 22 amino acids that make up protein. Nitrogen derived from aspartic acid is used to form ribonucleotides, precursors of both DNA and RNA, the substances that carry human hereditary patterns. Aspartic acid also helps in ammonia detoxification. (Ammonia can be highly toxic if it enters the circulatory system.) Of interest to bodybuilders, several experiments have shown that aspartic acid increases physical endurance, which can help increase the duration and intensity of your workouts.

L-carnitine is produced within the human body from the amino acids methionine and lysine in the presence of iron, vitamins C and B_6, and niacin. Carnitine assists the body in metabolizing fat and utilizing branched-chain amino acids. Many bodybuilders use carnitine supplements after a workout to facilitate recovery.

L-cysteine is a sulfur-containing amino acid that exists in protein in its disulfide form, L-cystine. Cysteine protects the body against radiation exposure and the damaging effects of alcoholism. L-cysteine is essential in the formation of skin and hair.

L-glutamic acid is an acidic amino acid that can be derived from many other aminos. It is essential in brain metabolism and neurotransmitter excitability. Glutamic acid has been used in the treatment of epilepsy and mental retardation.

L-glycine has been used to treat progressive muscular dystrophy, and it is a vital part of the ATP cycle for the metabolism of glycogen to produce energy for muscle function. Glycine has also been shown to play a role in pituitary function, which can affect a wide range of processes in the human body, including improvement in the basal metabolic rate. Finally, glycine has been used successfully in the treatment of hypoglycemia.

L-histidine has been used successfully to treat ulcers, cardiac insufficiency, angina pectoris, anemia, allergic diseases, and arthritis.

L-isoleucine is one of the three branched-chain amino acids so essential to muscle growth. It is also necessary in the formation of red blood cells. Isoleucine is an essential amino acid that must be supplied (often in supplement form) in a bodybuilder's diet.

L-leucine is another of the three branched-chain aminos necessary in building muscle tissue. It is also an essential amino acid. Leucine is used in the treatment of alcoholism, kidney problems, hyperglycemia, and in the healing of skin wounds and broken bones.

L-lysine is another essential amino acid, one of those recommended to enhance hGH release. It is also useful in the treatment of viral diseases, including cold sores and herpes simplex.

L-methionine is an essential amino acid containing sulfur. Along with choline, inositol, and betaine, methionine is a lipotropic agent, meaning that it helps in the metabolism and transport of fat within the system. Methionine is necessary for the formation of hemoglobin, and it helps treat some types of mental disorders, including schizophrenia.

L-ornithine is an amino acid that does not combine with others to form protein. It helps the body in detoxification and immune system stimulation. For several years, ornithine was considered to be an hGH stimulant, but research does not confirm this function.

L-phenylalanine is needed to form proteins such as those found in insulin and neurotransmitters. It is necessary for a positive mood and mental alertness, and it has been used to fight depression.

L-proline is a nonessential glycogenic amino acid. Proline is very important in forming collagen, which ensures strong joints and connective tissues in bodybuilders. And it is a necessary constituent of healthy cardiac muscle.

L-threonine is a glycogenic amino acid essential for normal growth. It is also important in lipid metabolism.

L-tryptophan is one of the essential amino acids, but it has taken on the role of villain in the early 1990s. Several deaths resulted from the use of tryptophan as a sleep aid. (It is essential in alleviating stress, insomnia, anxiety, and depression.) Whether or not the FDA allows tryptophan back on the general market will only be determined by the passage of time.

L-tyrosine can alter mood and has been used successfully to treat depression in place of traditional antidepressant drugs. Tyrosine has also been used to treat hay fever and other pollen allergies.

L-valine is the last of the three branched-chain amino acids necessary for the formation of muscle tissue. Each of the three branched-chain aminos should be consumed with and in proper proportion to the others. Valine is glycogenic and acts as a precursor for propionic acid. As with the other two branched-chain aminos, it is best taken after workouts to enhance recovery and muscle growth.

"The 1990 Mr. Olympia was the first drug-tested Olympia, and I was in my lifetime best shape," says Mike Christian, who placed fourth in the event. "Correct amino acid supplementation played a big role in my success formula."

THE LAST WORD ON AMINOS

Entire books have been written on the structure and function of individual amino acids, so it is difficult to cover the subject adequately in a chapter such as this. However, this chapter probably provides most of the information a bodybuilder needs to know about amino acids in his or her nutritional program.

Normally an endomorph (a naturally fat individual), Pro World Champ Laura Creavalle is able to consistently reach absolute peak condition by following the procedure she outlines in this chapter for hyping the BMR.

9

HYPING THE BMR

When viewing the lineup at the prejudging for any state- or regional-level bodybuilding competition, you will note athletes in widely varying degrees of physical condition. Some will be so sliced up that they look like skinned rabbits—and very skinny skinned rabbits at that. Others will appear as big and smooth as walruses. But the bodybuilders who invariably take home the heavy gold are those men and women who combine symmetry and proportional balance with a goodly degree of muscle mass and sharply defined muscles. They appear to be 100 percent muscle and 0 percent body fat, with skin as tightly fit over the muscles as plastic food wrap.

Wouldn't it be nice to be able to achieve this optimum contest condition every time you set foot onstage? Well, if you read and master the information presented in this chapter, you'll be able to hype up your basal metabolic rate (BMR) enough to burn off excess body fat without sacrificing hard-won muscle mass in the process.

It's not that difficult to get really ripped up. All you need to do is consume less than 1,000 calories per day (some bodybuilders call this "eating air") and spend four to six hours per day pumping iron and/or riding an exercise bike. It's certainly not a healthy practice—and some bodybuilders following this regimen have bordered on madness before they reached contest day—but it will make what little muscle you have left appear to have no skin covering it! You'll almost be able to see blood flowing through your surface vascularity.

No, the real trick to achieving championship condition is to build up a great degree of balanced muscle mass (see the instructions in Chapter 3) and then to maintain as much of that mass as possible when achieving contest shape. If you go about it correctly, you can still get sliced up to a near-limit degree while holding all of that mass you worked so hard for in the off-season. There's absolutely no sense in slaving away for months for muscle tissue and then starving it all off in a vainglorious attempt to achieve real contest shape.

DAILY CALORIC REQUIREMENT

One bodybuilder who seems to have a firm handle on achieving the type of condition we're discussing is Laura Creavalle (overall U.S. Champion, U.S. Mixed Pairs Champion, IFBB Amateur World Heavyweight Champion, and IFBB Pro Ms. International). "As a competitive bodybuilder," Laura instructs, "the first thing you must establish is your daily caloric requirement, of which there are three components."

The First Component: BMR

"The first and largest component is your BMR," Creavalle states. "Basal metabolic rate refers to the amount of calories needed to maintain all of the chemical reactions that take place within the body and its muscle tissues.

"The BMR is higher for larger bodybuilders. At 255 pounds on contest day, Lee Haney has a higher BMR than that of Lee Labrada, who weighs 185 onstage. Additionally, the BMR for men is higher than for women of the same weight, because males are naturally leaner and have much higher levels of testosterone, another BMR accelerator, in their bodies.

"The leaner a person is, the faster his BMR; and the fatter he grows, the slower the BMR becomes. This is why some large, naturally lean male bodybuilders—such as Franco Santoriello and Gary Strydom—can be completely sliced while consuming 5,000 calories or more each day.

"On the opposite side of the coin, I frequently hear obese individuals say they do not eat very much food, yet remain overweight. This *can* be true, since obese and inactive individuals have a small amount of lean body mass (muscle) and an overabundance of fat, both of which conditions actually slow down the BMR.

"Severely restricting calories will also decrease your BMR. As a defense mechanism against possible starvation, the body will slow its BMR and growth rate, because it is unsure when such a caloric restriction will end. Rather than starve, the body will slow down all

"I must have one of the highest BMRs in the sport," says Pro Ms. International, Jackie Paisley. "I can eat anything in the off-season and not gain fat. I actually have to force myself to eat more close to a show to go up in weight a couple of crucial pounds. I'm ripped all year!"

"The best part about bodybuilding is the fact that you can get paid for doing something you enjoy doing anyway," enthuses Pro World Champion, Mike Christian. "I'm lucky to have a fast BMR, so I'm always sliced, but it's hard for me to add muscle mass."

of its functions—including muscle growth—in order to preserve the status quo."

Big Mike Christian (IFBB Pro U.S. Champion) says, "Experienced bodybuilders also recognize that some individuals are just blessed with faster than normal metabolisms. Have you ever seen a male or female bodybuilder who could eat literally anything—pizza, beer, cake, pie, cheesecake—and still be sliced to doll rags on the day after a food binge?

"There are rare bodybuilders who are always sliced up at contest time, but they do have to pay a price for their massively fast BMRs. Just as it is absurdly easy for them to rip up for a show, it's unbelievably difficult for this metabolic type to pack on muscle mass. Sometimes they are able to gain only a pound or two of pure muscle each year, but it *is* pure muscle. They never seem to gain fat, and if they stick to a heavy training and dietary program long enough, this fast metabolic type of man or woman will one day be a superstar of the sport."

The Second Component: Physical Activity

"Physical activity is the second contributor to a bodybuilder's total daily caloric requirement," Creavalle states. "Bodybuilding workouts can increase caloric needs by 10 percent to 30 percent, while aerobic training sessions will increase caloric needs even further, depending on frequency and duration of the activity."

Seven-time Mr. Olympia Lee Haney observes, "Most serious bodybuilders hardly pay any attention to the calories they burn up in a bodybuilding training session. But you can and will burn up tremendous amounts of calories in a gym workout lasting 60 to 90 minutes at a time. I personally double-split my workouts even in the off-season, so my caloric expenditures during two daily weight sessions can mount up to more than an average lower-level bodybuilder doing one daily two-hour-long weight workout and 30 minutes on a stationary bike after the weight session.

"Where I really get down to business is over the final six weeks prior to a Mr. Olympia competition, when I actually triple-split my weight workouts, hitting the gym to pump iron a full three times daily. Inasmuch as I average about 1¼ hours per weight workout, I'm spending nearly 4 high-intensity hours per day in the gym three out of every four days. Need I clue you as to how many calories I'm expending each workout day just lifting iron? I'd estimate it at about 2,500 each day I'm in the gym three times.

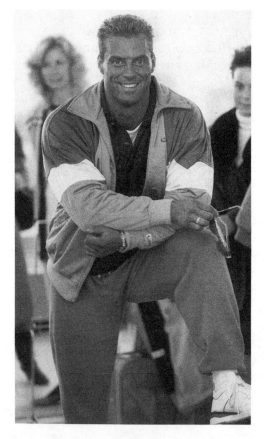

Bodybuilders like Berry de Mey don't spend all of their time in the gym, but they certainly spend plenty of it in gym clothing. Berry rides a stationary bike two or three times a day to increase his BMR prior to competition.

"When I'm burning up 2,500 calories per day three out of every four days I spend in the gym—don't forget, even though I double- or triple-split, I still follow the three-on/one-off split routine, resting from the gym every fourth day—you can see why I don't have to also do much aerobic training. I'll ride a stationary bike 15 to 30 minutes at a time occasionally, but mainly as a tool to fine-tune my degree of muscularity over the last couple of weeks leading up to an Olympia appearance. If I'm a tad behind schedule and need to quickly sharpen up, I'll jump on the bike, but otherwise the thing just gathers dust.

"By burning up so many calories in the gym triple-splitting, I can actually eat relatively normally each day, particularly in comparison to those poor guys on 1,500 calories per day before a major show. I seldom allow my body weight to travel more than 10 to 12 pounds over its competitive level, and start a moderate diet 12 weeks out from my contest. This way I can eat 4,000 to 4,500 calories per day during most of my preparatory cycle, and I *never* have to go under 3,000 per day. That type of diet is a pure pleasure for me to follow, and it leaves me with all of my muscle mass intact when I step onstage to be prejudged."

Creavalle comments, "Common sense tells you that a leg or back workout will require more calories to complete than a biceps or triceps session. The larger the muscles involved and the longer the duration of exercising one of them, the greater will be the total caloric expenditure. It doesn't take a Ph.D. degree to understand that a set of 10 squats with 400 pounds requires more calories to complete than a set of 10 with only 300."

The Third Component: SDE

"We rarely hear about a third component of energy expenditure, however," states Creavalle. "It is called SDE, short for specific dynamic effect. SDE is the energy produced chemically in the body in response to food intake, so that food can be properly digested, absorbed, and metabolized. Generally speaking, this stimulation of the digestive system increases your caloric expenditure requirement under normal circumstances by about 10 percent."

Andreas Cahling (IFBB Pro Mr. International) maintains that choice of food can increase the number of SDE calories expended: "There is a type of vegetable which I call 'negative-calorie foods.' These are fibrous carbohydrate foods such as celery, lettuce, rhubarb, cabbage, radishes, carrots, artichokes, and so forth, which literally require more calories to digest than they supply. When I'm a little short of my peak a few days out from a pro show, I'll increase my SDE caloric expenditure by adding two or three servings of my negative-calorie foods to my diet in place of starchy carb foods. This

"I begin taking cholins and inositol six weeks out from a show to help mobilize body fat and make me more sliced," says 1983 Mr. Olympia Samir Bannout. I recommend dosages of 1,000 to 1,500 milligrams a day of each element when in a peaking cycle."

works wonders at burning off the last vestiges of stored body fat, which might be slightly blurring out my deepest cuts and finest striations. A couple of days later, I'm ready to step onstage sliced!"

CALCULATING CALORIC EXPENDITURE

Using the foregoing information, you can make a fairly accurate representation of how many calories you are burning up on a contest diet. Assume that we are talking about a 220-pound male body-builder with 10 percent body fat, giving him 200 pounds of lean body mass. The formulas for calculating his energy levels are given in Table 9-1.

Pro Ms. International Jackie Paisley is one of many bodybuilders who find they achieve their best cuts by drinking large quantities of distilled water each day, often right up to the moment they step onstage to compete.

TABLE 9-1 CALCULATING CALORIC EXPENDITURE

Measurement	Formula	Example*
BMR requirement	100 calories times lean body mass in pounds	100 × 200 = 2,000 calories
Physical activity requirement	Calorie consumption per hour times hours in workout (training at high intensity consumes approximately 600 calories per hour)	600 × 1.5 (1½-hour workout) = 900 calories
SDE	Sum of first two caloric components multiplied by percentage of body fat	2,900 calories × 0.10 = 290 calories
Total daily caloric requirement	Add together the first three calculations	2,000 + 900 + 290 = 3,190 (or approximately 3,200 calories per day)

*Assume a 220-pound male bodybuilder with 10 percent body fat (200 pounds of lean body mass).

To keep blood sugar at relatively high levels throughout the day—and to keep blood amino acid levels and other nutrients relatively constant—it's best to eat six times per day, with the largest meal in the morning and the smallest latest in the day, usually not after 6:00 P.M. if you are really serious about winning your next contest.

"The timing of your last meal each day during a peaking cycle can be critical," reveals Anja Langer (IFBB Junior World Champion, IFBB Heavyweight European Champion, overall German Champion, 2nd/IFBB Pro World Championship, and fourth and second in two IFBB Ms. Olympia competitions). "Due to my busy schedule of training and coaching, I used to eat as late as 10:00 P.M., and I could never understand why I always missed peak condition by about 5 percent. But on the advice of my coach, I made an effort to consume my last meal no later than 6:00 P.M. That allowed me to reach my lifetime best condition for the 1989 Ms. Olympia, where I extended perennial Ms. Olympia winner Cory Everson before ultimately placing second.

"When you eat late and go right to sleep, much of the food in your stomach is turned into stored body fat. And no matter how much aerobic training you do, you never quite work off that excess adipose tissue. No, it's much better to eat prior to 6:00 P.M. and go to bed at 10:00 a little hungry. You'll look much sharper for your next competition as a result!"

Laura Creavalle adds, "Meal timing can be a critical factor. The reason breakfast should be the largest meal of the day is that's when the body's digestive enzymes and internal body chemistry are most ready and active to digest, absorb, and use a maximum level of calories and other nutrients for muscle growth and energy expenditure. But as the day progresses, the body's output of enzymes tends to slow down, as does the overall metabolism."

"Most serious bodybuilders hardly pay attention to the number of calories they burn up in a bodybuilding training session," reveals seven-time Mr. O Lee Haney. "But you can and will burn up tremendous amounts of calories in a gym session lasting 60 to 90 minutes at a time.

With our hypothetical 220-pound bodybuilder consuming 3,200 calories on a precontest diet each day, he could divide up his caloric consumption over six meals somewhat like this:

Meal Number	Total Calories
1	1,000
2	600
3	600
4	400
5	400
6	200

Approximately 2–2½ hours should elapse between each of the six meals.

Several specific types of diets can be followed, and they are outlined in Part III. Just keep in mind that individual bodybuilders will modify any diet to suit themselves, even if it is just a matter of substituting one food they like for a similar but less tasty food.

"Although it sounds very basic and coaches have preached about its value for years," notes Creavalle, "water is still the most important of all nutrients. It makes up 70 percent of the body's content and is responsible for millions of internal chemical reactions. It helps carry nutrients from one place to the next, transports oxygen to cells to promote energy and growth, and removes carbon dioxide from the cells as waste products after a set.

"Most bodybuilders are underhydrated at the cellular level, where growth takes place. Although 8 glasses of water daily are recommended for most individuals, I suggest an absolute minimum intake of 12 glasses daily. The typical 8-glass level is recommended for an inactive 154-pound male. Bodybuilders are more active and heavier on an average, so they require much more water. It is actually possible to be slightly dehydrated without experiencing any sensation of thirst whatsoever."

In practice, many champion bodybuilders—among them Lee Haney, Richie Gaspari, Lee Labrada, and Jackie Paisley—have recognized that drinking large quantities of distilled water right up to the hour of a show actually results in a much harder onstage appearance than if they followed the water-deprivation methods, carbo depleting-loading, and/or sodium loading-depleting currently in use by hundreds of competitive bodybuilders.

Let's hear what Lee Haney has to say about his own consumption of water: "Along with protein, fat, carbohydrate, vitamins, and minerals, water is an absolutely essential nutrient. It is the body's natural solvent and does yeoman work to detoxify the body's tissues. I'm careful to drink a great deal of water—probably a gallon or more—during the day, because it is so valuable in the bodybuilding process, and because I perspire so freely in the normally hot, humid weather we have in Atlanta over the summer when I'm training two or three times per day to prepare for an Olympia defense.

"During the bulk of the year, I drink bottled natural spring water, for its purity and mineral content. If you live in the country, well water is a good substitute, but I'd caution you against drinking tap water in large urban areas. It has so much chlorine, fluorine, and other toxins in it that it could conceivably harm your health and set your bodybuilding progress back many months. The only safe way to drink urban tap water is to first filter it. Most health food stores have home water filtration units available at reasonable prices. And they can also be mail-ordered through ads in health-oriented magazines.

"Prior to a show, I drink only distilled water, since it has zero sodium content. But unlike many bodybuilders, who deprive themselves of water before a competition, I drink it freely throughout the day, even on a contest day. Drinking plenty of water prior to an Olympia fully hydrates my muscles—making them appear as large as possible—*and* completely eliminates water rention, which might blur out my best cuts. Water power! Use it and win."

THE AEROBICS BUMP

By itself, caloric restriction can be counterproductive to dieting for a competition. It can slow down your BMR and cause loss of muscle tissue, as well. Considering the amount of time and effort that goes into building up new muscles, plus the importance of your metabolism, bodybuilders need to protect themselves against these situations. The best way to do this is by incorporating aerobic exercise into your own training program.

Whenever a person loses body weight, he or she is actually losing three things: fat tissue, muscle tissue, and water. Studies show this is especially evident when the dieter is simply reducing calories.

The proof is easy to see. Did you ever notice how the "before" and "after" photos of untrained individuals are simply smaller versions of their formerly fat selves? In the after photos, their arms are skinny but *fat*, their thighs are smaller but still full of that dimpled cellulite appearance. In effect, they go from a large pear-shaped physique to a smaller pear-shaped body.

This is because muscles give contour and shape to the body. These untrained folks don't work out, so they lose a significant amount of muscle, and with that goes all of their body shape.

In one particular study, two groups of people were analyzed: a group that only dieted, and another that combined diet with exercise. The exercise consisted of 45 minutes of aerobic activity at 70 percent

Swimming is an effective aerobic activity.

to 85 percent of their maximum heart rate, followed by light calis-
thenics. This was done for a period of eight weeks.

While both groups lost similar amounts of body weight—11.8
kilograms for the exercise-dieters and 9.2 kilos for the diet-only
group—the *type* of weight loss varied greatly. The exercising group's
weight loss came almost entirely from fat, and virtually no muscle
was lost. Conversely, the diet-only group lost a walloping 36 percent

Never deprive your body of water when dieting. A healthy sweat, such as that shown by Iron Man Pro Invitational Champion Shawn Ray, eliminates toxins from your body and makes your skin seem to glow at contest time.

of their weight total in the form of muscle. Ouch, talk about a serious muscle loss!

As you can see, aerobics are absolutely vital for the dieting body-builder, who needs to conserve as much muscle mass as possible. Furthermore, aerobics have the additional benefit of burning mostly fat as opposed to muscle glycogen for energy, and the activity keeps stimulating the metabolism long after exercise has ceased. In many cases, you can increase your caloric intake by up to 25 percent and *still* record a weight loss by the use of aerobics.

Although everyone seems to have an opinion, the "ideal" length of time to do aerobics is between 30 and 60 minutes at a time. If a session goes over 60 minutes, it's better to split it into another aerobic session, rather than plowing past the hour.

Keep in mind that aerobics is much more than sitting on a stationary bike and pedaling. You can substitute riding a free bike, using a rowing machine, hiking, running, speed walking, stair climbing, swimming, skating, cross-country skiing, and even treading water. Activities that have short bursts of movement of a start-and-stop nature—like tennis, handball, basketball, racquetball, touch football, volleyball, baseball, and martial arts—will not produce the necessary aerobic effect.

Just what is the "aerobic effect"? This is when your pulse rate is *between* 70 percent of your maximum heart rate and the cutoff figure of 85 percent of your max. Table 9-2 designates heart rate target zones for healthy individuals of various age groups.

When taking your pulse rate, try to keep moving slightly to get a

TABLE 9-2 TARGET HEART RATE ZONES FOR AEROBIC EFFECT IN HEALTHY INDIVIDUALS OF VARIOUS AGE GROUPS

Age	Target Heart Rate (70%)	Cutoff Heart Rate (85%)
20–25	140	167
26–30	134	163
31–35	131	159
36–40	127	155
41–45	124	150
46–50	120	146
51–55	117	142
56–60	113	138
61–65	110	133

Aerobic Effect Zone

more accurate reading. If you are well into the aerobic zone, you can slow down ever so slightly and still get the desired effect. If you are short of the mark, pick up your pace at whatever activity you're performing.

A good monitoring device is the "talk test." If you are biking or rowing so fast that you cannot converse with someone else, ease off! That extra speed will only dip into your reservoir of recuperation, and you won't see the difference from a cosmetic standpoint anyway.

For a bodybuilder, it's best to stay near the lower end of the aerobic zone. A rule to keep in mind is that if the activity you're doing starts to cause a burn in the muscles, then you are using carbohydrate as a source of fuel, not fat. It's the longer-lasting, lower-intensity efforts that use fat as a fuel source.

How often should you do aerobics? As often as your needs dictate. If you are falling behind on your projected weight loss schedule, step up the frequency from three to five times per week. If the weight is piling off quickly, either increase your caloric intake or cut down on the frequency of aerobics.

You should always do a *minimum* of three aerobic sessions per week, regardless of your schedule. This is the lowest you should go. We've seen some bodybuilders perform three aerobic sessions daily of one hour each and experience no appreciable signs of muscle loss (although, in these cases, they were playing catch-up with their physical conditions.)

Design your aerobics program exactly to your needs. To avoid those occasional bouts of boredom, you can read, watch a television placed strategically in front of you, or listen to a stereo headset while exercising.

As a general guideline, the average resting pulse rate is 60 to 80 beats per minute for men, 70 to 90 for women. An aerobically fit bodybuilder typically has a heart rate below 60 beats per minute.

The most accurate time to check your heart rate is in the morning. Simply touch the carotid artery on either side of your neck and feel the pulse on your fingertips. You don't need to squeeze hard at all. Count the beats for 10 seconds, then multiply the result by 6 to get the beats per minute.

Interestingly enough, a minisurvey we conducted on bodybuilders who typically did high-rep squats in their leg routines proved our hunch: they all had lower-than-normal pulse rates *regardless* of their body weight or body fat content. The facts are clear; put aerobics into your general training philosophy—today!

SUPPLEMENTS FOR THE RIPPED LOOK

"Food supplements are essential for all serious bodybuilders," emphatically states Eddie Robinson (NPC Overall U.S. Champion, IFBB Pro Gold's Classic Champion). "To lose fat and get ripped, you have to develop a caloric deficit, which in turn may lead to nutritional deficiencies when you drop particular foods from your diet. Therefore, I recommend one vitamin-mineral multipack for smaller bodybuilders and two for larger guys like myself. And you can gradually work out an individualized program of supplementation—such as extra vitamin B-complex, choline, inositol, desiccated liver, etc.—which you can consume along with your multipacks at mealtime."

Laura Creavalle observes, "Supplements are only as effective as your diet. That is, they work as catalysts in conjunction with food, *not* in place of it. Although it sounds as basic as drinking water in quantity, eating a variety of food on a peaking diet is of great importance.

"Most of us fall prey to consuming the same 10 to 12 foods day in and day out. Different foods have unique vitamins, minerals, and enzymes in them to promote growth and overall health, and a diet consisting of many different foods is automatically better balanced nutritionally than one limited to 10 to 12.

"Over the past few years, an array of fat-burning supplements has become popular with competitive bodybuilders. Two of the best are MCT oil and L-carnitine. Although I have used both of these products with great success, you should understand that weight-loss products will only work if you are eating fewer calories than you need to maintain your body weight. This is only good common sense!

"MCT oil, a medium-chain triglyceride, is a shorter-chain version of a typical dietary fat. It is absorbed by the body faster due to its shorter molecular length. In fact, it is absorbed almost as quickly as normal carbohydrate foods. Consuming any type of fat increases the secretion of lipases in the body. A lipase is a fat-burning enzyme that is produced in response to fat intake, for metabolism purposes. Since MCT oils are absorbed so quickly, the lipase has nothing to work on

"The timing of your last meal each day during a peaking cycle can be critical," says German angel Anja Langer. "I used to eat as late as 10 in the evening and couldn't get as sliced as I wanted to. It was only when I disciplined myself to consume my last meal of the day no later than 6 that I reached my best condition."

"I'm not the type who has to do a lot of aerobic training," says Robby Robinson. "I keep my weight well within 10 pounds of competitive level during the off-season and follow a sensible low-cal diet to zero in on contest shape. No riding an exercise bike all day for me!"

except stored body fat; hence it helps a bodybuilder to achieve an ultra-ripped-up appearance.

"L-carnitine is a nonessential amino acid that helps assist in transporting fat to the powerhouses of the cell—the mitochondria—where it can be used as energy. L-carnitine is present in protein foods, but in too small a quantity to be effective for fat metabolism. It is widely available in tablet form at health food stores, however.

"Both MCT oil and L-carnitine should be taken before aerobic training. If I am restricting my carbohydrate intake, I will take them both before and after my weight workout as well. This way, my glycogen is depleted, and my body will call upon fats for energy, rather than carbohydrate stores.

"As a final note, always remember to keep your weight under control between contests, start your preparations early for each competition, and always rely on common sense and moderation for best results. This approach will get you to the top far more rapidly than you would ever expect!"

Samir Bannout (the 1983 IFBB Mr. Olympia winner) says, "There are a couple of B vitamins—choline and inositol—which have been used as fat-burners since Larry Scott was winning the first Mr. Olympia title in 1965. Both choline and inositol work to metabolize stored body fat and transport it to cell mitochondria, where the fatty acids are burned to provide energy for workouts and a huge variety of other bodily functions. Choline and inositol can be purchased at moderate cost in capsule and tablet form at health food stores.

"I personally don't use choline or inositol in the off-season, because I believe laying off these supplements for several months gives them a greater effect when I begin taking them six weeks out from a competition. I suggest choline dosages of 1,000 to 1,500 milligrams for men and 750 to 1,000 milligrams for women, spread out during the day. And I recommend inositol dosages of 1,000 to 1,500 milligrams for men and 500 to 1,000 milligrams for women, with both supplements taken together at mealtimes."

SWIM FOR IT!

We once knew an M.D. who was a very good competitor, having placed in the top five overall at one Mr. America show back in the seventies. To keep from embarrassing his relatives or the superstar bodybuilder who coached him, we'll simply call him "Doc." Well, Doc was undeniably intelligent and fantastically well educated, and as is the case with some of the superintellects we've known, he was quite eccentric.

One of the authors used to room with Doc and was constantly amazed at the steady stream of seemingly fantastic bodybuilding theories he came up with. Since Doc had a habit of piling 35 to 40 pounds of blubber on his frame during each off-season ("It makes it easier to gain muscle mass, because the mere weight of the excess adipose causes muscle hypertrophy!"), he had scores of methods of ripping up for an upcoming competition. Some of his methods must have worked, because Doc routinely stepped onstage as ripped and vascular as anyone against whom he was competing.

One of Doc's precontest diets consisted of 20 whole almonds, 30 amino acid capsules, and 2 gallons of distilled water each day. "The whole secret is the almonds," he explained, "because they are almost pure fat and kill my appetite. The aminos feed the muscles and keep my mass up as I lose body fat from the lower caloric intake I'm on. And the water both cleanses my system and helps rid my body of excess water retention." We *did* say he was a tad eccentric!

One of Doc's other ripping-up systems did work quite well, even though on the surface it also seemed a bit from outer space. "If I'm ever coming up a little short of my peak, I go swimming in the cold Pacific surf," he said. "Nothing will cause the body to mobilize calories faster than being cold and trying to warm itself up. That's simple survival. And you have to swim like an otter to survive heavy surf, thereby using up even more calories. After 30 minutes thrashing around in the water, I'm completely exhausted and have nothing but sleep on my mind once I'm warmed up again. And when I do wake up in the morning, you simply wouldn't *believe* how much more cut up I am than I was the previous day."

"When it all comes together and you win one, it's the greatest feeling on earth," says Vince Taylor, who has won Night of the Champions and placed third in Mr. Olympia as a pro. At the end of his amateur career, he won the overall Nationals.

10

SUPPLEMENTS AND COSMETIC APPEARANCE

A few years ago, when Billy Crystal's comedy career became an overnight success, it was his imitations that left everyone in stitches. Of all the people he did, he got the greatest reaction to his rendition of Fernando Lamas uttering that now-famous line, "Remember, darling, it is better to look good than to feel good!"

Given the choice, most bodybuilders would rather take a supplement that will make them look good than take one that will make them feel good. After all, the success of your bodybuilding progress is measured by how you look, not how you feel. Of course, this in no way implies that bodybuilders don't care how they feel. Bodybuilding, by its very nature, makes you feel great. Bodybuilders are much healthier than the average person. Even their minds are healthier. Research has proved this point.

A team of researchers headed by Patty Freedson of the University of Massachusetts in Amherst studied female competitive bodybuilders to see how their psychological profiles matched those of other athletes. Their findings revealed that female bodybuilders were less anxious, neurotic, depressed, angry, and confused when compared with the general population. They were also more extroverted, vigorous, and self-motivated, stated the researchers in the publication *Physician and Sports Medicine*. The researchers also report, "This psychological profile reflects positive mental health and is remarkably congruent with the psychological profile of elite, world-class male athletes."

Still, bodybuilders want to look good. (We knew about those psychological benefits anyway.) In their quest for physical enhancement, bodybuilders will try all sorts of supplements to see which ones work. While many supplements work very well, giving increased energy levels that you can actually sense, many others don't seem to do anything that you can "feel." Yet bodybuilders won't disregard these types of supplements because taking them may provide some psychological assurance that they're getting valuable nutrients.

When it gets right down to which food supplements make you *look* better, however, many bodybuilders simply aren't aware. That's OK, because *we* are. This chapter deals with those few gold-plated supplements that actually make a detectable cosmetic difference. We will also take an in-depth look at the little-known mineral potassium. It plays a major role in giving your muscles that highly desired "full look."

Generally speaking, however, the greater the amount of body fat you have, the harder it is to notice changes. Fat obscures the appearance of a muscle. Also, some bodybuilders notice the tiniest details on their physiques, while others need huge and obvious results to draw a conclusion. Either way, the supplements work, and potassium is important. Your cosmetic appearance will definitely show it.

SKIN TONE

Skin is the largest organ of our body. It keeps microbial invaders out and stops us from leaking all over the place. As an active bodybuilder, you put your skin through torture. Tanning beds and direct sunlight, gaining and losing weight, pumping up your muscles, and sweating all over yourself—all have a stressful effect on skin. Skin needs constant nourishment because it is always shedding, in little amounts you can't pick up with the naked eye.

Typically speaking, dry, rough-looking skin is deficient in vitamin B. If this sounds like you, we advocate a high-potency vitamin B-complex supplement. Since vitamin B is water-soluble, you'll need to take it daily, even several times during the day. If you are concerned about premature wrinkling, studies show that deoxyribonucleic acid (DNA) and ribonucleic acid (RNA) can help slow down the effects of aging.

In many cases, we have actually seen the effect of B vitamins on the skin of a bodybuilder who was originally diagnosed as deficient. This is especially true if the B-complex product is high in niacin. Niacin makes your cheeks turn slightly red and brings color to your face when present in higher-than-normal levels.

While literally thousands of products claim to be good for your skin, and many of them are, you won't be able to detect the difference with them as you can with a good B-complex formula. A chem-

"I used to have a lot of trouble with looking flat and having my muscles cramp up on me onstage," reveals Vince Taylor, Night of the Champions victor. "Then someone pointed out that I wasn't using enough electrolyte supplements—particularly not enough potassium—to get the job done. I supplemented and got everything I wanted!"

Getting the full look. My arm appears to be full of glycogen.

ical called Retin-A will improve facial wrinkles to a marked degree, but that's a topical lotion—a drug, not a food supplement.

Another aspect of skin tone is bruising. Some bodybuilders bruise easily. Once they get bruised, it sometimes takes weeks for it to go away. You can really notice this on lighter-skinned individuals.

The solution to bruising is incredibly simple—take in more vitamin C. If you do bruise, this information may remind you that you don't take any C. You see, to get a bruise from a casual bump or bang, you actually have to be quite deficient in vitamin C. Keep in mind that we're talking about an average bump, not the kind of bump you get when a car tries to run you over.

When you bruise easily, it's your body's way of telling you that a vitamin C deficiency exists. Your body simply can't repair the damaged veins and surrounding cellular structure without the C. Vitamin C is the cellular cement in our bodies. Start taking two to three grams daily, and you'll see those discolored spots fade within days.

THE FULL LOOK

When your body fat is low and your muscles are full of glycogen, the slightest movement can send hordes of muscle fibers and wormlike veins pushing out against the skin and scattering everywhere. The effect is like an electrical storm. This is known as the "full look." It makes you look as though you're going to blow a gasket. How do you get it? Carbohydrates and water are certainly responsible, but you still need to hold the water inside the muscle. The answer to this is potassium.

Although potassium is the third most abundant element in the body, after calcium and phosphorus, its roles are weakly understood by the general bodybuilding population. Potassium is a silvery white metallic element that is never found as a pure metal; it always combines with other substances. About 98 percent of the mineral constituent within cells is potassium. The chief mineral outside the cell is sodium, and that's where the plot thickens.

Intracellular fluid has a potassium content of more than 30 times that of the potassium concentration outside the cell. Big differences like that tell you something. A chemical tug-of-war is constantly going on between potassium and sodium. Precisely at the point when potassium is winning, the highly desired full look is achieved. Of course, several conditions must be met.

First, you have to jimmy around with that sodium-potassium ratio so that water flows into the muscle cells like East Germans headed into West Germany. The safest way to do that is to take in zero sodium on the final three days before a contest. Restricting sodium sooner will cause aldosterone hormone levels to rise, and you'll end up holding more water than before. Cutting sodium one day out won't give it enough time to clear out of your system.

As you can see, the process is subtle and sensitive, which helps to explain why so many amateur and professional bodybuilders can miss their marks at contest time. It takes some trial and error to get it right.

Next, you must make sure that your incoming carbohydrates are high in potassium. With temporarily reduced sodium levels, that extracellular water will flow into the higher ionic gradient within the muscle cell. Normally, the sodium-to-potassium ratio is 1:10 inside the cell and 28:1 in the extracellular fluid. When the sodium levels are down, these ratios favor heavily toward potassium, and water fills up those muscles. Presto! Ballooned-up muscles.

Individual genetic variations cause bodybuilders to add their personal touches to this process. Some bodybuilders prefer to restrict water intake a day or so out for further tightening of the skin. Others have tried this method and found they went flat like a pancake. Instead, they achieved excellent results by drinking water all the way through the carbing up process, managing to keep their hard look.

You have to experiment ahead of time if you want to blueprint this process. Generally speaking, though, we have found that bodybuilders who love to drink water all day need also to drink during their carbing up cycle. Bodybuilders who are never motivated to consume much water do better on a fluid-restriction regimen.

Depletion and Surplus

Rob yourself of potassium, and all kinds of nasty things can happen. You could experience muscle weakness and atrophy, depression, edema, bone and joint pain, overall fatigue, constipation, insomnia, nervous disorders, and a galloping heart. Definitely not the ideal state for a chest and lat workout!

Do you think potassium shortage rarely occurs? NASA found out it didn't. James Irwin of the Apollo 15 mission suffered a series of abnormal heartbeats during three hours of transferring moon rocks to the Command Module. His partner, David Scott, had irregular heartbeats just before splashdown. The overly refined "foods" that were standard issue for space travel had vanishingly low potassium levels.

Starting with Apollo 16, astronauts had potassium-rich foods added to their diets, and also received a potassium-loaded preflight diet before the blast-off. Gee, you'd think NASA would know better. Joe Weider was promoting the importance of potassium and the pitfalls of food processing as early as the mid-1960s in his magazines. Sheesh!

A potassium deficiency can occur from any one of the following things: smoking, alcohol, laxative therapy, refined sugar, excessive intake of sodium chloride, diuretics, diarrhea, vomiting, aspirin, mental and physical stress. However, too much potassium can be bad as well. If you suddenly increased your intake to 18 grams, you could have a cardiac arrest. That's certainly not the best way to end up your posing routine.

In his book *Folk Medicine*, Dr. D. C. Jarvis writes that potassium is

Few people in the sport have experienced the highs and lows of Phil Hill. He won the overall Nationals and two weeks later was a washout at the World Championships. He won the Detroit Grand Prix one year and hasn't been in shape since. Perhaps he needs to raise his potassium IQ.

linked to growth. According to Dr. Jarvis, the soil in Vermont has always been deficient in potassium. He claims that's why Vermonters, as a rule, are shorter in stature than the national norm.

He states that babies not getting enough potassium chew the sides of their cribs to extract the mineral from wood. Horses gnaw at their stalls until potassium, in the form of apple cider vinegar, is added to their feed. And when potassium is missing from the diet of Vermont cows, calves of below-normal height are born. Without doubt, whether you're a cow, horse, or bodybuilder, potassium belongs on the essential list. Especially if you live in Vermont.

The Varied Roles of Potassium

Potassium is vital for the conversion of blood sugar into glycogen. Glycogen is the only fuel stored as a carbohydrate. That's what bodybuilders run on during their brutally hard workouts.

The potassium ion relaxes muscle. Hence, a high concentration in the heart relaxes the heart, as opposed to calcium, which stimulates the heart. Together they normalize the rhythm of your ticker and make sure that you don't end up "buying the farm" after several sets of high-rep squats.

Calcium and magnesium unite with potassium in order to regulate neuromuscular activity. It is interesting to note that serum potassium is very low during attacks of paralysis, and low potassium can cause the muscles to cramp when they are flexed hard.

I (Negrita) once stretched out my thighs during a long plane ride to a contest, and one of my thigh muscles cramped wickedly. The inner teardrop muscle above my knee looked like a three-car pileup. It was wildly disfigured. I immediately wolfed down some electrolytes, water, and a few cal-mag tabs, and shortly thereafter the bunched-up muscle returned to its original shape. The man sitting beside me thought I was much more interesting to watch than the onboard movie, which was *Little Shop of Horrors*.

Potassium functions as an activator of enzymes and is involved in the use of amino acids. Recent scientific evidence suggests that potassium is also involved in bone calcification. In short, potassium is a co-factor in many reactions, especially those involving energy production and muscle building.

Potassium and Blood Pressure

Years ago, our distant ancestors consumed at least 10 times more potassium than sodium each day. Unfortunately, modern techniques for food processing and preserving have inverted this balance. Today, most of us eat more sodium than potassium. For example, freshly picked corn has 280 milligrams of potassium and less than 1

"Mastering your body's potassium-sodium ratios within and without the muscle cells is what gives that full, skin-stretching look to your muscles," says Vince Comerford, an amateur National Middleweight Champion and current IFBB pro.

milligram of sodium per 100-gram portion. The same amount of canned corn has lost most of its potassium and gained 235 milligrams of sodium.

Process the corn further, and the results are wild. Cornflakes have 1,005 milligrams of sodium per 100 grams, and where the heck did the potassium go? One hundred grams of fresh grapes contain 158 milligrams of potassium, yet grape juice starts to pull the vanishing act and cranks out only 34 milligrams.

Check out the two primitive foods against the two modern creations, and see how people today have reversed their natural dietary pattern (per 100-gram edible serving):

	Sodium (mg)	Potassium (mg)
Hot dog	1,100	200
Venison steak	65	385
Apple pie	110	80
Apple	1	301

As you can see, we are the guinea pigs in a modern nutritional experiment, the results of which are starting to show up.

At a recent meeting of the American Physiological Society, researchers spoke of an important dietary link to high blood pressure. They suggested that we should deliberately avoid processed foods not only for their high sodium content but also because of their woefully low potassium content.

Hear Dr. Harold Battarbee of Louisiana State University: "We'd see some dramatic changes in incidence of hypertension [high blood pressure] if Americans cut their salt intake to three grams a day and started eating at least that much potassium."

He further noted, "Although potassium is plentiful in many fresh fruits and vegetables, it is almost entirely lost when they're canned or frozen." Other nutritionists have suggested that a potassium-sodium ration of 2:1 may be even better.

A British study has confirmed that a diet high in potassium and low in sodium has normalized blood pressure in patients having elevated blood pressure. Remember, though, not all high blood pressure has the same cause. Some people have a genetic predisposition to high blood pressure due to an improper sodium-potassium balance.

On the whole, bodybuilders eat better than the average person, so their diets are probably a lot closer to primitive people's, and are less likely to have whacked-out sodium-potassium ratios. Still, practically every contest we've been to has someone cramping, holding water, or looking flat, so never underestimate potassium's importance. It certainly does a lot more than simply reside in a banana.

Actually, bananas aren't even close to being the best source of potassium. To make sure you get enough, as a hard-training body-builder should, we've listed numerous sources of potassium in Table 10-1.

TABLE 10-1 SOURCES OF POTASSIUM

(Milligrams per 3½-Ounce Edible Portion)

Baking powder	10,948	
Seaweed, raw, dulse	8,060	5-star
Seaweed, raw, kelp	5,273	sources
Blackstrap molasses	2,927	★ ★ ★ ★ ★
Brewer's yeast, dry	1,700	
Wheat bran	1,121	
Sunflower seeds	920	
Almonds	773	
Raisins	763	4-star
Prunes, dried	694	sources
Peanuts	674	★ ★ ★ ★
Dates	648	
Figs, dried	640	
Avocados	604	
Halibut	540	
Spinach	470	3-star
Buckwheat	450	sources
Mushrooms	414	★ ★ ★
Salmon	410	
Potato (with skin)	407	
Broccoli	382	
Banana	370	
Carrots	341	
Celery	341	2-star
Nectarine	294	sources
Apricot, fresh	281	★ ★
Sweet corn	280	
Lettuce, all types except iceberg	264	
Cantaloupe	251	
Honeydew melon	251	
Tomato	244	1-star
Papaya	234	sources
Brown rice	214	★
Peaches, fresh	202	
Orange, peeled	200	

Important Potassium Pointers

To round out your knowledge of potassium, here are many pointers on how to eat to maximize dietary potassium intake:

- Don't push that parsley off your plate. It's more than a decoration; it has twice as much potassium as bananas per unit weight and one-twelfth the calories.
- A magnesium deficiency results in failure to retain potassium. This can lead to potassium deficiency.
- Studies show that the need for potassium increases when there is growth of lean muscle tissue.
- Excessive potassium buildup may result from kidney failure or from severe lack of fluid.
- Authorities suggest a minimum intake of 2,500 milligrams of potassium per day.
- Potassium is readily soluble. More than 90 percent of ingested potassium is absorbed.
- Potassium does not chelate. Therefore, tablets marked "chelated potassium" are incorrectly named, but are still good supplements.
- Heart patients taking digitalis are especially prone to adverse effects of potassium depletion.
- The weakness of the elderly is directly related to the severity of their potassium deficiency, so the next time you visit your grandparents, give them raisins, and watch them motor all over the place.
- The skins of foods such as potatoes are potassium-rich, so don't throw them away. Eat them instead. Soaking and cooking in water leaches out potassium.
- Coffee increases the urinary excretion of potassium, so pass on this drink when you start to diet down for your contest.
- Potassium chloride has proved itself effective in treating allergies.
- The hormone aldosterone stimulates potassium excretion, so drink six to eight glass of water daily to keep your aldosterone levels down.

Remember, potassium is vital for the bodybuilder. It makes you full-appearing, hard, and energetic, and it helps keep your nervous system cool under pressure. Now who wouldn't want that?

HARDNESS

Any ergogenic aid that increases your androgen levels will also make you look harder. The truth is, not too many food elements will actu-

"A muscle's cosmetic appearance is influenced by the degree of muscle pump you achieve before going onstage," notes Pro World Champ Ron Love. "To achieve a good pump, you'll need to have your systems loaded with glycogen before warming up."

ally increase androgen level. Mother Nature determines most of your natural level, not supplements.

Blacks have generally higher androgen levels than Caucasians, and Caucasians have higher androgen levels than Asians. That explains to a certain degree why blacks *generally* acquire hardness to a greater degree. But keep in mind that these differences are very small.

On the flip side, you *can* increase your estrogen levels. This is not desirable at all. You will become softer, hold water, and take on a

In this shot, I am in a cosmetically hard state.

harmless appearance, somewhat like a hamster. This is not a goal for a bodybuilder to shoot for.

Things that can raise your estrogen are marijuana, wheat germ in any form, whole-wheat bread, pasta (for some people), cold-pressed vitamin E, and wheat germ oils.

The following supplements can show a cosmetic improvement on some physiques:

- *Vitamin C*—Surprised? Don't be. Vitamin C has saved many bodybuilders from the dreaded "holding water" look. Taken in doses of 10 grams or higher, it can remove subcutaneous water. It also increases the tactile hardness of your physique. And when you feel harder, you look harder (although it is better to look hard than to feel hard).
- *Free-form amino acids*—These are fantastic for improving your appearance. Aminos can impart a full, rounded, better pumped-up look to the muscles. They are extremely valuable supplements during contest preparation, because they can increase the apparent density of the muscles. But they are not that cost-effective a supplement for use in the off-season.
- *Arginine*—Taken by itself, this amino acid gives you incredible pumps. You can see the difference it makes. To get this effect, take five grams of arginine one hour before your workout.
- *Carnitine*—Research indicates that carnitine is responsible for cellular fat transport. We feel that carnitine exerts its best effect when you already have low fat levels. At that point, you can discern the improved cuts in as little as two days.
- *GABA*—Short for glutamic acid aminobutyrate, this amino acid has been shown to act as a neurotransmitter in the central nervous system. GABA also increases the secretion of growth hormone and gives muscles a fuller, rounder appearance. You also acquire hardness with GABA. This is one of my (Negrita's) personal favorites.

There you have it: food supplements that add to your cosmetic appearance. As you can see, there aren't very many that do. The reason for this is simple. Food supplements are still foods. Taken by themselves, they play a very small part in the physical picture. The fact that even these supplements exert some degree of noticeable physical change is impressive indeed.

The biggest part of the physical picture at contest time is *diet*. It always was and always will be. For getting the physique you want, there is absolutely no substitute for calorie counting, aerobics, and sound nutrition. This is an important point and seems to bear out something Arnold Schwarzenegger once said: "I won the Mr. Olympia while using food supplements, and I won the Mr. Olympia using none at all, so for me it didn't really make that much difference."

Keeping things in proper perspective, we should remember that Arnold did compete in the early 1970s and early 1980s, having retired between 1976 and 1980. Physiques have changed a lot since then. Still, the major reason why bodybuilders look so much better now is that dieting methods have improved dramatically. Bodybuilding nutrition is literally down to a science.

In closing, we would like to touch briefly on the synergism of supplements. When they are used *all together* the total effect can undeniably accelerate your bodybuilding progress. The unique features of each supplement add up. Many bodybuilders have reported *impressive* improvements in their physiques during periods when they were taking a wide variety of food supplements. The bottom line is this: If it works for you, use it. If it doesn't do anything, lose it!

11

NUTRITION AND ENERGY LEVELS

Seasoned competitive bodybuilders have tortured their bodies for years in daily—often twice-daily—workouts. In the process, they have developed massive, sliced-to-ribbons muscles. They have also gradually built up exceptional ability for between-workouts recovery and for summoning up huge amounts of energy to blast through each scheduled training session.

You know the type of workout that develops quality muscle mass, don't you? It's heavy and fast, as you move near-maximum weights for 10 to 15 total sets per muscle group, resting as little as possible between sets. The demand on your cardiorespiratory system is terrific as you scorch your working muscles each set by pushing to the painful point of muscle failure. It takes a very special person to push this hard—a bodybuilder!

There is a direct, linear relationship between heavy breathing (actually the volume of oxygen consumed in a particular period of time) and the amount of energy expended in a specific workout. It takes plenty of oxygen to burn the fuel stores held in your muscles to produce the energy you expend in training those muscles.

When working a large and complex muscle group like legs or back, you end up breathing like a locomotive powering uphill. In fact, your breathing becomes so deep and frantic that your rest intervals between sets are necessarily longer than those between sets done for a smaller body part like biceps.

If you didn't take comparatively long rest intervals between sets of squats, you'd go so deeply into oxygen debt that your body would literally *force* you to stop exercising. No matter how great your will to perform another heavy set of squats, you'd still be lying on your back on the gym floor, gasping for air.

Some relatively inexperienced bodybuilders find it difficult to summon up the energy reserves necessary for back or leg workouts. As a result, these key areas are trained less intensely than they should be, eventually becoming chronic weak points because of such neglect. We've known many experienced bodybuilders who so abhorred the fatigue pain associated with heavy squats that 10 to 15 years after taking up bodybuilding they would do anything to avoid a squat workout. Needless to say, each of these individuals has chronically weak leg development.

Body heat is another indication of how much energy is being expended in a workout. Heat is generated in the process, which releases energy for use in muscle contractions, and it can be easily perceived by feelings of overheating or excessive perspiration. If you

"I always carry all of my food on the road, plus a hot plate and cooking utensils,'" notes Michael Ashley, who won the first drug-tested World Championships (light-heavyweight division) in 1986. "This way I can consume the precise foods that give me the most workout energy and best muscle growth."

One very hot amateur competitor—whether competing alone or with her husband, Gordon, in mixed pairs—Drorit Kearns is a medical student at UCLA. She's only been training four years.

train regularly in a gym with several top bodybuilders, you've no doubt felt heat radiating off of them from five feet away during a hard workout. They are literally walking, working-out furnaces, as their bodies burn fuel in the presence of oxygen to provide energy.

The human body has a system of peripheral blood circulation in the form of capillary beds beneath the skin. That system is intended to efficiently dissipate built-up body heat and is what causes the sensation of heat radiating from a hard-working bodybuilder. It is responsible for the pores opening and exuding perspiration, which rapidly evaporates and aids in the body-cooling process. Nature never reckoned with bodybuilders, however, because they often become overheated despite this system of peripheral circulation and the perspiration process.

CAUSES OF FATIGUE

Sports scientists have done considerable research on causes of physical fatigue. As a result of this research, many interesting theories have been presented, some of them conflicting. One probable reason for the conflict is the fact that there are several clearly defined causes of fatigue, most of which overlap one or more other causes.

The most cogent listing of causes of fatigue that we've seen was

"I used to eat M&Ms all of the time but noticed they were causing abrupt fluctuations in workout energy," says National Middleweight Champ Lisa Lorio. "Now I'm more intelligent and concentrate on complex carbs as my main sources of energy for both workouts and daily life."

presented by Christian Zauner, a researcher at the University of Florida. Dr. Zauner categorizes contemporary fatigue research into five groups:

1. Fatigue resulting from depletion of energy sources
2. Fatigue resulting from body dehydration
3. Fatigue resulting from an elevated body core temperature
4. Fatigue resulting from exhaustion of the cardiorespiratory system
5. Fatigue resulting from psychological factors

Nutritionally speaking, we can directly reduce fatigue and/or increase energy stores by working with the first two of these factors—depletion of energy sources and body dehydration. Indirectly, nutrition also plays a role in reducing exhaustion of the cardiorespiratory system.

CARDIORESPIRATORY EFFICIENCY

"I'm going past the pain barrier on this set!" If you train in a public gym, we're sure you've heard this statement—or something similar to it—hundreds of times. Pain-barrier training produces superstar bodybuilders, and everyone in the sport knows it. What they often don't know is why and how smashing past the pain barrier builds big, sliced muscles.

As you push a heavy set toward completion, fatigue toxins build up rapidly in the working muscles. The main two fatigue by-products that accumulate are carbon dioxide and lactic acid, both of which are flushed out of the fatigued muscles by the circulatory system between sets.

The relative efficiency of your circulatory system dictates how quickly these fatigue by-products are removed from your muscles. And the efficiency of your entire cardiorespiratory system affects the speed at which new supplies of oxygen are infused into your fatigued muscles, readying them for another hard set.

The health of your body in general affects cardiorespiratory efficiency. The healthier you are, the more efficient your lungs, heart, and entire circulatory system will be, and the faster you'll recover between sets. Obviously, good nutrition affects general health. But even the most efficient circulatory system sometimes can't keep up with the massive lactic acid buildup commonly experienced during a heavy bodybuilding workout.

Lactic acid buildup is what causes that familiar burn in your muscles and sets up the pain barrier that top bodybuilders are always interested in smashing past during a hard set. With experience and proper mental commitment, it's possible to ignore muscle burn and continue pushing a set past the point where fatigue pain stops mere mortals in their tracks. Literally, the further you push a set toward absolute exhaustion, the more muscle hypertrophy results from that set, provided, of course, sufficient calories are present in your diet.

You'll never become a massively developed, sliced bodybuilder until you develop an ability to successfully contend with the pain barrier. You only build this championship type of muscular development by pushing several notches past the pain barrier set after set and workout after workout for several years.

If your circulatory system can't remove lactic acid as quickly as you'd like—or you prefer to retard the buildup of lactic acid during a set—we can help you achieve this with a simple food supplement. This supplement is called a blood buffer, and it was discussed in Chapter 5.

Briefly, blood buffers include phosphate, bicarbonate, and carnosine, which act to varying degrees to reduce lactic acid levels in fatigued muscles. For a more detailed discussion of these supplements, see the section on blood buffers in Chapter 5.

DEHYDRATION AND ENERGY

Science has clearly demonstrated that dehydration is directly linked to fatigue. The more dehydrated you become during a sustained workout, the less energy you have, the weaker you become in terms of handling exercise poundages, and the less mental drive you will exhibit as you attempt to force yourself to continue your workout. Therefore, it's absolutely essential to drink fluids both before and during a training session.

Despite all of the fancy claims for carbohydrate drinks and electrolyte replacement drinks—to say nothing of good, old-fashioned beer—water is the best workout drink on the face of the earth. For bodybuilders, the recommended level of water intake is 10 to 12 glasses per day, depending on body mass and level of daily physical activity. Try drinking two or three glasses during the hour before your workout, and another two or three during a training session, and you should have no trouble with dehydration.

It's best to drink water out of a glass or plastic water bottle, because drinking out of a fountain causes you to take in air with the water. This air can bloat your stomach and interfere with the comfort of a good workout.

FOOD AND ENERGY

Biochemistry researchers have identified three sources of energy used in physical work: muscle glycogen, blood glucose, and free fatty

"Dehydration is a very real problem to hard-training bodybuilders," says Rich Gaspari, three times a second-place finisher in Mr. Olympia. "When the body becomes too dehydrated, you'll lose training energy. It's best to keep frequently drinking liquids—particularly pure water—throughout your workout."

acids (FFAs). Having each of these nutrient derivatives—particularly the first two—at optimum level before a bodybuilding workout will increase perceived energy levels and delay the onset of fatigue.

Glycogen and glucose are both derived from dietary carbohydrate foods. Most bodybuilders pay some attention to carb intake, but few do so to an optimum level. The Multiple-Carbohydrate Leverage Loading (MCLL) technique presented in Chapter 7 is the optimum method for producing maximum and sustained levels of muscle glycogen and blood glucose.

MCLL was devised by Negrita Jayde as one means of producing a pro-level physique for her in near record time. When MCLL was first introduced to the bodybuilding public via an article in *Flex* magazine, the mag's editors were flooded for several months with mail testifying to the technique's effectiveness. Of the many instructional

Getting sliced begins with gut-busting training to build a high degree of pure muscle mass. Mr. Universe Tom Platz shows how it's done with a heavy set of T-bar rows to thicken up his back musculature.

articles Negrita has had published in *Flex* and other muscle mags, the one on MCLL has probably affected a larger segment of the serious bodybuilding population than any other.

MCLL combines several different carbo sources—each of which metabolizes into glycogen and glucose at a different rate of speed— at each meal. This combination of different carbo sources is what produces a sustained and even flow of energy throughout the day, particularly during a hard pumping iron session.

If you have a busy schedule each day, you'll have to plan meals ahead and carry food with you to work and other obligatory functions. But regardless of where you consume your meals—at home, in your car, in the gym—MCLL will give you *great* results in producing workout energy. For a complete outline of MCLL, turn to Chapter 7.

In bodybuilding weight workouts, FFAs are an insignificant source of energy. Pumping iron is an anaerobic activity, which draws almost completely from carbohydrates for its energy sources. Where FFAs come into play is during aerobic training sessions, which tend to burn primarily FFAs past the 15-minute point. Indeed, bodybuilders include aerobic workouts in their general training philosophies— particularly during a precontest cycle—primarily to burn up stored body fat.

As blood-borne FFAs are burned up during aerobic sessions, they are replaced from body fat stores and dietary sources. In the relative absence of dietary fat consumption during a peaking cycle, FFAs are mainly replaced from fat stores. You can facilitate this conversion of stored body fat into FFAs by taking "fat burners," or food supplements that mobilize body fat and turn it into FFAs. Fat burners include choline, inositol, methionine, and L-carnitine.

SUPPLEMENTS FOR ENERGY

Of the supplements that increase workout energy, the newest and trendiest is MCT (medium-chain triglycerides), which can be purchased at health food stores or via mail order from Parrillo Performance, 8031 Hamilton Ave., Cincinnati, OH 45231 (or phone 513-521-0040 for prices and ordering information).

Here's what seven-time Mr. Olympia Lee Haney says about MCTs: "If you're the type of bodybuilder who always seems to run out of gas toward the end of a high-intensity workout, you've probably experimented with a variety of methods for improving sustained workout energy flow. Some of these no doubt included the use of preworkout carb-loading combinations, or strategies such as taking inosine tablets or capsules by the handful, gulping wheat germ oil, or popping down fistfuls of desiccated liver tablets.

"Your next step should be to try MCTs, which have appeared widely on the health food market and are drawing rave reviews from athletes who use them regularly. In essence, MCTs are a very concentrated source of liquid-form energy, which is readily and quickly available to the bloodstream.

"Scientifically speaking, MCTs are lipids assembled into medium-chain (rather than the more common long-chain) triglycerides. As such, they have more than twice the potential for releasing energy into the body for use during a workout than carbohydrates. And crucially, MCTs are less likely to be turned into body fat stores than are long-chain triglycerides.

"Since MCTs aren't carbohydrates—yet do supply abundant amounts of workout energy—they are ideal for a bodybuilder following a low-carb diet, especially when he's depleting a few days out from a show prior to a carb-loading cycle. But MCTs are also a great preworkout energy source when taken 30 to 60 minutes prior to commencing any training session. You'll find yourself bursting with energy that will last those few minutes of a hard workout, blasting through that period in the past when you've wanted to just pack it in and take a shower. Since bodybuilding is a game of millimeters, this product could ultimately spell the difference between winning and losing."

The amino acid L-carnitine will delay the onset of aerobic fatigue, so it's most appropriate for use during a peaking cycle when you're spending hours per week on an exercise bike. Still, many top body-builders take L-carnitine during the off-season, too, believing that it noticeably affects anaerobic energy production as well. Suggested daily dosages vary from one to five grams, depending on body mass and relative daily activity levels.

Proper electrolyte supplementation also can markedly affect energy levels, since a shortage of any of the four electrolytes (sodium, potassium, calcium, magnesium) causes physical lassitude. Normally, sodium is at higher than necessary levels in most body-builders' diets, so think more in terms of taking good calcium and potassium-magnesium supplements.

Desiccated liver has long had a reputation for improving workout energy levels, an undeserved rep. In one often-cited study, three groups of lab rats were fed varying diets (group 1 received the normal lab-rat diet, group 2 that diet plus synthetic B-complex vitamins, and group 3 the lab-rat diet plus desiccated liver) and then thrown into drums of water to see how long they could swim before drowning. Since group 3 swam significantly longer than the other two groups, the researchers concluded that desiccated liver caused the increase in endurance.

That experiment is a good example of what can happen if variables are not strictly controlled during an experiment. In this case, there was nothing mysterious about desiccated liver, except that it provided a superior supply of protein in comparison to the ordinary lab-rat diet. This protein (plus the 30 percent carbohydrate content of desiccated liver) is what caused the increase in energy. If you lack protein or carbohydrate intake—as the normal lab rats did—then by all means include a ton of desiccated liver in your diet.

There is one final supplementary source of energy: those popular carbohydrate drinks taken before and during a hard workout. As long as you don't mind the extra calories—and you read the labels— most of these drinks are helpful to athletes whose energy falls off during a workout, as is the case with hypoglycemic individuals.

Avoid any product that contains high-fructose corn syrup or sucrose, since these are the simplest possible sugars, and they cause severe energy fluctuations. Take one, and you initially feel like a multistage rocket on a moon trajectory, since the initial effect of such a nutrient is an upward energy spike. But this spike is so abrupt that the body releases insulin to drive it downward, and you end up feeling as though the second stage of your moon rocket is driving you back to earth even more quickly than the first one that sent you aloft. You might as well eat a candy bar.

Most of the best carbo drinks come in powder form and have to be mixed with water before consumption. Look for one that contains electrolytes as well as carbs, and you'll have an ideal preworkout drink. These minerals tend to make energy drinks taste a little raunchy, however, so it's difficult to find them. The grandfather of all energy drinks (it's been around since the early 1970s) is called ERG (electrolyte replacement with glucose). You might be able to find some at a running-oriented sporting goods store. Otherwise, run through the energy drinks section in a health food store, reading all of the labels before choosing your product.

The best sources of carbohydrate for energy drinks are glucose polymers and crystalline fructose, with the glucose polymers preferred due to their more complex structure and slower rate of breakdown in your digestive system. Mix up enough to give yourself about 40 grams of supplementary carbohydrates, and you should be able to blast through any bodybuilding workout!

Ageless Albert Beckles didn't win his first pro title until he was 50 years old. Now 60, he's still mixing it up at virtually every IFBB pro show with kids less than half his age, and he's still placing high!

PART II
RECIPES

12

POULTRY

Most bodybuilders view plain, dry chicken breast as their number one source of protein when dieting for a show. But the truth is that chicken doesn't have to be that plain. As a rule, domestic fowl blend very well with a wide variety of flavorings and spices. Spend a few extra minutes preparing the tasty recipes presented in this chapter, and your poultry dishes will never be boring again.

When preparing chicken or other poultry, remove the skin, because the majority of a bird's fat is stored just below the skin. Also, poultry fat is less saturated than beef or pork fat. So, go ahead and enjoy your next chicken meal!

SPARTAN ROAST CHICKEN

This primitive recipe comes in handy for the time-conscious bodybuilder. It yields six tasty portions of chicken that can be eaten throughout the day, thus negating the practice of eating fast-food chicken and trimming the fat, a popular habit with bodybuilders, who are particularly hooked on El Pollo Loco chicken in southern California.

1 3-pound chicken
Seasonings as desired: chervil, curry,
    dill, marjoram, mustard, oregano,
    rosemary, sage, tarragon, thyme,
    turmeric

1. Preheat oven to 425°F.
2. Cut chicken into six equal portions.
3. Trim away all visible fat.
4. Apply seasoning of preference to each chicken piece, then wrap pieces individually in aluminum foil.
5. Roast for 45 to 55 minutes.

Serves 6

Per serving (calculated on 50% dark and 50% light meat): 215 calories, 24 grams of protein, 0 grams of carbohydrate, 3 grams of fat, 16 milligrams of sodium

TANDOORI CHICKEN

2 chicken breasts, skinned and deboned
¾ teaspoon low-sodium Dijon mustard
1 tablespoon lemon juice
½ teaspoon MCT oil
⅛ cup nonfat yogurt
¾ teaspoon ginger
Dash each of cumin powder, coriander, turmeric
1 tablespoon white wine
1½ teaspoons chili powder

1. Place chicken in a bowl. Mix together remaining ingredients, and pour over chicken breasts. Let sit overnight in refrigerator.
2. Barbecue the chicken breasts 6 inches away from coals for 20 minutes, or until done.

Serves 2

Per serving: 162 calories, 27 grams of protein, 2 grams of carbohydrate, 3 grams of fat, 111 milligrams of sodium

Note: There will be many references to MCT oil. The one we recommend is CapTri, available from Parrillo Performance. See page 198.

MAMA'S MARINATED CHICKEN

2 chicken breasts, about 4½ ounces
   each, skinned and deboned
Juice of ½ lemon
½ teaspoon lemon rind, grated
1 teaspoon olive oil
½ garlic clove, crushed
½ teaspoon each of oregano, paprika,
   parsley, cayenne pepper

1. Place chicken in a bowl. Mix remaining ingredients together, and pour over chicken. Cover and let chicken marinate overnight in the refrigerator.
2. Remove from marinade, and cook on barbecue until done, approximately 12 to 15 minutes.

Serves 2

Per serving: 164 calories, 26 grams of protein, 1 gram of carbohydrate, 5 grams of fat, 58 milligrams of sodium

KILLER CHICKEN CACCIATORE

Leftover servings can be wrapped and frozen for use up to one week or tightly wrapped and refrigerated for up to one day.

Nonstick vegetable oil spray
1 3½-pound chicken, skinned, defatted,
   cut into 8 pieces
3 onions, quartered
1 garlic clove, crushed
½ cup dry red wine
6 ripe tomatoes, pureed
½ cup tomato sauce, no salt added
1 cup mushrooms, sliced
1 bay leaf, crushed
¼ teaspoon pepper
¼ cup chopped fresh parsley

1. Spray large saucepan with nonstick vegetable oil. Heat the pan, and add chicken. Cook over low heat, browning both sides. Remove chicken, and add onions and garlic to saucepan. Cook 3 minutes, then return chicken to pan.

2. Add wine to chicken, and bring mixture to a boil. Cook 2 more minutes, then add tomatoes, tomato sauce, mushrooms, bay leaf, pepper and parsley. Let simmer for 45 minutes. Stir occasionally.

Serves 8

Per serving: 179 calories, 21 grams of protein, 13 grams of carbohydrate, 4 grams of fat, 203 milligrams of sodium

ONIONS GALORE CHICKEN

1 2-pound chicken, skinned, all visible
    fat removed, cut in quarters
Juice of 1 lemon
¼ teaspoon black pepper
½ teaspoon garlic powder
¼ teaspoon oregano
¼ teaspoon red pepper
¼ teaspoon rosemary
¼ teaspoon paprika
Nonstick vegetable oil spray
2½ pounds onions, peeled and sliced
    (approximately 6 onions)
2 cloves garlic, crushed
1 cup dry white wine
1 tablespoon red wine vinegar
1 bay leaf, crushed
Parsley

1. Sprinkle chicken with lemon juice, black pepper, garlic powder, oregano, red pepper, rosemary, and paprika.
2. Spray frying pan with nonstick vegetable oil, and add chicken pieces. Cook over medium heat until brown.
3. Add remaining ingredients except parsley, and simmer, covered, for 40 minutes, stirring occasionally. Or bake at 375°F for 40 minutes. Serve chicken on a bed of onions.

Serves 4

Per serving: 200 calories, 15 grams of protein, 25 grams of carbohydrate, 2 grams of fat, 68 milligrams of sodium

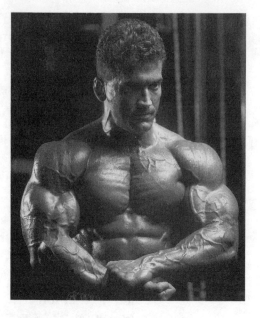

Lee Labrada is the fastest-rising IFBB pro, having won a host of professional Grand Prix shows and placed second twice in Mr. Olympia. As an amateur, he was the National and World Middleweight Champion. He works as a personal trainer in Texas.

BIANCA'S CHICKEN BREASTS

1 teaspoon lemon juice
½ clove garlic, crushed
1 teaspoon Worcestershire sauce
Dash each of black pepper, paprika,
    celery seed, low-sodium mustard, red
    pepper
3 tablespoons nonfat yogurt
1 whole chicken breast, cut in half and
    flattened
2 cherry tomatoes, cut in half
Fresh parsley
3 tablespoons whole-wheat bread
    crumbs

1. Combine lemon juice, garlic, Worcestershire sauce, seasonings, and yogurt in a bowl. Mix. Add chicken, and let marinate overnight in the refrigerator.
2. Remove chicken from marinade, and place in a nonstick baking dish. Bake uncovered at 350°F for 45 to 55 minutes.
3. To serve, garnish with cherry tomatoes, and sprinkle with fresh parsley and bread crumbs.

Serves 2

Per serving: 233 calories, 38 grams of protein, 11 grams of carbohydrate, 3 grams of fat, 144 milligrams of sodium

MARINATED TARRAGON CHICKEN

2 chicken breasts, skinned and boned
2 tablespoons sherry
2 tablespoons lemon juice
¼ teaspoon dried tarragon
1 onion, quartered
Dash each of pepper and garlic powder
2 tablespoons fresh parsley, chopped
½ lemon

1. Marinate chicken in the sherry, lemon juice, and tarragon. Keep overnight in a covered bowl in the refrigerator.
2. Remove the chicken from the marinade, reserving the liquid. Broil the chicken for 10 to 15 minutes.
3. Arrange onion quarters in a baking dish, placing chicken breasts on top. Pour in marinade. Sprinkle with pepper and garlic powder.
4. Bake uncovered in a preheated 375°F oven for 1 hour. Baste occasionally.
5. Garnish with lemon and parsley.

Serves 2

Per serving: 243 calories, 29 grams of protein, 22 grams of carbohydrate, 2 grams of fat, 74 milligrams of sodium

CHILLED CHICKEN DRUMSTICKS

1½ teaspoons MCT oil
1 tablespoon raspberry wine vinegar
¼ cup water
1½ teaspoons sherry (optional)
¾ pound chicken drumsticks, skinned
Lettuce
Fresh parsley, chopped

1. In a skillet, heat MCT oil, vinegar, water, and sherry (optional) together. Stir in chicken drumsticks, and bring to boil. Reduce heat, and simmer for 25 to 30 minutes.
2. Chill drumsticks for 4 hours before serving.
3. To serve, arrange drumsticks attractively on a bed of lettuce, and garnish with parsley.

Serves 2

Per serving: 236 calories, 33 grams of protein, trace of carbohydrate, 7 grams of fat, 141 milligrams of sodium

CHICKEN SALAD ROLL-UPS

½ pound chicken, cooked, skinned, and
  deboned
2 tablespoons sunflower seeds
2 tablespoons dried fruit bits
2 tablespoons celery, sliced
⅓ cup nonfat yogurt
Fresh iceberg lettuce leaves

1. Dice chicken, and place in mixing bowl. Combine with sunflower
   seeds, fruit bits, celery, and yogurt.
2. Spread a little chicken mixture on a lettuce leaf, and roll up
   tightly. Repeat until mixture is used up.
3. Serve immediately, or wrap roll-ups in plastic wrap for later use.

Serves 2

**Per serving: 241 calories, 30 grams of protein, 16 grams of carbohydrate,
6 grams of fat, 101 milligrams of sodium**

RETURN OF THE CHICKEN SALAD ROLL-UPS

1 medium onion, sliced
¼ green bell pepper, chopped
1 tablespoon MCT oil
½ bay leaf, crushed
1 8-ounce chicken breast, cooked,
  skinned, deboned, and diced
Dash of pepper
2 tablespoons cognac
2 tablespoons unsweetened pineapple
  juice
¼ cup blanched slivered almonds
¼ cup fresh parsley, chopped
Fresh iceberg lettuce leaves

1. Sauté onion and green pepper in MCT oil.
2. Add bay leaf, chicken, pepper, cognac, and pineapple juice to the
   skillet. Cover and simmer for 5 to 7 minutes.
3. To serve, arrange lettuce leaves on a serving platter. Mound the
   chicken mixture on top. Sprinkle with almonds and parsley. Place
   lettuce leaves around the mound. Let each person spoon the
   chicken on lettuce and roll up tightly.

Serves 2

**Per serving: 420 calories, 32 grams of protein, 21 grams of carbohydrate,
12 grams of fat, 74 milligrams of sodium**

HUNGARIAN CHICKEN PAPRIKASH

2 tablespoons dry white wine
1 chicken breast, cut into 1-inch cubes
1 small onion, chopped
½ cup fresh mushrooms, sliced
2 teaspoons Hungarian paprika
Dash of pepper
¾ cup water
2 teaspoons whole-wheat flour
¼ cup nonfat yogurt
4 ounces spinach noodles, cooked and
    drained

1. Heat wine in saucepan, and add chicken and onion. Cook over medium heat until chicken is brown on all sides.
2. Add mushrooms, paprika, and pepper, and cook for 3 minutes.
3. Add ½ cup of water. Bring to a boil. Reduce heat, and let simmer for 15 minutes.
4. Stir whole-wheat flour into remaining water, then mix in yogurt. Pour mixture slowly into saucepan with chicken, stirring frequently. Heat through, then serve on noodles.

Serves 2

Per serving: 295 calories, 44 grams of protein, 18 grams of carbohydrate, 3 grams of fat, 114 milligrams of sodium

A former California Champion, Carol Mock has tried in vain in recent years to win a pro card. She has a well-balanced, muscular physique and should win soon at the national level.

ONE-PAN CHICKEN DISH

Nonstick vegetable oil spray
2 chicken breasts, skinned and boned
1 large sweet potato, peeled and cut into
    ½-inch slices
1 apple, cored and quartered
½ onion, sliced in rings
3 ounces apple cider
¼ teaspoon each thyme, rosemary, sage
Dash of pepper
¼ cup water
1 teaspoon whole-wheat flour

1. Spray large skillet with nonstick vegetable oil. Add chicken, and brown on both sides. Remove, set aside.
2. Add sweet potatoes and apples to skillet. Cook over medium heat until browned, stirring occasionally. Remove to plate.
3. To skillet, add onion. Cook, stirring until tender. Return chicken to pan. Add apple cider, herbs, and pepper. Bring to a boil. Reduce heat, and let simmer for 15 minutes, covered.
4. Return potatoes to skillet, and simmer, covered, for 10 minutes.
5. Add apples to pan, and simmer for 10 minutes.
6. Stir wheat flour into cold water. Gradually pour into skillet while stirring. Cook another 10 minutes, stirring frequently.

Serves 2

Per serving: 250 calories, 16 grams of protein, 42 grams of carbohydrate, 2 grams of fat, 57 milligrams of sodium

BLACKIE'S CHICKEN BROCCOLI

1 teaspoon MCT oil
½ onion, chopped
½ red bell pepper, chopped
1 cup chopped broccoli
1½ teaspoons whole-wheat flour
1 cup skim milk
¼ cup mozzarella cheese, shredded
1 8-ounce chicken breast, cubed
1 cup macaroni elbows or shells
Dash of black pepper
1 teaspoon chopped fresh parsley
1 tablespoon slivered almonds

1. Preheat oven to 375°F. In a skillet, sauté onions, red pepper, and broccoli in MCT oil until crispy-tender.
2. Sprinkle flour on vegetables, and stir. While stirring, pour in milk.
3. Place chicken in a nonstick baking dish, and pour sauce on top.
4. Sprinkle with parsley and almonds. Bake uncovered for 30 minutes.
5. Cook macaroni. Spoon cooked chicken and sauce over macaroni. Season with black pepper.

Serves 2

Per serving: 466 calories, 44 grams of protein, 27 grams of carbohydrate, 11 grams of fat, 241 milligrams of sodium

CHICK-PEA CHICKEN CHARGER

Nonstick vegetable oil spray
½ red onion, sliced
2 chicken breasts, skinned, deboned, cut
   into thin strips
½ teaspoon ground cumin
Dash each of pepper, cinnamon, paprika
4 dried apricot halves, quartered
1 tablespoon raisins
½ head of escarole, cut into bite-sized
   pieces
¾ cup chick-peas, cooked
¼ cup nonfat yogurt (optional)

1. Spray skillet with nonstick vegetable oil. Sauté onions for 2 minutes, stirring occasionally.
2. When onions are tender, add chicken, and sprinkle with cumin, pepper, cinnamon, and paprika. Stir and cook over low heat another 4 minutes.
3. Stir in apricots and raisins. Cook for 2 minutes, then add the escarole a bit at a time until all is mixed well.
4. Add chick-peas. Stir to mix. Cover and cook for another 3 minutes.

Serves 2

Per serving: 310 calories, 40 grams of protein, 34 grams of carbohydrate, 4 grams of fat, 72 milligrams of sodium

ORANGE-GLAZED CHICKEN

½ onion, chopped
½ green onion, chopped
¼ clove garlic, minced
1 tablespoon finely chopped fresh
   parsley
½ cup fresh orange juice
Grated rind of ½ orange
½ teaspoon low-sodium soy sauce
1 small chicken, halved, fat removed
Juice of ½ lemon
Ground pepper to taste
¼ teaspoon thyme
¼ teaspoon rosemary
2 tablespoons raisins
1 tablespoon chestnuts, chopped
1½ teaspoons cornstarch
2 tablespoons cold water
1 cup cooked brown or wild rice
2 navel oranges, sliced ¼-inch thick
Watercress

1. Combine onion, green onion, garlic, parsley, orange juice, orange rind, and soy sauce in a bowl. Add chicken, then marinate for 4 hours or overnight in refrigerator.
2. Preheat oven to 400°F.
3. Remove chicken from marinade. Place in a casserole dish skin side up, and season with lemon juice, pepper, thyme, and rosemary. Bake uncovered for 30 minutes.
4. Heat remaining marinade, and pour over chicken. Sprinkle with raisins and chestnuts. Cover and bake 30 minutes.
5. Remove chicken from casserole, reserving marinade. Keep warm.
6. Blend cornstarch with cold water. Mix into baking dish. Cook over medium heat until sauce thickens.
7. To serve, arrange chicken halves over a bed of rice decorated with orange slices and watercress. Pour sauce on top, and serve immediately.

Serves 2

Per serving: 259 calories, 26 grams of protein, 56 grams of carbohydrate, 4 grams of fat, 126 milligrams of sodium

CHICKEN SALAD WITH CURRY

½ cup nonfat yogurt
2 tablespoons lemon juice
¼ teaspoon curry powder
¼ teaspoon pepper
1 8-ounce chicken breast, cooked and
　　diced
¼ cup celery, diced
2 tablespoons raisins
1 tablespoon sunflower seeds
Lettuce leaves

1. Combine yogurt, lemon juice, curry powder, and pepper in a mixing bowl.
2. Add remaining ingredients except lettuce. Toss (not too high, though!).
3. Arrange lettuce leaves on salad plates, and pile chicken salad on top.

Serves 2

Per serving: 238 calories, 31 grams of protein, 19 grams of carbohydrate, 8 grams of fat, 188 milligrams of sodium

CHICKEN-VEGETABLE DELIGHT

1 teaspoon MCT oil
2 tablespoons white wine
½ cup mushrooms, sliced
½ cup onion, chopped
½ red bell pepper, chopped
2 teaspoons whole-wheat flour
½ cup skim milk
1 8-ounce chicken breast, cooked and
　　diced
½ cup fresh peas, blanched
¼ teaspoon pepper

1. Heat MCT oil and wine in a skillet. Add mushrooms, onion, and red pepper. Sauté until crispy-tender, stirring occasionally.
2. Sprinkle flour over mixture. Mix. Stir in milk, making sure to stir constantly.
3. Bring to a boil. Cover. Let simmer until sauce thickens. Add remaining ingredients, and heat through.

Serves 2

Per serving: 268 calories, 33 grams of protein, 20 grams of carbohydrate, 3 grams of fat, 101 milligrams of sodium

GINGERED CHICKEN WITH PEACHES

2 tablespoons orange juice concentrate
1 clove garlic, crushed
1 tablespoon grated fresh ginger root
2 tablespoons dry white wine
1 1-pound chicken breast, skinned,
   deboned, sliced
1 onion, chopped
1 teaspoon cornstarch
1 cup fresh snow peas, blanched for 1
   minute
3 fresh peaches, sliced, blanched for 1
   minute

1. Mix orange juice concentrate and garlic together in a bowl. Stir in ginger root, then wine. Add chicken slices. Let chicken marinate overnight in refrigerator.
2. Remove chicken, and set aside, reserving the liquid.
3. In a skillet, heat 2 tablespoons of marinade. Add onion, and cook for 3 minutes. Add chicken, and brown on all sides.
4. Mix cornstarch with remaining marinade, and add to chicken mixture. Let simmer for 10 minutes.
5. Add snow peas and peaches. Stir and cook for 5 minutes more.

Serves 3

Per serving: 316 calories, 37 grams of protein, 26 grams of carbohydrate, 4 grams of fat, 82 milligrams of sodium

WALDORF CHICKEN SALAD

1 ¾-pound chicken breast, cooked and
   diced
½ Granny Smith apple, cored and diced
1 celery stalk, sliced
½ green pepper, diced
½ cup seedless red grapes
½ cup raisins
¼ cup walnut pieces
⅓ cup orange juice
¼ cup nonfat yogurt
Dash of nutmeg
Dash of cinnamon
Lettuce

1. In a mixing bowl, combine chicken, apple, celery, green pepper, grapes, raisins, and half of the walnuts.
2. In a small bowl, mix orange juice, yogurt, nutmeg, and cinnamon until blended. Pour over chicken mixture, and toss. Mound mixture on a bed of lettuce. Sprinkle with the remaining walnuts.

Serves 2

Per serving: 492 calories, 44 grams of protein, 55 grams of carbohydrate, 11 grams of fat, 150 milligrams of sodium

CHICKEN-PRUNE CASSEROLE

1 onion, sliced
2 chicken breasts, skin and fat removed,
   quartered
Dash of oregano
Dash of pepper
4 ounces pitted prunes
1 3½-ounce can low-sodium tomato
   sauce
2 tablespoons dry red wine

1. Preheat oven to 350°F.
2. Put onion slices in a 2-quart casserole dish. Arrange half of the chicken on top of the onions. Season with half the oregano and pepper.
3. Sprinkle half the prunes on top of the chicken. Pour half the tomato sauce and half the wine on the mixture. Repeat layers with remaining ingredients.
4. Cover and bake for 1 hour (or until chicken is very tender).

Serves 2

Per serving: 242 calories, 16 grams of protein, 36 grams of carbohydrate, 4 grams of fat, 198 milligrams of sodium

Competition doesn't always have to be, well, competitive. Anja Langer (left) and Marjo Selin (both are former European Champions) compare side-chest poses at a recent Ms. Olympia competition.

PARRILLO'S CHICKEN FINGERS

This recipe is courtesy of John Parrillo, from the *CapTri Cookbook*. Available from Parrillo Performance, 8031 Hamilton Avenue, Cincinnati, Ohio 45231.

> 1 5-ounce chicken breast, partially
>   frozen
> 1 tablespoon MCT oil
> ¼ cup oatmeal (rolled oats)
> Garlic
> Paprika
> Chili powder
> Pepper
> Nonstick vegetable oil spray

1. Cut chicken into thin slices (1 inch × ½ inch). Put in a bowl, and toss with other ingredients, adding spices to taste.
2. Place chicken strips on a cookie sheet that has been sprayed with nonstick vegetable oil and bake at 400°F for 15 minutes.

Serves 1

Per serving: 387 calories, 39 grams of protein, 17 grams of carbohydrate, 5 grams of fat, 76 milligrams of sodium

ORANGE CORNISH HENS

2 oranges
Nonstick vegetable oil spray
½ onion, chopped
½ carrot, chopped
½ cup water
⅓ cup brown rice
¼ cup cranberries, chopped
1 1½-pound Rock Cornish hen
½ teaspoon thyme
½ teaspoon rosemary
Dash of pepper
Dash of paprika

1. Grate peel of oranges to make 1 teaspoon. Set aside. Squeeze juice from oranges to make ½ cup of juice. Set aside.
2. Spray large skillet with nonstick vegetable oil, and sauté onion and carrot until soft, about 5 minutes. Pour in water and orange juice, and bring to boil. Stir in rice, and let simmer for 45 minutes, covered. When rice is cooked, add cranberries and the teaspoon of grated orange peel. Mix and remove from heat.
3. Preheat oven to 350°F. Rinse hen and dry. Fill cavity of hen with rice mixture. Any leftover rice should be covered and kept warm.
4. With string, tie the legs and tail together, and fold wings back and tie to the neck skin. Place hen in a roasting pan, breast side up. Spray with nonstick vegetable oil, and sprinkle with herbs, pepper, and paprika. Roast for 65 minutes. Baste occasionally with pan drippings.
5. Cool hen, then remove strings and empty bird. Put all the rice on a serving platter, and place bird attractively on top. Decorate with orange slices.

Serves 2

Per serving: 550 calories, 47 grams of protein, 48 grams of carbohydrate, 18 grams of fat, 96 milligrams of sodium

ORANGE-TURKEY SALAD

12 ounces turkey breast, cooked and
  cubed
¼ cup celery, sliced
¼ cup water chestnuts, sliced
½ cup nonfat yogurt
2 oranges, peeled and segmented
½ onion, chopped
Lettuce
Parsley

1. Combine turkey, celery, water chestnuts, and yogurt in a salad bowl. Marinate for 1 hour.
2. Just before serving, add half the orange segments and all the onions. Toss.
3. Pile salad on a bed of lettuce. Garnish with remaining orange segments and parsley.

Serves 2

Per serving: 222 calories, 20 grams of protein, 28 grams of carbohydrate, 5 grams of fat, 132 milligrams of sodium

TURKEY SALAD

8 ounces turkey meat, cooked and diced
½ cup rice, cooked and chilled
1 tomato, diced
½ cup celery, diced
¼ onion, diced
½ red bell pepper, diced
2 tablespoons nonfat yogurt
1 tablespoon chopped fresh parsley
Dash each of dry mustard, black
  pepper, garlic powder
1 tablespoon lemon juice

1. Combine turkey, rice, tomato, celery, onion, and red pepper in a salad bowl.
2. In a separate bowl, mix together remaining ingredients. Pour over turkey mixture. Chill and serve.

Serves 2

Per serving: 313 calories, 15 grams of protein, 46 grams of carbohydrate, 4 grams of fat, 98 milligrams of sodium

TURKEY-APPLE CURRY

½ onion
1 celery stalk, sliced
2 tablespoons dry white wine
⅓ pound fresh mushrooms, sliced
Juice of ½ lemon
½ clove garlic, crushed
1 apple, peeled, cored, diced
1 tablespoon raisins
¼ teaspoon curry powder
⅓ cup apple juice
¼ cup water
½ pound turkey breast, cooked and
    diced
1 tablespoon fresh parsley, chopped

1. Braise onion and celery in white wine until tender. Add mushrooms, lemon juice, and garlic. Mix and cook for 3 minutes.
2. Add apple, raisins, curry powder, apple juice, and water. Cook for 15 minutes.
3. Add turkey and parsley. Simmer until turkey is thoroughly heated.

Serves 2

Per serving: 179 calories, 31 grams of protein, 18 grams of carbohydrate, 4 grams of fat, 61 milligrams of sodium

SUPER-EASY TURKEY/PINEAPPLE SALAD

½ pineapple, peeled and cored, cut into
    bite-sized pieces
½ pound turkey breast, cooked and
    cubed
1 celery stalk, sliced
2 tablespoons nonfat yogurt
½ teaspoon ginger
¼ teaspoon pepper

1. Toss all ingredients together.
2. Chill or serve immediately.

Serves 2

Per serving: 145 calories, 12 grams of protein, 17 grams of carbohydrate, 4 grams of fat, 84 milligrams of sodium

TURKEY AND SWEET POTATO CARB LOADER

½ turkey breast (about ½ pound),
    skinned and deboned
1 tablespoon MCT oil
1 large sweet potato, cooked and
    quartered
2 tablespoons dry sherry
¼ cup nonfat yogurt
¼ cup orange juice
Dash of rubbed sage
1 orange, sliced
Chopped parsley

1. Pound turkey breast flat, and cut into 2 pieces.
2. In a skillet, heat MCT oil. Sauté turkey for 4 minutes.
3. Stir in sweet potatoes, sherry, yogurt, orange juice, and sage. Cover and simmer for 25 minutes, until turkey is tender. Garnish with orange slices and parsley.

Serves 2

Per serving: 338 calories, 13 grams of protein, 42 grams of carbohydrate, 4 grams of fat, 56 milligrams of sodium

TURKEY-ALMOND STIR-FRY

½ pound turkey breast cutlets cut into
    ¼-inch thicknesses
3 tablespoons water
2 teaspoons cornstarch
1 tablespoon dry sherry
Dash of ground ginger
½ clove garlic, crushed
2 stalks celery, sliced
2 carrots, chopped
¼ cup whole blanched almonds
½ cup fresh spinach, washed and
    drained
½ cup rice, cooked and kept hot

1. In a bowl, combine water, cornstarch, sherry, ginger, and garlic.
2. In a nonstick skillet, cook celery and carrots until crispy-tender. Stir in almonds and spinach. Remove from heat. Transfer vegetable mix to separate dish. Add turkey and sherry mixture to the skillet. Cook until turkey is tender, about 4 to 5 minutes.

3. Add vegetable mix back to skillet. Warm evenly.
4. Serve turkey mixture on a bed of rice.

Serves 2

Per serving: 433 calories, 18 grams of protein, 55 grams of carbohydrate, 13 grams of fat, 92 milligrams of sodium

TITANIC TURKEY-NOODLE CASSEROLE

1½ teaspoons whole-wheat flour
⅓ cup skim milk
¼ cup nonfat evaporated milk
Dash each of thyme, parsley, black
    pepper, oregano, and crumbled bay
    leaf
2 tablespoons dry sherry
1 teaspoon MCT oil
¼ cup mushrooms, sliced
1 teaspoon onion flakes
½ stalk celery, sliced
¼ green pepper, sliced
¼ cup fresh green peas
3 ounces whole-wheat noodles, cooked
    and drained
½ cup broccoli cut into florets, cooked
    and drained
7 ounces turkey, cooked and diced
2 teaspoons bread crumbs
¼ teaspoon each basil and thyme

1. Stir flour into cold skim and evaporated milk in a saucepan. Heat over medium stove, stirring constantly. Add dash each of thyme, parsley, pepper, oregano, bay leaf, and the sherry. Let simmer for 5 minutes. Cover and set aside.
2. In a skillet, heat MCT oil, and sauté mushrooms and onion flakes. Add celery, green pepper, and peas, stirring occasionally. Reduce heat, and cook for 3 minutes.
3. Preheat oven to 350°F. In a large nonstick casserole dish, spread cooked noodles evenly. Pour mushroom mixture on top of noodles. Layer casserole with broccoli, then diced turkey. Pour sauce on top. Sprinkle with bread crumbs, basil, and thyme.
4. Bake for 35 minutes.

Serves 2

Per serving: 245 calories, 18 grams of protein, 32 grams of carbohydrate, 3 grams of fat, 106 milligrams of sodium

13

FISH

Fish is a unique food group. It is low in calories, low in fat, and contains enough high-grade protein to satisfy any bodybuilder. Fish is very adaptable to the various flavorings available and is easy to prepare. Although the general public may consume fish only occasionally, it is a staple food in the diet of every bodybuilder who wishes to get sliced.

Fish contains fatty acids called omega III. In particular, one of its components, called eicosapentanoic acid (or EPA for short), is known to lower serum cholesterol levels in the blood. It also increases the number of high-density lipoproteins (HDL), the *good* cholesterol, which reduces the risk of blood clots and strokes. The best sources of omega III are albacore tuna, pollack, halibut, swordfish, cod, and orange roughy. You will find tasty recipes using all of these fish in this chapter.

Just a few quick pointers when buying fish: Make sure the eyes of the fish are bright and shiny. If they appear dull and sunken and the fish doesn't smell fresh, move on. Also, pay close attention to the cooking times. Otherwise, that fish in your pan will dissolve before you know it!

FISH IN FOIL

½ pound halibut, cut in 2 pieces
1 tomato, chopped
1 green onion, chopped
4 small zucchini, julienned
1 carrot, julienned
¼ cup dry white wine
½ teaspoon each fresh dill and parsley
Dash of freshly ground pepper

1. Preheat oven to 400°F. Cut 2 12-inch-square pieces of foil.
2. Place a piece of fish on each square of foil. Top each piece of fish with tomato, green onion, zucchini, and carrot.
3. Sprinkle each with wine, herbs, and pepper. Fold foil edges together, sealing with a pleat.
4. Bake for 15 minutes.

Serves 2

Per serving: 180 calories, 25 grams of protein, 11 grams of carbohydrate, 2 grams of fat, 78 milligrams of sodium

ALL-OUT BARBECUED SOLE FINGERS

Juice of 1 lemon
1 teaspoon onion flakes
½ teaspoon each oregano, basil, paprika
4 fillets of sole (approximately 1 pound)
2 tablespoons chopped fresh parsley
Lemon quarters for garnish

1. In a mixing bowl, combine lemon juice, onion flakes, oregano, basil, and paprika. Add sole, and marinate for 1 hour in the refrigerator.
2. Line grill with foil, and grill fillets for 10 minutes or until fish flakes with a fork.
3. Sprinkle fish with parsley, and garnish with lemon wedges.

Serves 2

Per serving: 178 calories, 40 grams of protein, 4 grams of carbohydrate, 2 grams of fat, 160 milligrams of sodium

"GO FOR IT NOW!" FILLET OF COD

2 fillets of cod (about 5 ounces each)
Dash of oregano
Dash of parsley
3 tablespoons nonfat yogurt
2 teaspoons lemon juice
1 teaspoon low-sodium Dijon mustard
1 teaspoon grated horseradish
Fresh parsley for garnish

1. Place fillets on an aluminum-covered grill.
2. Combine remaining ingredients except parsley, and pour over fish.
3. Grill for 5 minutes. Garnish with parsley, and serve.

Serves 2

Per serving: 130 calories, 28 grams of protein, 2 grams of carbohydrate, 1 gram of fat, 123 milligrams of sodium

MEGAHEAVY SALMON FILLETS

Nonstick vegetable oil spray
2 salmon fillets
1 tablespoon lemon juice
1 tablespoon dry white wine
¼ teaspoon each of onion powder,
    oregano, pepper, paprika
Parsley
Lemon wedges

1. Preheat oven to 350°F. Spray baking dish with nonstick vegetable oil spray, and place salmon inside.
2. Combine lemon juice, wine, onion powder, oregano, pepper, and paprika. Pour over fish.
3. Bake for 12 minutes, basting occasionally.
4. Garnish with parsley and lemon wedges.

Serves 2

Per serving: 260 calories, 26 grams of protein, 1 gram of carbohydrate, 15 grams of fat, 58 milligrams of sodium

"THROUGH THE PAIN BARRIER" HALIBUT STEAKS

1½ teaspoons low-sodium soy sauce
½ teaspoon garlic powder
Juice of ¼ lemon
2 5-ounce halibut steaks
Paprika
Parsley
Lemon wedges

1. Combine soy sauce, garlic powder, and lemon juice, and pour over fish in a plastic bag. Marinate for 1 hour in the refrigerator.
2. Drain fish, and place on grill pan. Sprinkle with paprika, and grill for 10 minutes. Baste if necessary.
3. Garnish with parsley and lemon. Serve immediately.

Serves 2

Per serving: 175 calories, 40 grams of protein, 1 gram of carbohydrate, 2 grams of fat, 222 milligrams of sodium

Winner of the 1983 Ms. Olympia title, Carla Dunlap was the star of the film *Pumping Iron II: The Women*. She's also won two National titles and a Pro World Championship and has long been one of the most innovative posers on the pro circuit.

FILLET OF POLLACK WITH YOGURT SAUCE

2 fillets of pollack (bluefish)
3 tablespoons nonfat yogurt
2 teaspoons lemon juice
2 teaspoons low-sodium Dijon mustard
Dash each of oregano, celery seed,
   onion flakes

1. Place fish on an aluminum-covered grill.
2. Mix together remaining ingredients, and spread evenly on fish.
3. Grill until fish flakes with fork. Serve immediately.

Serves 2

Per serving: 135 calories, 24 grams of protein, 2 grams of carbohydrate, 1 gram of fat, 100 milligrams of sodium

At the age of 19, Shane DiMora recorded an interesting bodybuilding triple play, taking the Teenage, Junior, and Senior Nationals in the middleweight division. He was also the overall winner at the Teen Nats.

POACHED SWORDFISH WARM-UP

1 cup dry white wine
1 cup water
1 bay leaf
Dash of pepper
2 5-ounce swordfish steaks
2 carrots, cut in 1-inch pieces
1 onion, sliced
1 green pepper, cut in 1-inch pieces
1 tablespoon chopped fresh parsley
1 tablespoon fresh dill
6 lemon slices for garnish

1. In a frying pan, bring to boil wine, water, bay leaf, and pepper.
2. Add swordfish, carrot, onion, green pepper, parsley, and dill.
3. Bring to boil again. Lower heat, and simmer for another 15 minutes. Garnish with lemon slices.

Serves 2

Per serving: 337 calories, 31 grams of protein, 21 grams of carbohydrate, 6 grams of fat, 200 milligrams of sodium

SUPERPOWER TROUT ALMANDINE

2 small trout
¼ cup white wine
¾ teaspoon butter
Juice of ½ lemon
⅛ cup slivered almonds
1 tablespoon fresh parsley, chopped

1. Braise trout in white wine until done.
2. Remove trout, and drain off fat.
3. In the skillet, add butter and lemon juice, and sauté almonds until lightly browned.
4. Mix in chopped parsley, and pour almond mixture over trout. Serve immediately.

Serves 2

Per serving: 322 calories, 26 grams of protein, 5 grams of carbohydrate, 20 grams of fat, 78 milligrams of sodium

STUFFED BASS SURPRISE

To freeze leftovers, wrap tightly in freezing paper, and use within 1 month.

1 6-pound bass
1 tablespoon lemon juice
1 onion
1 garlic clove
1 tomato
3 celery stalks
1 green pepper
2 egg whites
½ teaspoon thyme
½ teaspoon basil
2 tablespoons whole-wheat bread
    crumbs
1 tablespoon butter

1. Clean fish, and prepare for stuffing. Preheat oven to 400°F.
2. In a food processor, grind together lemon juice, onion, garlic, tomato, celery, green pepper, egg whites, thyme, basil, and bread crumbs. Stuff the mixture in the fish.
3. Grease baking dish with butter, and add fish. Bake for 1 to 1½ hours, basting frequently with the fish's own juices. Fish is done when it flakes easily.

Serves 8

Per serving: 333 calories, 55 grams of protein, 5 grams of carbohydrate, 8 grams of fat, 253 milligrams of sodium

TUNA SALAD WITH FRESH DILL

1 7-ounce can of water-packed low-
    sodium tuna, rinsed and drained
¼ cup chopped celery
¼ cup chopped fresh dill
2 tablespoons chopped fresh parsley
¼ cup nonfat yogurt
½ teaspoon low-sodium Dijon mustard
Pepper

1. Combine all ingredients in a mixing bowl.
2. Serve on lettuce, pita bread, Rykrisp, baked potato, pasta, or rice.

Serves 2

Per serving: 158 calories, 21 grams of protein, 7 grams of carbohydrate, 1 gram of fat, 158 milligrams of sodium

ISO-TENSION TUNA

3 boiled egg whites
1 6½-ounce can low-sodium water-
 packed tuna, rinsed and drained
2 tablespoons low-calorie, low-sodium
 mayonnaise
1 stalk celery, sliced
½ small cucumber, chopped
1 tomato, chopped
Dash of pepper

Mix all ingredients. Serve in a pita pocket if desired.

Serves 2

Per serving: 217 calories, 35 grams of protein, 7 grams of carbohydrate, 5 grams of fat, 193 milligrams of sodium

A newcomer to IFBB pro ranks, Arizonan firefighter Sandy Riddell took second place in her first Ms. Olympia competition. She has a sensational future ahead of her.

FRUITY TUNA-PASTA SALAD

6 ounces rotini pasta, cooked, drained,
  and chilled
1 7-ounce can low-sodium water-packed
  tuna, rinsed and drained
1½ ripe peaches, sliced
½ cucumber, chopped
½ stalk celery, sliced
½ cup nonfat yogurt
1 tablespoon grated orange rind
2 tablespoons orange juice
  (unsweetened)
¼ teaspoon celery seed
Dash of curry powder
Toasted sliced almonds (optional)

1. In a large salad bowl, toss together pasta, tuna, peaches, cucumber, and celery.
2. To make dressing, whisk together remaining ingredients, and pour over salad. Chill to blend flavors.
3. Toss dressing with salad before serving.

Serves 2

Per serving: 312 calories, 16 grams of protein, 40 grams of carbohydrate, 2 grams of fat, 130 milligrams of sodium

MUSCLE PRIORITY TUNA-STUFFED PEPPERS

2 green peppers, cut in half and cleaned
1 7-ounce can low-sodium water-packed
  tuna, rinsed and drained
2 tablespoons chopped onion
2 tablespoons chopped celery
2 egg whites, hard-boiled and chopped
1 tablespoon MCT oil
½ teaspoon dill
½ teaspoon fennel

1. Preheat oven to 350°F. Place green pepper halves on a nonstick baking pan.
2. Combine remaining ingredients, and stuff into pepper halves.
3. Bake for 10 minutes.

Serves 2

Per serving: 240 calories, 33 grams of protein, 9 grams of carbohydrate, 1 gram of fat, 143 milligrams of sodium.

CRABMEAT RISOTTO

Nonstick vegetable oil spray
½ onion, chopped
½ garlic clove, crushed
½ cup rice
1 cup water
2 small tomatoes, pureed
8 ounces crabmeat, cooked
1 tablespoon chopped fresh parsley

1. Spray a large nonstick skillet with nonstick vegetable oil. Add onion and garlic, and sauté until tender.
2. Add rice, water, and pureed tomatoes to skillet, stirring to mix. Bring to a boil, reduce heat, and simmer for 15 minutes uncovered.
3. Add crabmeat, and let simmer for another 10 minutes. Mix in parsley, and serve.

Serves 2

Per serving: 340 calories, 25 grams of protein, 49 grams of carbohydrate, 3 grams of fat, 262 milligrams of sodium

HAWAIIAN SKEWERED SCALLOPS

2 tablespoons lemon juice
1 tablespoon olive oil
½ pound fresh sea scallops
¼ fresh pineapple, cored, peeled, and cubed
4 ounces fresh whole mushroom caps
½ red pepper, diced
½ green pepper, diced
½ onion, chopped
6 cherry tomatoes
1 celery stalk cut into 1¾-inch pieces

1. Combine all ingredients, and let marinate for 1 hour in the refrigerator.
2. Drain marinade and reserve. Thread scallops, pineapple, and vegetables alternately on skewers.
3. Grill on both sides, brushing with reserved marinade.

Serves 2

Per serving: 224 calories, 20 grams of protein, 20 grams of carbohydrate, 7 grams of fat, 177 milligrams of sodium

GARDEN AND TUNA PASTA SALAD

½ cup nonfat yogurt
1 tablespoon MCT oil
4 teaspoons each oregano, thyme, garlic
    powder
½ tablespoon each chopped fresh
    parsley and dill
4 ounces fusilli, cooked al dente and
    drained
1 3½-ounce can of low-sodium water-
    packed tuna, rinsed and drained
½ cup fresh peas, cooked
½ tomato, diced
1 stalk celery, sliced
¼ red pepper, sliced
¼ red onion, chopped

1. In a salad bowl, combine yogurt, oil, oregano, thyme, garlic
   powder, parsley, and dill. Mix well.
2. Add remaining ingredients to the bowl. Mix, and chill to blend
   flavors.

Serves 2

**Per serving: 209 calories, 21 grams of protein, 22 grams of carbohydrate,
1 gram of fat, 109 milligrams of sodium**

PRE-EXHAUSTION WHITEFISH WITH VEGGIES

Nonstick vegetable oil spray
¼ cup chopped onion
2 whitefish fillets
⅓ cup dry white wine
¼ teaspoon oregano
¼ teaspoon basil
2 potatoes, peeled and cubed small
2 carrots, peeled and sliced
6 green beans, cut into 1-inch pieces
6 large mushrooms, sliced
¼ teaspoon thyme
¼ teaspoon paprika
¼ cup nonfat yogurt
Lemon juice
Fresh parsley

1. Preheat oven to 350°F. Spray casserole dish with nonstick vegetable oil. Place chopped onion in the dish, then lay fillets on top. Sprinkle with wine, oregano, and basil.
2. Bake fish for 12 minutes, or until flaky.
3. In ⅓ cup liquid from baked fish, braise the vegetables until done. Add thyme, paprika, yogurt, and lemon juice to vegetable mixture. Serve fish with vegetable mixture. Garnish with parsley.

Serves 2

Per serving: 395 calories, 28 grams of protein, 41 grams of carbohydrate, 4 grams of fat, 126 milligrams of sodium

OVERLOAD PRINCIPLE RIGATONI

4 ounces rigatoni pasta, cooked and drained
½ cup green beans, steamed for 5 minutes
1 sweet potato, peeled, cooked, and diced
½ cup fresh peas, cooked
1 7-ounce can of low-sodium water-packed tuna, rinsed and drained
½ pineapple, cored, peeled, and diced
2 tomatoes, pureed
2 egg whites, hard-boiled
4 teaspoons paprika

1. In a salad bowl, combine pasta, beans, sweet potato, peas, tuna, pineapple, and tomatoes.
2. Mix together chopped egg whites and paprika. Sprinkle on top of pasta mixture. Chill.

Serves 2

Per serving: 421 calories, 34 grams of protein, 56 grams of carbohydrate, 8 grams of fat, 106 milligrams of sodium

Arizona's newest pro, Vince Comerford (left) fights for first against Nimrod King (Dean Tornabene is doing the side-chest shot between the two) at a recent Los Angeles Pro Grand Prix event. King won the overall title and Comerford placed second.

SALMON WITH BROCCOLI AND PASTA

½ bunch broccoli, cut into florets
1 cup medium pasta shells, cooked and
  drained
1 3½-ounce can low-sodium salmon,
  rinsed and drained
¼ cup nonfat yogurt
2 tablespoons dry sherry
1 tablespoon lemon juice
1 teaspoon low-sodium Dijon mustard
1½ teaspoons each chopped fresh
  parsley and dill
Dash of nutmeg
Dash of black pepper
¼ red bell pepper, seeded and chopped

1. Preheat oven to 350°F. In a casserole dish, mix together broccoli, pasta, and salmon.
2. Combine remaining ingredients, and pour over pasta mixture.
3. Bake for 25–30 minutes.

Serves 2

Per serving: 286 calories, 19 grams of protein, 29 grams of carbohydrate, 8 grams of fat, 87 milligrams of sodium

CASEY VIATOR JAMBALAYA

1½ teaspoons MCT oil
¼ cup dry red wine
½ onion, chopped
½ cup sliced celery
½ each green and red bell pepper, diced
½ clove garlic, crushed
2 ripe tomatoes, pureed
8 ounces shrimp, cooked
¼ cup rice, cooked
Dash each of crushed bay leaf, chili
    powder, thyme, and black pepper

1. In a large skillet, heat MCT oil. Add onion, celery, red and green pepper, and garlic. Sauté until crispy-tender.
2. Add remaining ingredients, cover, and let simmer until heated through.

Serves 2

Per serving: 306 calories, 25 grams of protein, 37 grams of carbohydrate, 1 gram of fat, 214 milligrams of sodium

U.S. and National Lightweight Champ Susie Jaso has repeatedly experienced difficulty gaining muscular body weight. Strict attention to consuming six meals a day and plenty of heavy training on basic movements solved her problem.

SAUTEED OYSTERS

1 pound oysters
1 garlic clove, crushed
3½ ounces white wine
¼ cup chopped fresh parsley

1. Sauté oysters and garlic in white wine until done.
2. Add parsley. Serve immediately.

Serves 2

Per serving: 194 calories, 20 grams of protein, 10 grams of carbohydrate, 4 grams of fat, 173 milligrams of sodium

ORANGE ROUGHY

2 ounces dry white wine
2 ounces unsweetened orange juice
1 ½-pound orange roughy fillet, cut in 2
    pieces
½ onion, chopped
½ green pepper, chopped
½ clove garlic, chopped
1½ teaspoons MCT oil
½ large carrot, shredded
4 ounces nonfat yogurt
1½ teaspoons grated orange rind
Dash each of dry mustard, tarragon,
    black pepper
½ orange, sliced for garnish

1. Preheat oven to 350°F. Combine wine and orange juice, and pour over fillet. Marinate in the refrigerator for 1 hour.
2. Sauté onion, green pepper, and garlic in MCT oil until vegetables are tender.
3. Place fillets on a nonstick baking dish, reserving the marinade.
4. In a blender, whirl together carrot, yogurt, orange peel, herbs, and 2 tablespoons of marinade. Pour over fish.
5. Bake for 30 minutes

Serves 2

Per serving: 231 calories, 21 grams of protein, 19 grams of carbohydrate, 5 grams of fat, 292 milligrams of sodium

14

BEEF

If you are hesitant to eat meat while dieting for a competition, it's time to beef up your knowledge about this nutritious food.

Beef has a "bad-boy" image for several reasons. The first is cosmetic. The standard slab of beef reveals a high amount of white fat, which contrasts sharply against the red muscle meat. To someone dieting, it looks terrifying, like beef's an alien creature from another planet, waiting . . . to enter your body and rob you of your cuts.

The next reason has to do with beef cuts and fat percentages. Not all beef is created equal. Due to a wide variety of beef cuts, quoted fat percentages can vary by as much as 25 percent. That's a serious difference, and one you should be aware of.

Lastly, there exists a feeble understanding about fat in general, which leads to an overreaction within the bodybuilding community. In fact, fats provide the most concentrated source of energy in your diet—approximately nine calories per gram of fat. They supply essential fatty acids, contribute to the feeling of fullness after eating, are carriers for fat-soluble vitamins, and make other foods more palatable.

The term *lipids*, also used to describe fats, refers to a variety of chemical substances. In addition to triglycerides, they include mono- and diglycerides, phosphatides, cerebrosides, sterols, terpenes, fatty alcohols, fatty acids, and other substances.

Physical characteristics of fat depend upon degree of unsaturation, length of the carbon chains, and the isomeric form of the fatty acids,

With a chest measurement more than double that of his waist, Britain's Brian Buchanan impressed many IFBB veteran pros for a couple of years but couldn't put everything together for the bigger shows. He's now retired and living in Australia, where he owns a gym.

as well as the molecular configuration. Fats that are hard at room temperature primarily come from animal sources. Fats that are liquid at room temperature tend to be more unsaturated and are derived from vegetable, nut, or seed sources like corn, sunflowers, and olives.

Fat in meats is commonly grouped as saturated, although saturated acids actually account for less than 50 percent of the total fatty acids in red meats. Stearic acid constitutes one-quarter to one-third of the saturated fatty acids in beef.

Classifying foods as hypercholesterolemic, or cholesterol-raising, based on the amount of saturated fatty acid, rather than considering constituent fatty acids, tends to overstate the potential of red meats to raise cholesterol. Oleic acid, a monounsaturated fatty acid that makes up 45 percent of total fatty acids in beef, has actually been shown to have a cholesterol-*lowering* effect.

Studies of healthy subjects showed that there was no difference, in the blood levels of total and HDL cholesterol, between those who ate beef and those who did not. Other research demonstrated that diets containing moderate amounts of lean red meat were effective in lowering serum total and LDL cholesterol levels in men.

What all of this means to you as a bodybuilder is simply that avoiding red meat because you think it's too fat is vastly simplifying a truly complex food item. The truth is, if you choose a lean cut like round steak and trim all visible fat before cooking, it ends up having the same fat content as chicken. If we had to choose, we'd pass on the bird any day.

TABLE 14–1 FAT CONTENT OF VARIOUS FOODS

(Grams of Fat in a 90-Gram, or 3-Ounce, Serving)

Lean eye-of-round	4	Broiled cod	5
Lean rump roast	7	Canned tuna (packed in water)	7
Roast chicken (no skin)	7	Eggs (2)	12
Fried chicken (no skin)	11	Peanut butter (60 milliliters)	32

Table 14-1 bears out what we have been saying about the fat content of beef. As the facts indicate, beef is right in there with chicken and tuna, which of course trashes any theory about avoiding beef during a diet.

TABLE 14–2 CHOLESTEROL CONTENT OF VARIOUS FOODS

(Milligrams of Cholesterol in a 90-Gram, or 3-Ounce, Serving)

Beef	82	Cheddar cheese	63
Chicken	80	Peanut butter	0
Cod	73	Shrimp	135
Eggs (2)	548	Pork liver	394

In Table 14-2, you can take a look at cholesterol and see how beef fares in that department. Once again, beef is lower in cholesterol than you might expect. However, that's no accident. Recent weight consciousness by the public has created a demand for leaner beef. To produce animals with a higher percentage of lean meat, cattle ranchers have altered feeding rations, the weight at which animals are marketed, and the genetic makeup of the herd. All of that effort is reflected in recent nutritional findings on beef, so a lot of less than up-to-date charts can now be made into paper airplanes. Now you know beef is a lean and mean food machine.

That's only the beginning. Beef is crammed full of valuable nutrients, such as iron. Several studies have reported evidence of iron depletion and iron deficiency in highly trained athletes. Actually, iron deficiency is the most common nutritional deficiency in the United States, Canada, and western Europe.

TABLE 14–3 IRON CONTENT OF VARIOUS FOODS

(Milligrams of Iron in a 90-Gram, or 3-Ounce, Serving)

Beef	3.3
Chicken	1.1
Cod	0.9
Eggs (2)	2.0
Cheddar cheese	0.4
Peanut butter	1.2

Although iron is only a trace element, the small quantity needed in the diet is essential for the formation of hemoglobin, myoglobin, the cytochromes, and iron-containing enzymes. They give a bodybuilder energy and vitality.

But not all iron is created equal. According to nutrient tables, spinach appears to have more iron than beef. However, iron in foods is present in two forms: heme iron found in meat sources, and non-heme iron from vegetables, nuts, and grains. The majority of iron in beef is in the form of heme iron, a form more easily utilized by the body. Specifically, absorption rates of heme iron can be as high as 25 percent, whereas nonheme absorption rates range between 3 percent and 10 percent. So while the nutrient tables indicate the iron content of spinach is higher than that of beef, most of it goes unabsorbed. No wonder Popeye only had good forearms; he should have eaten beef (see table 14-3)!

Beef leaves the rest behind! Put another way, cod isn't the way to go for your iron needs.

Also worthy of note is the fact that heme iron improves the absorption of nonheme iron. Therefore, if you combine beef with a vegetable, the overall iron absorption is much better. That's an especially important point for women bodybuilders, as their iron needs are often not being met. Start up the barbie!

When it comes to the high-tech, every-detail-counts sport of bodybuilding, you can't overlook even the smallest details. So without zinc, you just might sink. Studies show that a zinc deficiency could impair energy metabolism or decrease protein synthesis due to inadequate amounts of necessary enzymes.

Recent reports suggest that athletes may have increased zinc requirements, since strenuous exercise leads to significant urinary losses and sweat losses of zinc. It just so happens that beef is brimming with zinc. Check out the data in Table 14-4, and you'll come away convinced of the value of beef as a zinc-containing food.

TABLE 14–4 ZINC CONTENT OF VARIOUS FOODS

(Milligrams of Zinc in a 90-Gram, or 3-Ounce, Serving)

Beef	4.8
Chicken	1.3
Cod	0.4
Eggs (2)	1.2

Incidentally, the zinc in meat is biologically available and better absorbed than the zinc in plants. Consequently, vegetarians may be prone to the development of marginal zinc deficiencies due to the limited availability of dietary zinc.

Are you starting to feel foolish for avoiding beef? Great, because there's more. Let's move on to the B-complex vitamins. Studies have shown that the requirements for the many B vitamins are directly proportional to energy expenditures and stress levels. Of particular note is B_{12}. This water-soluble vitamin is the one that contains essential mineral elements. It's necessary for metabolizing protein, fats, and carbohydrates; aids in the production of DNA and RNA, the body's genetic materials; helps vitamin A placement into bodily tissues; and closely relates to many other biochemical action pathways. You can find evidence of the value of beef as a source of B_{12} in Table 14-5.

TABLE 14–5 VITAMIN B_{12} CONTENT OF VARIOUS FOODS

(Milligrams of Vitamin B_{12} in a 90-Gram, or 3-Ounce, Serving)

Beef	1.6
Chicken	0.3
Cod	0.4
Eggs (2)	1.3

Notice the absence of vegetables on the list in Table 14-5? That's because they'd all receive zeros, and it wouldn't appear too impressive for the salad lovers out there. You see, animal protein is the only source in which B_{12} occurs in substantial amounts.

The beat goes on further for the B vitamins. Significant amounts of niacin, riboflavin, and B_6 are also locked into beef. Meat also contains a good portion of potassium and phosphorus, the former being especially important for maintaining law and order within the bodily fluids.

But what about calories? With all those goodies crammed into beef, you'd think it's just gotta be high in calories. Well, let's take a look at Table 14-6.

TABLE 14–6 CALORIE CONTENT OF VARIOUS FOOD ITEMS

(Number of Calories in a 90-Gram, or 3-Ounce, Serving)

Lean beef	133
Lean rump roast	176
Lean sirloin steak	196
Fried chicken (no skin)	210
Roast chicken (no skin)	171
Broiled cod	153
Fish sticks	158
Canned tuna (packed in water)	177
Eggs (2)	158
Peanut butter (60 milliliters)	396

Game over! Clearly, beef does not pile on the calories as you might have expected.

But there's a tenth inning to this game. And beef's up to bat, with its home run king, Mr. Phenylalanine. It's not enough that beef's low in calories, and obviously an ideal food for dieting bodybuilders, but phenylalanine adds a bonus.

Found abundantly in beef, phenylalanine increases the norepinephrine levels in the brain. This helps keep you "up" and alert, and is therefore something every dieter should use. Also, phenylalanine causes the brain to release a hormone caused CCK, which inhibits the eating urge. This means that although beef is low in calories, it'll make you feel fuller after a meal than if you ate a bird or a fish. Craaak, Mr. Phenylalanine just hit a home run out of the nutritional stadium.

Another heavy hitter is creatine phosphate. It's an organic chemical that's a short-term energy buffer involved in the ATP/ADP energy cycle. Creatine phosphate makes an anaerobic exercise last more than just a few seconds. Without it, a bodybuilder could do only one or two repetitions before frying his or her muscles. Beef contains plenty of creatine phosphate.

Methionine, glycine, and arginine can be combined in the body to make creatine phosphate. Beef's loaded with those aminos too.

The more creatine phosphate that you can eat, the stronger you'll be, which explains why we feel stronger when we eat beef. We've tried heavy-duty workouts on chicken and fish exclusively, but felt like a sparrow or a minnow, and our cuts weren't any better.

That brings us to another important finding. It has to do with muscular density. Although we can't back it up with convincing scientific evidence, we firmly believe that beef increases apparent muscle density. Every time we insert it into a bodybuilder's contest diet, he or she reports an enhanced density, or we can clearly see it for ourselves. Why this occurs is not fully understood, but its occurrence is something you should incorporate into your physique. Try it and see.

Well, that's the big picture on beef. As you can see, beef is a very important addition to a dieting regimen. If you are concerned about the tenderness of lean meat, numerous hammer curls, performed over the meat with a mallet, should handle the needs of the most discriminating palate.

How often should you eat meat? About twice a week is what we'd consider a minimum intake during a calorie-restricted period. Remember, we're not advising you to consume two Texas-sized steaks that spill over your plate and onto the table. The standard portion size we recommend is $3\frac{1}{2}$ ounces—a piece of meat roughly the size of a deck of playing cards.

Another important tip for maximum nutritional benefit is to use a digestive aid when eating beef. Simply adding one hydrochloric acid tablet greatly speeds up the breakdown and subsequent uptake of beef's plethora of important nutrients. Of course, that means you must thoroughly chew your beef. We've seen many a starving bodybuilder gulp down meat like a mad dog; be careful not to do this. It doesn't look good on a date.

Beef satisfies—physically, psychologically, and nutritionally. Add it to your eating regimen today, and you'll be carrying more beef around tomorrow!

Like fine wine, bodybuilders get better with age. Nearing 50, Dave Draper is the owner of a World Gym in Santa Cruz, California. He's won every major title but Mr. Olympia.

BARBECUED STEAK TERIYAKI

½ clove garlic, crushed
½ onion, chopped
2 tablespoons dry white wine
1 tablespoon low-sodium Worcestershire sauce
1½ teaspoons powdered ginger
¾ pound lean steak, cut into thin strips against the grain

1. In a mixing bowl, combine garlic, onion, wine, Worcestershire sauce, and ginger.
2. Add meat, and marinate for 4 hours or overnight in the refrigerator.
3. Skewer ribbons of steak on a stick, and grill for 3–5 minutes.

Serves 2

Per serving: 240 calories, 34 grams of protein, 5 grams of carbohydrate, 9 grams of fat, 305 milligrams of sodium

DESCENDING SETS STEAK

½ pound flank steak, cut into 2 portions
Pepper and seasonings to taste

1. Season steak.
2. Grill on the barbecue or in your broiler oven until done.

Serves 2

Per serving: 163 calories, 25 grams of protein, 0 grams of carbohydrate, 6 grams of fat, 86 milligrams of sodium

Toppings for Steak

MUSHROOM ONION DELIGHT

½ onion, sliced
¼ cup sliced mushrooms
1 tablespoon MCT oil

In a saucepan, sauté onions and mushrooms in MCT oil for 7 minutes.

Serves 2

Per serving: 75 calories, 1 gram of protein, 4 grams of carbohydrate, 7 milligrams of sodium

HORSERADISH-YOGURT TOPPING

¼ cup nonfat yogurt
1½ teaspoons horseradish
¼ teaspoon dill

Combine all ingredients. Use on top of steak or potatoes.

Serves 2

Per serving: 24 calories, 3 grams of protein, 3 grams of carbohydrate, 0 grams of fat, 47 milligrams of sodium

Shawn Ray, a former overall National Amateur Champ, began showing outstanding bodybuilding potential in his middle-teen years. His first big success was a Junior World Championship at age 19, two years before he won the Nationals.

SUPERSETS STEAK 'N' TOMATOES

2 lean steaks, about 5 ounces each
1 tablespoon dry white wine (or water)
½ green onion, sliced
1 tomato, sliced
½ tablespoon fresh parsley
½ tablespoon fresh basil

1. Brown steaks in the broiler for 10 minutes.
2. Heat wine in a nonstick skillet, and braise green onion until soft.
3. Add tomato slices and herbs. Heat through. Serve on steaks.

Serves 2

Per serving: 353 calories, 34 grams of protein, 5 grams of carbohydrate, 13 grams of fat, 121 milligrams of sodium

BURGUNDY STEAK AND PEPPERS

⅛ cup burgundy wine
5 ounces lean steak, cubed
1½ teaspoons MCT oil
1½ teaspoons arrowroot starch
½ celery stalk, sliced
½ small onion, sliced
½ clove garlic
1 tablespoon water
¼ teaspoon oregano
¼ teaspoon thyme
½ red pepper and ½ green pepper,
    seeded and diced

1. Bring wine and MCT oil to a boil in skillet. Add meat cubes, and brown.
2. While stirring, add arrowroot to steak mixture.
3. Add celery, onion, and garlic. Mix in water, and let simmer for 15 minutes covered, stirring occasionally.
4. Add oregano, thyme, and diced peppers. Cook covered another 15 minutes.

Serves 2

Per serving: 217 calories, 33 grams of protein, 34 grams of carbohydrate, 8 grams of fat, 128 milligrams of sodium

FORCED REPS BEEF STEW

½ pound lean beef stew meat, cut into
  1½-inch cubes
1 teaspoon MCT oil
1 teaspoon whole-wheat flour (if allergic
  to wheat, use rye flour)
Dash of pepper
¼ cup onion, finely chopped
½ garlic clove
⅓ cup red wine
1 ripe tomato, pureed
1 teaspoon fresh parsley
1 teaspoon low-sodium Dijon mustard
½ bay leaf, crushed
1 cup carrots, diced
1½ potatoes, peeled and diced
½ cup fresh corn

1. Place beef cubes in a dutch oven that has been brushed with MCT oil. Sprinkle with flour and pepper.
2. Bake in a 350°F oven until beef pieces are browned (about 20 minutes), turning over once.
3. Stir onion and garlic into wine, and pour into the dutch oven. Bake another 20 minutes.
4. Add remaining ingredients to the stew, and bake another 45 minutes, or until the potatoes are done.

Serves 2

Per serving: 441 calories, 34 grams of protein, 40 grams of carbohydrate, 14 grams of fat, 108 milligrams of sodium

Tom Platz shows extreme knee and ankle flexibility during this set of hack squats. But he's long had a rep for possessing the sport's greatest all-time leg development, so who's going to argue with his formula for success?

MEATY GREEN BEANS AND ALMONDS

1½ teaspoons MCT oil
3 ounces round steak, cut into ribbons
1 cup fresh green beans, cut on a bias
2 tablespoons slivered almonds
Dash of garlic powder

1. Heat MCT oil in a nonstick skillet. Add steak, and brown on both sides.
2. Add remaining ingredients, and cook for 5 minutes.

Serves 2

Per serving: 304 calories, 18 grams of protein, 5 grams of carbohydrate, 14 grams of fat, 56 milligrams of sodium

POPEYE'S SPINACH HELPER

1½ teaspoons MCT oil
½ onion, chopped
½ clove garlic, crushed
½ green onion, sliced
½ green pepper, chopped
½ pound lean ground beef
½ pound fresh mushrooms, sliced
5 ounces fresh spinach, washed and
    drained
½ cup nonfat yogurt
1 ounce Weight Watchers dry-curd,
    unsalted cottage cheese
1 ounce water
1½ teaspoons fresh oregano

1. Heat MCT oil in skillet. Sauté onion, garlic, green onion, and green pepper until tender.
2. Add ground beef, and cook until just browned.
3. Add mushrooms and spinach. When spinach is limp, add remaining ingredients. Heat through and serve.

Serves 2

Per serving: 349 calories, 34 grams of protein, 37 grams of carbohydrate, 12 grams of fat, 151 milligrams of sodium

DOUBLE-SPLIT BEEF-TOMATO SALAD

8 ounces cooked roast beef, cut into
    strips
3 chopped tomatoes
2 chopped green onions
2 tablespoons MCT oil
1 tablespoon chopped fresh basil

1. Combine all ingredients in a bowl.
2. Chill before serving.

Serves 2

Per serving: 338 calories, 25 grams of protein, 15 grams of carbohydrate, 14 grams of fat, 172 milligrams of sodium

STEAK SAVORY

2 lean steaks, about 5 ounces each
2 tablespoons dry white wine
1 apple, peeled, cored, and sliced
½ cup sliced onion
½ teaspoon savory

1. Broil steak on both sides until browned.
2. In a skillet, heat wine. Add apples and onions, and braise until soft. Sprinkle with savory. Reduce heat, and cook until apples are done. Spread apple mixture on top of steaks.

Serves 2

Per serving: 270 calories, 32 grams of protein, 30 grams of carbohydrate, 8 grams of fat, 112 milligrams of sodium

FRUITY FLANK FEAST

½ cup lemon juice
Rind of 1 lemon
Juice of 1 orange
Rind of 1 orange
1 garlic clove, crushed
1 teaspoon Worcestershire sauce
10 ounces cubed flank steak

1. Mix together all ingredients except meat. Add steak cubes, and marinate overnight in refrigerator.
2. Remove steak cubes from marinade. Broil, basting with marinade, until done.

Serves 2

Per serving: 252 calories, 32 grams of protein, 11 grams of carbohydrate, 8 grams of fat, 245 milligrams of sodium

BETWEEN-SETS CHILI

Keep leftover Between-Sets Chili covered in the refrigerator. To reheat, add water to desired consistency, and stir occasionally until heated through.

1 pound lean ground beef
1 onion, chopped
1 green pepper, chopped
3 tomatoes, chopped
1 teaspoon chili powder
½ teaspoon cumin powder
Dash ground red pepper
1 16-ounce can red kidney beans, rinsed
  and drained
1 15-ounce can chick-peas, rinsed and
  drained
1 15-ounce can corn, rinsed and
  drained
1 8-ounce can low-sodium tomato paste
6 ounces water

1. Cook ground beef in large skillet until no longer pink. Drain fat.
2. Add remaining ingredients, stirring to ensure equal distribution. Cover and simmer for 1 hour, stirring occasionally.

Serves 8

Per serving: 329 calories, 23 grams of protein, 44 grams of carbohydrate, 8 grams of fat, 192 milligrams of sodium

BARBELL-DUMBBELL SURPRISE

½ pound lean stewing beef
3 tablespoons red wine
1 tablespoon lemon juice
1½ tablespoons MCT oil
2 small onions, cut in half
4 small potatoes, cut in half
4 cherry tomatoes
1 cup mushroom caps
½ sweet potato, cut into 1¼-inch cubes

1. Cut meat into 1¼-inch cubes.
2. Combine wine, lemon juice, and MCT oil to form marinade.
3. Marinate meat and vegetables for 1 hour.
4. Thread meat and vegetables attractively on skewers. (Make them look like little barbells, if you like.) Grill for 15 minutes, or until done.

Serves 2

Per serving: 352 calories, 29 grams of protein, 32 grams of carbohydrate, 7 grams of fat, 106 milligrams of sodium

BEEF 'N' VEGGIES MEDLEY

¼ pound ground beef
3½ tablespoons white wine
1 green bell pepper, seeded and diced
1 medium onion, sliced
½ garlic clove, crushed
½ eggplant, cut in 1-inch cubes
⅔ cup water
1 medium zucchini, diced
3 tomatoes, diced
½ cup fresh mushrooms, chopped
½ teaspoon oregano
½ teaspoon basil

1. Brown ground beef in a nonstick skillet, and drain the fat. Set fat aside.
2. Pour 3 tablespoons wine in a saucepan, and sauté bell pepper, onion, and garlic for 5 minutes. Remove with a slotted spoon, and set aside.
3. In the same pan, place eggplant, water, and ½ tablespoon wine. Braise until tender. Return all vegetables and beef to saucepan, and stir in remaining ingredients.

4. Bring to a boil, reduce heat, and let simmer for 20 minutes.

Serves 2

Per serving: 227 calories, 19 grams of protein, 29 grams of carbohydrate, 8 grams of fat, 72 milligrams of sodium

SAUTEED VEAL

1 tablespoon MCT oil
10 ounces veal chuck, sliced
1 cup sliced fresh mushrooms
¼ cup chopped onion
¼ teaspoon garlic powder
½ cup sherry or marsala
Dash of pepper

1. Heat MCT oil in skillet. Sauté veal until browned, and set aside.
2. To the skillet, add mushrooms, onion, and garlic powder. Cook until vegetables are tender, stirring occasionally.
3. Add wine, and cook for 2 minutes. Add veal and pepper. Cook until veal is heated. Serve immediately.

Serves 2

Per serving: 309 calories, 23 grams of protein, 9 grams of carbohydrate, 11 grams of fat, 90 milligrams of sodium

THREE-MORE-REPS BURGER

1 egg white, beaten until fluffy
½ pound lean ground beef
½ cup fresh mushrooms, sliced
1½ tablespoons chopped fresh parsley
Dash of garlic powder
2 tablespoons red wine

1. Mix all ingredients together. Divide into two portions.
2. Form patties, and grill, broil, or fry in a nonstick pan until done.

Serves 2

Per serving: 223 calories, 26 grams of protein, 1 gram of carbohydrate, 11 grams of fat, 102 milligrams of sodium

PINEAPPLE AND BEEF PITA PIZZA

¼ pound lean ground beef
½ green pepper, sliced
4 ounces low-sodium tomato sauce
2 pita bread pockets, toasted
2 ounces fresh mushrooms, sliced
2 ounces low-sodium mozzarella cheese,
   shredded
¼ pineapple, diced
¼ teaspoon each black pepper, oregano,
   garlic powder

1. In a skillet, cook ground beef and green pepper together. Drain fat.
2. Add tomato sauce to beef mixture. Spread sauce on pita pockets.
3. Sprinkle each pita pocket with remaining ingredients.
4. Broil for 3 to 4 minutes. Watch carefully not to burn the cheese.

Serves 2

Per serving: 379 calories, 23 grams of protein, 31 grams of carbohydrate, 13 grams of fat, 164 milligrams of sodium

ITALIAN BEEF AND PASTA

¼ pound lean ground beef
¼ onion, chopped
1 cup fresh mushrooms, chopped
1 tablespoon white wine
Dash each of basil, celery seed, oregano,
   chili powder, pepper, dry mustard
¼ cup tomato paste
1 tomato, pureed
⅔ cup macaroni, cooked
2½ ounces Weight Watchers low-sodium
   cottage cheese
½ tomato, thinly sliced

1. Preheat oven to 350°F. Sauté ground beef until browned. Drain fat. Put beef aside.
2. Braise onion and mushrooms in wine until tender. Add ground beef and all of the spices. Mix well.
3. Stir in tomato paste and pureed tomatoes.
4. Add macaroni and stir.
5. In a casserole dish, arrange layers of macaroni, meat mixture, and

cheese. Repeat layers, ending with macaroni. Place tomato slices on top.
6. Bake covered for 15 minutes. Remove cover; then bake for 15 more minutes.

Serves 2

Per serving: 247 calories, 20 grams of protein, 25 grams of carbohydrate, 7 grams of fat, 142 milligrams of sodium

NEGRITA'S SPINACH NOODLE LASAGNA

This lasagna freezes well. Just cover with plastic wrap and freeze. To use again after frozen, double the cooking time.

    1 pound artichoke or spinach noodles
    2 large onions, chopped
    1 clove garlic, crushed
    ¼ cup dry white wine or sangria or
        water
    2 pounds lean ground beef
    4 large ripe tomatoes, pureed
    7 ounces salt-free tomato paste
    2 tablespoons each chopped fresh
        parsley, basil, oregano
    32 ounces Weight Watchers unsalted
        cottage cheese
    2 egg whites
    1 pound fresh spinach, chopped, cooked,
        and drained
    1 large tomato, thinly sliced for garnish

1. Boil noodles until tender. Drain.
2. Braise onions and garlic in white wine for 4 minutes. Add ground beef. Cook until no longer pink. Drain fat.
3. Add pureed tomatoes, tomato paste, and herbs. Simmer for 20 minutes.
4. In a blender, mix cottage cheese, egg whites, and spinach. Puree.
5. Preheat oven to 350°F. Place a layer of meat sauce in a large baking pan. Layer with noodles and spinach mixture. Repeat layers, ending with noodles. Arrange tomato slices on top. Bake for 45 minutes.

Serves 12

Per serving: 253 calories, 34 grams of protein, 18 grams of carbohydrate, 8 grams of fat, 84 milligrams of sodium (If you use low-fat cottage cheese, the sodium level will be 383 milligrams.)

MUSCLE DENSITY BROCCOLI SALAD

½ pound cooked steak, cut in strips
1 cup broccoli, cooked and chopped
1 cup green beans, cooked and cut
1 stalk celery, sliced
½ cup mushrooms, sliced
1 green onion, sliced
½ tablespoon red wine vinegar
1½ tablespoons lemon juice
¼ cup nonfat yogurt
½ teaspoon salt-free mustard
¼ teaspoon ground pepper
½ head of lettuce
½ tomato, sliced
Fresh parsley

1. In a large salad bowl, combine steak, broccoli, green beans, celery, mushrooms, and onion.
2. In a screw-top jar, combine the vinegar, lemon juice, yogurt, mustard, and pepper, and shake until thoroughly mixed for the salad dressing.
3. Arrange salad on a bed of lettuce leaves. Garnish with tomato slices and parsley.

Serves 2

Per serving: 240 calories, 30 grams of protein, 20 grams of carbohydrate, 7 grams of fat, 188 milligrams of sodium

At 5'9" and 155 pounds, Dorothy Herndon is one of the largest—and leanest—women competing on the pro circuit. After placing last at the 1987 USA, she came back to win the overall title a year later to qualify for her pro card.

15

STARCHY AND FIBROUS CARBS

Whether they take the form of potatoes, rice, pasta, or salads, complex carbohydrates have a way of tasting great. Their variety and ability to mix with all other food groups make them a staple in the diet of every bodybuilder.

As Chapter 7 pointed out, the differences between starchy and fibrous carbs are significant. It's as if Mother Nature herself is a fan of bodybuilding, because she has provided carbs for size and carbs for cuts. Add to that the amazing range of tastes found within the complex-carb group, and there's never a dull moment with carbohydrate foods.

Always interesting and always tasty—that's carbohydrates! Try out this mouth-watering delight for your eager palates, as well as for your bodybuilding goals. Truly, carbs are king.

POWER ROASTED POTATO

1 potato, peeled and quartered
½ teaspoon MCT oil
Dash each of pepper, oregano, paprika

1. Preheat oven to 325°F.
2. Boil potato for 10 minutes. Drain.
3. Brush potato with MCT oil, and place it on a baking sheet.
4. Sprinkle with seasonings, and roast for 45 minutes, or until crispy. Turn once to brown all sides.

Serves 1

Per serving: 128 calories, 3 grams of protein, 26 grams of carbohydrate, trace of fat, 5 milligrams of sodium

Variations

Cut potatoes in a stick shape, making french fries, or slice thinly, making roasted scalloped potatoes.

POTATO PANCAKES

1½ potatoes, grated
1 egg white, beaten until fluffy
½ onion, grated
2 tablespoons oatmeal
Dash of pepper
1 tablespoon MCT oil

1. Puree potatoes, egg white, onion, oatmeal, and pepper in a blender.
2. Heat MCT oil in a nonstick skillet.
3. Spoon potato mixture onto hot skillet. Make five or six pancakes at a time. Turn over once to brown both sides.

Serves 2

Per serving: 204 calories, 4 grams of protein, 24 grams of carbohydrate, trace of fat, 59 milligrams of sodium

PARSLEYED POTATO JACKETS

2 medium baking potatoes
1 tablespoon fresh parsley
1 tablespoon fresh dill
¼ cup nonfat yogurt

1. Bake potatoes in a 400°F oven for 1 hour.
2. Slice each potato in half lengthwise. Scoop out insides, leaving skin intact.
3. Mash potato insides. Add parsley, dill, and yogurt, and mash thoroughly. Spoon back into skins. Garnish with parsley.
4. Bake at 425°F for another 10 minutes. Serve hot.

Serves 2

Per serving: 128 calories, 5 grams of protein, 28 grams of carbohydrate, trace of fat, 32 milligrams of sodium

GERMAN POTATO SALAD

¾ pound potatoes, boiled, cooled, and
  diced
½ cup peeled and diced cucumber
1 egg white, boiled and sliced
½ cup sliced celery
¼ cup diced green pepper
½ green onion, chopped
½ teaspoon fresh parsley, chopped
Dash each of black pepper, paprika,
  thyme, rosemary, dill, celery seed
¼ cup nonfat yogurt
1½ teaspoons wine vinegar
½ teaspoon prepared mustard

1. In a salad bowl, combine potatoes, cucumber, egg white, celery,
   green pepper, green onion, parsley, and seasonings.
2. Separately mix together yogurt, vinegar, and mustard. Pour over
   potato mixture.
3. Chill for 4 hours or overnight to blend flavors.
4. Toss before serving.

Serves 2

**Per serving: 127 calories, 6 grams of protein, 35 grams of carbohydrate,
trace of fat, 142 milligrams of sodium**

PECTORAL POTATO AND PEA CURRY

1 tablespoon MCT oil
1 large potato, diced small
2 tomatoes, pureed
¼ pound fresh peas
½ teaspoon curry powder
¼ cup dry white wine

1. In a skillet, heat MCT oil. Sauté potato cubes for 6 minutes.
2. Add remaining ingredients. Cover and simmer for 30 minutes. Add
   water if necessary.

Serves 2

**Per serving: 198 calories, 5 grams of protein, 26 grams of carbohydrate,
trace of fat, 9 milligrams of sodium**

POTATO-PEPPER SAUTE

1 tablespoon MCT oil
¼ onion, chopped
½ garlic clove, crushed
3 potatoes, peeled, cooked, diced
½ green bell pepper, diced
½ red bell pepper, diced
Dash of black pepper

1. Heat MCT oil in skillet. Add onion and garlic. Sauté until onion is soft.
2. Add remaining ingredients, and sauté until peppers are limp.

Serves 3

Per serving: 164 calories, 4 grams of protein, 27 grams of carbohydrates, trace of fat, 10 milligrams of sodium

TRAPEZIUS TZIMMES

2 teaspoons MCT oil
2 large carrots, sliced
1 potato, peeled and quartered
⅓ cup water
1 cup orange juice
3 tablespoons pitted prunes
2 tablespoons raisins
2 tablespoons quartered dried apricots
2 teaspoons apple juice concentrate
½ teaspoon grated lemon peel
2 teaspoons lemon juice
¼ teaspoon cinnamon
Dash of ground cloves
1 teaspoon cornstarch
1 teaspoon cold water

1. In a large skillet, bring to boil MCT oil, carrots, potato, water and orange juice. Reduce heat and simmer for 20 minutes.
2. Add prunes, raisins, apricots, apple juice concentrate, lemon peel, lemon juice, cinnamon, and cloves. Cook covered for 25 minutes.
3. Whisk cornstarch into cold water, and pour into stew, stirring gently. Cook for 5 additional minutes, until thickened.

Serves 2

Per serving: 239 calories, 4 grams of protein, 44 grams of carbohydrate, trace of fat, 28 milligrams of sodium

TRICEPS TOFU-TATERS

1½ teaspoons MCT oil
1½ teaspoons lemon juice
1½ teaspoons water
½ teaspoon Dijon mustard
⅛ cup chopped celery
1½ teaspoons onion flakes
1½ potatoes, boiled, cooled, cubed
½ cup tofu, cubed

1. To make salad dressing, in a screw-top jar, shake together MCT oil, lemon juice, water, and mustard.
2. In a salad bowl, mix together celery, onion flakes, and potatoes. Toss.
3. Gently add tofu cubes to potato mixture. Chill.
4. Just before serving, gently stir in salad dressing.

Serves 2

Per serving: 152 calories, 5 grams of protein, 24 grams of carbohydrate, 1 gram of fat, 123 milligrams of sodium

LAST REP FRUIT AND POTATO SALAD

1 large potato, cooked and diced
1 tablespoon chopped onion
¼ cup sliced celery
½ apple, diced
⅛ fresh pineapple, cored and diced
½ peach, diced
⅛ cup nonfat yogurt
Pepper to taste
Lettuce

1. In a salad bowl, combine all ingredients except lettuce. Chill.
2. When ready to serve, arrange potato salad on a bed of lettuce.

Serves 2

Per serving: 110 calories, 3 grams of protein, 26 grams of carbohydrate, trace of fat, 28 milligrams of sodium

Mike Quinn, a solid IFBB pro if there ever was one, utilizes a special rowing bar to improve midback thickness. Standing on the box allows him to achieve a full stretch position at the bottom point of the movement.

DECLINE BENCH CARROT HASH BROWNS

3 carrots, grated
3 potatoes, grated
½ small onion, grated
¼ teaspoon pepper
1 tablespoon MCT oil

1. Puree carrots, potatoes, onion, and pepper in a blender.
2. Heat MCT oil in a large skillet. When hot, add potato mixture in three scoops at a time. Turn once, browning each side.

Serves 3 (6 hash browns)

Per serving: 278 calories, 4 grams of protein, 32 grams of carbohydrate, trace of fat, 25 milligrams of sodium

STUFFED SWEET POTATO

1 medium yam
1 tablespoon honey
Dash of cinnamon
Dash of nutmeg

1. Pierce yam, and bake until tender, 45 minutes in a 400°F oven.
2. Cut yam in half, and scoop out the insides, leaving skin intact.
3. Mash yam with honey and spices, and stuff back into jackets.
4. Bake another 15 minutes.

Serves 2

Per serving: 137 calories, 3 grams of protein, 33 grams of carbohydrate, trace of fat, 7 milligrams of sodium

SPICED BAKED YAMS

1 medium yam
2 teaspoons MCT oil
Dash of pepper
Dash of nutmeg

1. Bake yam for 45 minutes in a hot oven (400°F).
2. Slice yam, and arrange in a baking dish.
3. Mix together MCT oil, pepper, and nutmeg, and brush on yam slices.
4. Broil for 3 minutes.

Serves 2

Per serving: 134 calories, 3 grams of protein, 24 grams of carbohydrate, trace of fat, 7 milligrams of sodium

Variation

Make yam fries by cutting yams into sticks.

RAISINED SWEET POTATO WITH PEAR

1 medium sweet potato
3 tablespoons orange juice
1 tablespoon pear brandy or pear juice
1 tablespoon apple juice concentrate
½ teaspoon cornstarch
3 tablespoons mixed raisins
1 pear, cored and sliced ¼ inch thick

1. Preheat oven to 350°F. Boil sweet potato until not yet tender, approximately 10 minutes. Peel and slice in ¼-inch thicknesses.
2. In a saucepan, heat together orange juice, brandy, and apple juice concentrate. Whisk in cornstarch. Stir constantly until sauce is thick and smooth.
3. Add raisins.
4. In a casserole dish, arrange sweet potato slices alternately with pear slices. Pour sauce on top, and bake for 40 minutes.

Serves 2

Per serving: 160 calories, 2 grams of protein, 35 grams of carbohydrate, 1 gram of fat, 102 milligrams of sodium

YAM MASH

1 tablespoon raisins
2 tablespoons orange juice
2 teaspoons sherry (optional)
1 medium yam, peeled, cooked, and
   diced
Dash of allspice
Dash of nutmeg

1. Plumb raisins in a mixture of orange juice and sherry for 20 minutes. Reserve liquid and raisins.
2. Mash yam. Add the reserved liquid, raisins, and spices. Mash until smooth. Serve warm.

Serves 2

Per serving: 139 calories, 3 grams of protein, 28 grams of carbohydrate, trace of fat, 9 milligrams of sodium

BEGINNING BODYBUILDER'S BASIC RICE

1¼ cups water
½ cup long-grain rice

1. Bring water to boil in large saucepan.
2. Add rice to boiling water. Reduce heat, and simmer covered for 35 minutes.

Serves 3

Per serving: 117 calories, 2 grams of protein, 35 grams of carbohydrate, trace of fat, 3 milligrams of sodium

CHAMP'S ORANGE RICE

1¾ cups water
⅓ cup orange juice
¼ teaspoon grated orange peel
¾ cup long-grain rice

1. Bring water, orange juice, and orange peel to a boil in a large saucepan.
2. Add rice to boiling liquid. Reduce heat and simmer covered for 35 minutes.

Serves 2

Per serving: 127 calories, 3 grams of protein, 27 grams of carbohydrate, 1 gram of fat, 3 milligrams of sodium

SPINACH AND RICE

⅓ cup rice, cooked
3 tablespoons Weight Watchers low-fat
  cottage cheese
1 egg white, beaten until fluffy
2 teaspoons chopped fresh parsley
2 teaspoons chopped fresh dill
Dash of pepper
2 cups fresh spinach, chopped
3 teaspoons whole-wheat bread crumbs

1. Preheat oven to 350°F.
2. In a mixing bowl, combine rice and cottage cheese.
3. In a small bowl, mix together egg white, parsley, dill, and pepper.
4. Add spinach and egg white mixture to rice mixture. Mix well. Pour into casserole dish, and sprinkle bread crumbs on top.
5. Bake for 40 minutes.

Serves 2

Per serving: 157 calories, 7 grams of protein, 29 grams of carbohydrate, 1 gram of fat, 113 milligrams of sodium

RICE, TOMATO, AND BEAN SALAD

1 small tomato, diced
¼ green bell pepper, chopped
¼ onion, chopped
¼ cup celery, sliced
¼ cup rice, cooked and chilled
1 cup red kidney beans, cooked
2 teaspoons cider vinegar
2 teaspoons MCT oil
Dash of chili powder
Dash of black pepper

1. In a salad bowl, combine tomato, green pepper, onion, celery, rice, and kidney beans.
2. In a screw-top jar, combine the remaining ingredients, and shake thoroughly.
3. Pour dressing over salad, and toss.

Serves 2

Per serving: 156 calories, 5 grams of protein, 30 grams of carbohydrate, 1 gram of fat, 30 milligrams of sodium

OFF-SEASON RICE DELIGHT

1 cup cooked rice, chilled
½ cup nonfat yogurt
2 tablespoons mixture of nuts and
   raisins
Dash of cinnamon
Dash of nutmeg

1. Combine in a bowl. Serve cold.

Serves 2

Per serving: 145 calories, 5 grams of protein, 26 grams of carbohydrate, 2 grams of fat, 40 milligrams of sodium

Variations

Instead of rice, use pasta or cubed leftover potatoes, sliced apples, pineapple chunks, sliced banana, or cooked oatmeal. Use your imagination!

SPANISH RICE FIESTA

1½ teaspoons MCT oil
¼ red bell pepper, chopped
¼ green bell pepper, chopped
¼ onion, chopped
¼ cup sliced celery
1¼ cups water
¼ cup rice
¼ cup low-sodium tomato paste
¼ teaspoon chili powder
Dash of black pepper
Dash of ground cumin

1. In a large skillet, sauté vegetables in MCT oil until tender.
2. Stir in remaining ingredients, and bring to a boil. Reduce heat, and simmer for 20 minutes until rice is done.

Serves 2

Per serving: 160 calories, 4 grams of protein, 30 grams of carbohydrate, trace of fat, 37 milligrams of sodium

PEAK CONTRACTION FRUITED CURRY RICE

1 cup water
1½ ounces apple juice
1½ ounces pineapple juice
Dash of curry powder
¼ red apple, diced
1 teaspoon raisins
⅓ cup rice

1. In a saucepan, bring to a boil water, juices, curry powder, apple, and raisins.
2. Add rice. Reduce heat, and simmer over very low heat for 35 minutes until rice is done.

Serves 2

Per serving: 146 calories, 2 grams of protein, 33 grams of carbohydrate, trace of fat, 3 milligrams of sodium

CHINESE FRIED RICE

1 egg white
1 teaspoon MCT oil
1 teaspoon mild, low-sodium soy sauce
⅓ onion, chopped
⅓ green pepper, chopped
⅓ red pepper, chopped
⅓ garlic clove, crushed
1 green onion, sliced
⅓ cup instant rice
⅓ cup boiling water

1. Cook egg whites in a nonstick skillet, chop, and set aside.
2. Heat MCT oil and soy sauce in a skillet. Add vegetables, and sauté for 5 minutes.
3. Add rice and water. Cover and simmer for 1 minute.
4. Add chopped egg whites. Mix and cover. Let stand for 3 minutes before serving.

Serves 2

Per serving: 150 calories, 5 grams of protein, 34 grams of carbohydrate, trace of fat, 119 milligrams of sodium

MUSHROOMS WITH WILD RICE

2 cups water
¼ teaspoon onion flakes
Dash each of thyme, crumbled bay leaf,
   and paprika
3 tablespoons brown rice
3 tablespoons wild rice
¼ cup mushrooms, sliced
1 green onion, chopped
¼ cup celery, sliced
1½ teaspoons dry white wine
1½ teaspoons lemon juice

1. In a small saucepan, mix together water, onion flakes, and herbs.
   Bring to a boil.
2. Add brown and wild rice. Cover and let simmer at a reduced heat
   for 45 minutes.
3. While rice is cooking, braise mushrooms, green onion, and celery
   in wine for 10 minutes. Stir occasionally.
4. Blend the mushroom mixture with the rice. Stir in lemon juice,
   and serve.

Serves 2

**Per serving: 137 calories, 4 grams of protein, 29 grams of carbohydrate,
trace of fat, 20 milligrams of sodium**

JIFFY'S RICE SALAD

¼ cup rice, cooked and chilled
2 tablespoons fresh peas, cooked
½ cup sliced celery
¼ red pepper, chopped
1 green onion, chopped
1 tablespoon chopped fresh parsley
1 tablespoon red wine vinegar
⅛ cup nonfat yogurt
¼ teaspoon salt-free mustard
2 cherry tomatoes
Lettuce leaves

1. In a salad bowl, combine rice, peas, celery, red pepper, green
   onion, and parsley.
2. Separately mix vinegar, yogurt, and mustard. Fold into rice mixture. Chill for 1 hour or overnight.

3. Before serving, toss salad, and pile on a bed of lettuce. Garnish with cherry tomatoes.

Serves 2

Per serving: 116 calories, 3 grams of protein, 25 grams of carbohydrate, trace of fat, 41 milligrams of sodium

MARINATED GARDEN PASTA SALAD

1 cup broccoli florets
1 cup diagonally sliced asparagus
1 cup sliced zucchini
1½ teaspoons MCT oil
½ green onion, sliced
½ cup mushrooms
1½ teaspoons fresh lemon juice
1 tablespoon red wine vinegar
1 tablespoon fresh lemon juice
¼ teaspoon each oregano, basil, thyme,
   garlic powder
½ cup pasta or vegetable fusilli, cooked
   and chilled
⅛ cup thin red pepper strips
5 small olives
2 tablespoons fresh parsley, chopped

1. Steam broccoli for 3 minutes in a steamer. Add asparagus and zucchini, and steam another 4 minutes.
2. Heat MCT oil in a skillet, and add green onion and mushrooms. Sauté for 4 minutes. Sprinkle with 1½ teaspoons of lemon juice, and set aside.
3. Mix vinegar, 1 tablespoon lemon juice, and the herbs in a jar. Shake well.
4. Combine the cooked vegetables, and pour marinade on top. Toss and chill.
5. When ready to serve, add pasta. Sprinkle with red pepper strips, olives, and parsley.

Serves 2

Per serving: 160 calories, 8 grams of protein, 20 grams of carbohydrate, 3 grams of fat, 90 milligrams of sodium

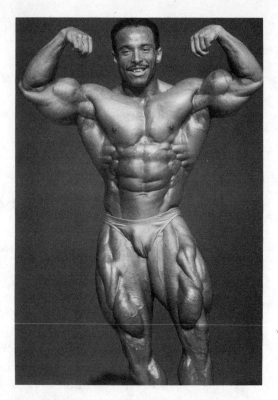

One of the new breed of pro competitors, mighty mite Mohammed Benaziza won the World Lightweight Championship in his first competition. An Algerian living in Marseilles, France, Benaziza notched his first pro win at the Night of the Champions in 1990.

RAINBOW PASTA SALAD

1 cup multicolored macaroni, cooked
½ tomato, diced
½ green onion, sliced
½ red pepper, chopped
4 black olives, pitted and sliced
1½ teaspoons MCT oil
1½ teaspoons red wine vinegar
1½ teaspoons each fresh basil, parsley,
    oregano
Black pepper to taste

1. In a salad bowl, combine macaroni, tomato, green onion, red pepper, and olives.
2. In a screw-top jar, combine remaining ingredients. Shake, pour over salad, and toss. Chill before serving.

Serves 2

Per serving: 136 calories, 3 grams of protein, 20 grams of carbohydrate, 2 grams of fat, 59 milligrams of sodium

GEORGE'S RIGATONI SPECIAL

4 ounces rigatoni pasta
1 tablespoon MCT oil
1½ teaspoons olive oil
½ onion, chopped
½ garlic clove, crushed

1. Cook rigatoni in boiling water until tender. Drain. Set aside.
2. While pasta is boiling, heat MCT oil and olive oil in a skillet.
3. Add onion and garlic, and sauté until onions are browned.
4. Combine onion mixture with rigatoni, and serve.

Serves 2

Per serving: 142 calories, 2 grams of protein, 12 grams of carbohydrate, 4 grams of fat, 5 milligrams of sodium

Variation:

5. Add ½ cup low-fat cottage cheese to the rigatoni mixture.
6. Heat for 2 minutes more, then serve.

Serves 2

Per serving: 187 calories, 9 grams of protein, 14 grams of carbohydrate, 5 grams of fat, 235 milligrams of sodium

ORANGE CUKE SALAD

1 cucumber, peeled and sliced
1 orange, peeled and sliced
½ onion, chopped fine
1 tablespoon lemon juice
1 tablespoon MCT oil
Dash of pepper
Dash of nutmeg

1. Combine all ingredients in a salad bowl.
2. Chill for 2 hours.

Serves 2

Per serving: 114 calories, 2 grams of protein, 19 grams of carbohydrate, trace of fat, 8 milligrams of sodium

SPINACH, ONION, ORANGE SURPRISE

5 ounces fresh spinach
3 large oranges, peeled and sliced
½ onion, sliced in rings
½ ounce orange juice
½ ounce apple juice
1 tablespoon red wine vinegar
½ clove garlic, crushed
⅛ teaspoon each of thyme, paprika, dry
    mustard, celery seed, pepper

1. Arrange spinach leaves to cover the bottom of a large salad bowl.
2. Place orange slices and onion rings alternately on top of spinach leaves.
3. Combine remaining ingredients in a screw-top jar, and shake.
4. Pour dressing over salad, and serve.

Serves 2

Per serving: 121 calories, 3 grams of protein, 30 grams of carbohydrate, 1 gram of fat, 12 milligrams of sodium

SUMMER GARDEN SALAD

4 cups mixed lettuce greens
12 cherry tomatoes, cut in half
1 stalk celery, sliced
1 carrot, grated
2 green onions, sliced
2 egg whites, hard-boiled and chopped
5 radishes, sliced
1 tablespoon MCT oil
1 tablespoon lemon juice
1 tablespoon red wine vinegar
¼ teaspoon garlic powder
1 tablespoon chopped fresh parsley

1. In a salad bowl, combine greens, tomatoes, celery, carrot, green onions, egg whites, and radishes.
2. In a screw-top jar, shake the remaining ingredients together. Pour over salad. Toss.

Serves 2

Per serving: 156 calories, 8 grams of protein, 19 grams of carbohydrate, trace of fat, 125 milligrams of sodium

BREADED CAULIFLOWER

¼ cup whole-wheat bread crumbs
2 cups cauliflower florets, blanched and
   cooled
1 egg white, beaten for 10 seconds
1 tablespoon MCT oil
Dash of pepper

1. Put bread crumbs in a plastic bag.
2. Coat cauliflower with egg white, and shake in the plastic bag until coated with the bread crumbs.
3. Heat MCT oil in a nonstick skillet. Add cauliflower, and brown all sides. Season with pepper.

Serves 2

Per serving: 141 calories, 6 grams of protein, 15 grams of carbohydrate, 1 gram of fat, 130 milligrams of sodium

CARROT-BROCCOLI-MUSHROOM SAUTÉ

1 tablespoon MCT oil
½ cup grated carrot
½ cup broccoli florets
½ clove garlic, crushed
½ cup mushrooms, sliced

1. Sauté carrots, broccoli, and garlic in MCT oil for 3 minutes.
2. Add mushrooms to the skillet, and sauté for another 6 minutes. Serve warm.

Serves 1

Per serving: 190 calories, 8 grams of protein, 14 grams of carbohydrate, 1 gram of fat, 47 milligrams of sodium

Amino acids prevent muscle tissue loss during periods of low carbohydrate intake.

SPINACH-MUSHROOM-EGG SALAD

3 cups spinach leaves, washed, drained,
   torn
1 cup mushrooms, sliced
2 egg whites, hard-boiled, sliced
2 tablespoons lemon juice
1 tablespoon MCT oil
½ teaspoon each basil, garlic powder,
   low-sodium mustard

1. In a salad bowl, combine spinach, mushrooms, and egg whites.
2. In a screw-top jar, shake together remaining ingredients. Pour over salad. Toss and serve.

Serves 2

Per serving: 108 calories, 7 grams of protein, 11 grams of carbohydrate, trace of fat, 133 milligrams of sodium

GREEN BEAN SALAD

½ cup sliced cucumber
½ cup green beans, cooked
½ cup kidney beans, cooked
¼ green bell pepper, chopped
½ onion, chopped
½ clove garlic, crushed
½ tablespoon fresh parsley, chopped
½ tablespoon fresh basil, chopped
1 tablespoon red wine vinegar
2 teaspoons MCT oil
6 cherry tomatoes

1. In a large salad bowl, combine all ingredients except cherry tomatoes.
2. Marinate salad a couple of hours in the refrigerator.
3. Toss before serving. Garnish with cherry tomatoes.

Serves 2

Per serving: 143 calories, 7 grams of protein, 23 grams of carbohydrate, 1 gram of fat, 15 milligrams of sodium

APPLE SLAW

1 cup green cabbage, finely shredded
2 carrots, grated
1 stalk celery, chopped
¼ teaspoon onion flakes
Dash of garlic powder
Dash of thyme
1 ounce raisins
1 green apple, cored and sliced
1 tablespoon raspberry vinegar
1 tablespoon apple juice concentrate
¼ cup nonfat yogurt

1. In a salad bowl, combine cabbage, carrots, celery, onion flakes, garlic powder, thyme, raisins, and apple.
2. Separately combine vinegar, apple juice concentrate, and yogurt. Pour over cabbage mixture.
3. Chill for a few hours or overnight.

Serves 2

Per serving: 128 calories, 3 grams of protein, 32 grams of carbohydrate, trace of fat, 85 milligrams of sodium

"COOL" CUCUMBER SALAD

2 ounces white wine vinegar
1½ teaspoons grated fresh ginger
1 cup peeled and sliced cucumber
1 carrot, grated
1 tomato, quartered
2 green onions, chopped
2 tablespoons chopped fresh parsley

1. Toss all ingredients together in a salad bowl. Chill to blend flavors.
2. Toss again before serving.

Serves 2

Per serving: 108 calories, 3 grams of protein, 25 grams of carbohydrate, trace of fat, 38 milligrams of sodium

Now better known as Gold on the "American Gladiators" television program, Tonya Knight is a highly respected competitive bodybuilder who has won pro titles and placed fifth in her first Olympia attempt.

CARROT-RAISIN-PINEAPPLE SALAD

1 cup shredded carrots
1 ounce raisins
½ cup pineapple chunks
2 tablespoons nonfat yogurt
1 tablespoon chopped walnuts

1. Mix all ingredients together in a salad bowl. Chill.
2. Toss before serving.

Serves 2

Per serving: 125 calories, 3 grams of protein, 21 grams of carbohydrate, 4 grams of fat, 48 milligrams of sodium

ROMAINE ROLL-UPS

½ avocado, mashed
½ tomato, diced
½ cucumber, peeled and sliced
1 cup alfalfa sprouts
1½ teaspoons lemon juice
4 large romaine lettuce leaves

1. Mix together avocado, tomato, and cucumber.
2. Stir in sprouts.
3. Place a heaping spoonful of avocado mixture in center of each lettuce leaf, and roll up.

Serves 2

Per serving: 117 calories, 4 grams of protein, 7 grams of carbohydrate, 8 grams of fat, 10 milligrams of sodium

FIONA'S FENNEL SALAD

2 cups fennel, sliced
1 cup diced red bell pepper
2 green onions, sliced
1 tablespoon red wine vinegar
1 tablespoon MCT oil
¼ garlic clove, crushed
Dash of oregano
Dash of black pepper

1. In a salad bowl, combine fennel, red pepper, and green onion.
2. In a screw-top jar, shake together vinegar, MCT oil, garlic, oregano, and black pepper. Pour contents on salad.
3. Marinate for 2 hours in the refrigerator.

Serves 2

Per serving: 103 calories, 2 grams of protein, 11 grams of carbohydrate, trace of fat, 153 milligrams of sodium

WORKOUT ENERGY SALAD

1 cup lettuce, torn into bite-sized pieces
⅓ cup spinach, torn into bite-sized
  pieces
⅓ cucumber, peeled and sliced
⅓ tomato, sliced
¾ cup sprouts
⅓ cup shredded carrots
⅓ cup sliced mushrooms
⅓ avocado, cubed
1 tablespoon raw sunflower seeds
1 tablespoon MCT oil
2 teaspoons lemon juice
Dash each of thyme, parsley, basil

1. In a medium-sized salad bowl, combine lettuce, spinach, cucumber, tomato, sprouts, carrots, mushrooms, avocado, and sunflower seeds.
2. In a screw-top jar, mix MCT oil with lemon juice and herbs. Shake vigorously, and pour over salad.

Serves 2

Per serving: 167 calories, 5 grams of protein, 9 grams of carbohydrate, 9 grams of fat, 22 milligrams of sodium

16
FRUIT DESSERTS

Due to their simple chemical structure, fruits are easily absorbed, provide a quick energy pickup, and help bridge the energy gap before complex carbohydrates break down in the digestive system. The sugar in fruit is called fructose, and it yields about half of the calories of other sugars.

When fruit sugar and protein are consumed together, they complement each other. The fructose can spare the protein from being used for energy, allowing its amino acids to be used to build and repair tissues, particularly muscle. Also, fructose can facilitate the absorption of amino acids into the muscles.

Best of all, fruits taste great, come in a variety of flavors, and are truly a healthy taste treat for a dieting bodybuilder.

FRESH APPLESAUCE

¼ cup fresh apple juice
1 apple, peeled, cored, and quartered
Dash each of nutmeg and cinnamon
½ frozen banana

Place all ingredients in a blender. Blend until smooth.

Serves 2

Per serving: 81 calories, 1 gram of protein, 21 grams of carbohydrate, trace of fat, 2 milligrams of sodium

PERFECT PEAR

1 ripe pear, cut in half including stem,
  cored
1 tablespoon orange juice
Dash each of nutmeg and cinnamon
2 prunes

1. Preheat oven to 350°F. Place pear halves in a baking dish, and
   sprinkle with orange juice.
2. Place 1 prune in each pear half.
3. Bake for 30 minutes. Serve warm.

Serves 2

**Per serving: 77 calories, 1 gram of protein, 20 grams of carbohydrate,
1 gram of fat, 1 milligram of sodium**

MELT-IN-YOUR-MOUTH FRUIT PIE

1 pound ripe strawberries, hulled and
  sliced (save 10 for garnishing)
½ pound fresh blueberries
2 tablespoons banana or strawberry
  liqueur or Grand Marnier
5 egg whites
¼ teaspoon cream of tartar
1½ teaspoons vanilla
2 ripe bananas, mashed
1 tablespoon lemon juice

1. Preheat oven to 225°F. Sprinkle strawberries and blueberries with
   liqueur, and let marinate for 3 hours.
2. Beat egg whites until foamy. Add cream of tartar, and beat until
   soft peaks form. Gradually add vanilla and mashed banana. Continue beating.
3. Place egg mixture in a 9-inch nonstick pie plate, and spread evenly
   (like a crust).
4. Bake for 1½ hours. Turn off oven, and let the pie shell sit in the
   oven for 2 hours to harden.
5. Gently place the marinated fruit in the pie shell, and garnish with
   remaining strawberries.

Serves 10

**Per serving: 60 calories, 3 grams of protein, 6 grams of carbohydrate,
trace of fat, 27 milligrams of sodium**

WORTH-SQUATTING-HEAVY-FOR STRAWBERRY SOUP

½ pound ripe strawberries, hulled and
    cut in half
1 teaspoon cornstarch
¼ cup, plus 1 tablespoon squeezed
    orange juice
¼ cup, plus 1 tablespoon red wine
2 tablespoons orange juice concentrate
¼ cup nonfat yogurt
Mint leaves for garnish

1. Save 4 perfect strawberries for garnish.
2. Puree the remaining strawberries.
3. In a saucepan, dissolve cornstarch in 3 tablespoons of orange juice.
4. Add remaining orange juice, red wine, orange juice concentrate, and pureed strawberries. Heat over medium heat. When mixture boils, remove from heat, and cool.
5. Mix in yogurt, then cover and refrigerate 4 hours.
6. Ladle into bowls, and garnish each bowl with 2 strawberries and a mint leaf.

Serves 2

Per serving: 102 calories, 3 grams of protein, 17 grams of carbohydrate, 1 gram of fat, 33 milligrams of sodium

BLUEBERRY-CANTALOUPE SUPREME

¼ cantaloupe, diced
½ mango, diced
1 peach, sliced
½ cup blueberries
½ banana, sliced

Mix together and serve.

Serves 2

Per serving: 122 calories, 7 grams of protein, 29 grams of carbohydrate, 1 gram of fat, 9 milligrams of sodium

Some athletes, such as Pro Ms. International Jackie Paisley, were blessed with superb BMRs, making it very easy to rip up for competition. Jackie can eat literally anything the last few days prior to competition and still end up in winning form.

FRUIT COMPOTE

½ cup water
½ cup sherry
Peel from ¼ lemon
1 tablespoon lemon juice
2 whole cloves
¼ cinnamon stick
¼ teaspoon vanilla extract
1 apple, peeled, cored, halved
1 pear, peeled, cored, halved
¼ cup cranberries, cooked
2 tablespoons raisins

1. In a large saucepan, mix water, sherry, lemon peel, lemon juice, cloves, cinnamon stick, vanilla, apple, and pear. Heat to boiling. Reduce heat, and simmer, covered, for 20 minutes.
2. Add cranberries and raisins. Simmer for 5 minutes.
3. Serve hot or cold.

Serves 2

Per serving: 142 calories, 1 gram of protein, 29 grams of carbohydrate, trace of fat, 5 milligrams of sodium

STRAWBERRY SUNDAE SALAD TREAT

1 cup nonfat yogurt
6 strawberries, hulled and sliced
1 tablespoon orange juice concentrate

1. Combine yogurt and strawberries in a small bowl.
2. Pour orange juice concentrate on top.

Serves 1

Per serving: 142 calories, 10 grams of protein, 26 grams of carbohydrate, trace of fat, 120 milligrams of sodium

CINNAMON WINK

1 cup nonfat yogurt
1 banana, sliced
Dash of cinnamon

1. Drop slices of banana on top of yogurt.
2. Sprinkle with cinnamon.

Serves 1

Per serving: 195 calories, 10 grams of protein, 41 grams of carbohydrate, trace of fat, 119 milligrams of sodium

STRAWBERRY-KIWI SALAD

1 orange, peeled and sliced
1 cup sliced strawberries
1 kiwi, peeled and sliced
½ ripe banana, peeled and sliced
2 teaspoons blueberries
4 ounces pineapple juice

Mix gently and serve.

Serves 2

Per serving: 125 calories, 2 grams of protein, 30 grams of carbohydrate, 1 gram of fat, 4 milligrams of sodium

17

PROTEIN SUPPLEMENT DRINKS

Now more than ever, protein powders—and the drinks mixed from them—have become a food group unto themselves. Crammed full of growth-promoting nutrients, they represent what bodybuilding is all about. They are incredibly quick to make, can be made in a staggering array of combinations, and best of all, they digest quickly to go where they're needed most: the muscles.

A quickly whipped up protein shake can also be quite valuable as a meal replacement when a bodybuilder is too busy to cook and consume a full meal. A protein drink can even be taken to work or school in a thermos bottle, shaken a bit, and quaffed as either a meal replacement or a supplement to a meal that might otherwise be nutritionally under par.

Typically speaking, a one-ounce serving of protein powder has 24 grams of muscle-building protein and only 0.8 grams of fat. Depending on the various bases mixed, you dial the amount of carbohydrate exactly to your bodybuilding needs at the moment.

Biologically speaking, the best quality of protein powder comes from egg whites, followed closely by calcium or sodium caseinate from milk. Whey from milk is a secondary source of supplementary protein, as are all vegetable-source protein powders (such as those made from soy isolates).

Try these 20 tasty treats, and see for yourself why protein powders are sold the world over, and making bodybuilders grow bigger for it!

ORANGE JULIUS

2 tablespoons lemon juice
2 egg whites
1 cup freshly squeezed orange juice
1 cup crushed ice
2 tablespoons protein powder

1. Pour everything into a blender.
2. Whip and enjoy!

Serves 1

Per serving: 200 calories, 33 grams of protein, 20 grams of carbohydrate, 1 gram of fat, 25 milligrams of sodium

CRANBERRY-PINEAPPLE COCKTAIL

1¼ cups cranberry juice
2 tablespoons lemon juice
½ cup pineapple chunks
1 cup crushed ice
2 tablespoons protein powder

1. Pour everything into a blender.
2. Whip and enjoy!

Serves 2

Per serving: 165 calories, 13 grams of protein, 30 grams of carbohydrate, 1 gram of fat, 23 milligrams of sodium

"EGG"STRA POTENT POTION

1 cup grape juice
2 tablespoons lime juice
2 egg whites
1 very ripe banana
1 cup crushed ice
2 tablespoons protein powder

1. Pour everything into a blender.
2. Whip and enjoy!

Serves 2

Per serving: 208 calories, 18 grams of protein, 36 grams of carbohydrate, 1 gram of fat, 96 milligrams of sodium

HONEYDEW HUDDLE

  1 cup orange juice
  1 tablespoon lemon juice
  1 cup honeydew pieces
  1 cup crushed ice
  2 tablespoons protein powder

1. Pour everything into a blender.
2. Whip and enjoy!

Serves 2

Per serving: 137 calories, 13 grams of protein, 22 grams of carbohydrate, 1 gram of fat, 24 milligrams of sodium

PEACH POWER

  1 cup peaches
  1 cup orange juice
  1 ripe banana
  1 cup crushed ice
  2 tablespoons protein powder

1. Pour everything into a blender.
2. Whip and enjoy!

Serves 2

Per serving: 177 calories, 14 grams of protein, 32 grams of carbohydrate, 1 gram of fat, 14 milligrams of sodium

PINEAPPLE PUNCH

  1 cup pineapple juice
  1 ripe banana
  6 frozen strawberries
  1 cup crushed ice
  2 tablespoons protein powder

1. Pour everything into a blender.
2. Whip and enjoy!

Serves 2

Per serving: 152 calories, 13 grams of protein, 27 grams of carbohydrate, 1 gram of fat, 14 milligrams of sodium

"Heavy basic exercises build up muscle mass, while a sensible low-calorie diet and plenty of aerobic activity get you sliced," instructs seven-time Mr. Olympia Lee Haney, shown here doing a warm-up set of barbell bent-over rows with 225 pounds.

BANANA SMOOTHIE

1 cup skim milk
1 ripe banana
1 cup crushed ice
2 tablespoons protein powder

1. Pour everything into a blender.
2. Whip and enjoy!

Serves 2

Per serving: 146 calories, 17 grams of protein, 20 grams of carbohydrate, 1 gram of fat, 76 milligrams of sodium

STRAWBERRY SMOOTHIE

1 cup skim milk
10 strawberries
1 ripe banana
1 cup crushed ice
2 tablespoons protein powder

1. Pour everything into a blender.
2. Whip and enjoy!

Serves 2

Per serving: 168 calories, 17 grams of protein, 26 grams of carbohydrate, 1 gram of fat, 77 milligrams of sodium

BLUEBERRY SMOOTHIE

1 cup pineapple juice
½ cup blueberries
1 ripe banana
1 cup crushed ice
2 tablespoons protein powder

1. Pour everything into a blender.
2. Whip and enjoy!

Serves 2

Per serving: 193 calories, 13 grams of protein, 37 grams of carbohydrate, 1 gram of fat, 16 milligrams of sodium

CRANBERRY SMOOTHIE

1 cup cranberry juice
1 cup skim milk
2 egg whites
½ teaspoon vanilla extract
1 cup crushed ice
2 tablespoons protein powder

1. Pour everything into a blender.
2. Whip and enjoy!

Serves 2

Per serving: 183 calories, 20 grams of protein, 26 grams of carbohydrate, 1 gram of fat, 130 milligrams of sodium

YOGURT-PEACH SMOOTHIE

1 cup frozen peach slices
1 cup nonfat yogurt
1 cup crushed ice
2 tablespoons protein powder

1. Pour everything into a blender.
2. Whip and enjoy!

Serves 1

Per serving: 227 calories, 34 grams of protein, 24 grams of carbohydrate, 1 gram of fat, 199 milligrams of sodium

YOGURT-PINEAPPLE SMOOTHIE

1 cup nonfat yogurt
1 cup crushed pineapple
1 tablespoon lemon juice
1 cup crushed ice
2 tablespoons protein powder
2 drops peppermint extract (optional)

1. Pour everything into a blender.
2. Whip and enjoy!

Serves 2

Per serving: 138 calories, 17 grams of protein, 17 grams of carbohydrate, 1 gram of fat, 101 milligrams of sodium

CHOCOLATE SMOOTHIE

1 cup nonfat yogurt
1 tablespoon carob powder
1 ripe banana
1 cup crushed ice
2 tablespoons protein powder

1. Pour everything into a blender.
2. Whip and enjoy!

Serves 2

Per serving: 160 calories, 17 grams of protein, 20 grams of carbohydrate, 1 gram of fat, 100 milligrams of sodium

APPLE CIDER SMOOTHIE

2 egg whites
1 cup apple cider
1 cup nonfat yogurt
Dash of mace
1 cup crushed ice
2 tablespoons protein powder

1. Pour everything into a blender.
2. Whip and enjoy!

Serves 2

Per serving: 169 calories, 20 grams of protein, 16 grams of carbohydrate, trace of fat, 153 milligrams of sodium

PARSLEY PICKUP

½ cup fresh parsley
1 cup pineapple juice
1 cup crushed ice
2 tablespoons protein powder

1. Pour everything into a blender.
2. Whip and enjoy!

Serves 1

Per serving: 188 calories, 26 grams of protein, 23 grams of carbohydrate, 2 grams of fat, 38 milligrams of sodium

BANANA DAIQUIRI

1 banana
1 cup grapefruit juice
1 cup crushed ice
2 tablespoons protein powder

1. Pour everything into a blender.
2. Whip and enjoy!

Serves 2

Per serving: 150 calories, 13 grams of protein, 26 grams of carbohydrate, 1 gram of fat, 14 milligrams of sodium

APPLE-CARROT SHAKE

1 cup apple juice
¼ cup carrot juice, freshly made
1 cup crushed ice
2 tablespoons protein powder

1. Pour everything into a blender.
2. Whip and enjoy!

Serves 1

Per serving: 205 calories, 25 grams of protein, 29 grams of carbohydrate, 1 gram of fat, 52 milligrams of sodium

PAPAYA-MANGO SHAKE

1 cup papaya juice
1 cup mango chunks
1 cup crushed ice
2 tablespoons protein powder

1. Pour everything into a blender.
2. Whip and enjoy!

Serves 2

Per serving: 188 calories, 13 grams of protein, 37 grams of carbohydrate, 1 gram of fat, 43 milligrams of sodium

GRAPE SHAKE

1 cup seedless grapes
1 cup apple juice
1 cup crushed ice
2 tablespoons protein powder

1. Pour everything into a blender.
2. Whip and enjoy!

Serves 2

Per serving: 148 calories, 13 grams of protein, 26 grams of carbohydrate, 1 gram of fat, 15 milligrams of sodium

Tom Terwilliger won the NPC Light-Heavyweight National Championships in 1987, opened a couple of gyms on Long Island, New York, and became a television commentator for bodybuilding events on cable TV.

PART III
PRECONTEST DIETS

Posing for the judges in contest condition.

18
SIX MONTHS TO COUNTDOWN

Whoever said, "Work smarter, not harder," was obviously not a bodybuilder. In some overly simplified way, this idea implies that by working harder you'll only get so far in your efforts, but if you work smarter instead, you will achieve much more in the end. While this idea may apply to a paper delivery routine, there's no easy way out when your goal is to achieve a minimum amount of body fat while retaining a maximum amount of muscle mass. The truth is, you must work smarter *and* harder!

There are no corner-cutting techniques in bodybuilding. You have a right way of getting ready for a show and a misinformed way. The work you do in the gym is always hard, and you must constantly push yourself even *harder* every successive workout. We'd love to see the creator of that initial quote train thighs with very high reps while taking in very low calories. He or she would *never* have come up with that ridiculous statement as a result.

Continuing in our tradition of truth, let's be brutally honest about bodybuilding genetics. The fact is, it's *very difficult* to defeat great genetics. Genetic superiors grow quicker, recuperate faster, and get more muscle response during an exercise than their less gifted gym mates. It can seem unfair if you plan to compete against one of these Goliaths. But we have seen *many* contests where David has handily defeated Goliath.

The downside for genetic superiors is that they tend to coast. Sure, they train hard and eat right, but they have never needed to go all

Never one to neglect details, John Hnatyschak parlayed one of history's most sliced midsections to National and Middleweight Championships, followed by a solid pro career. A severe lower-back injury suffered while serving as a police officer had frequently hampered him over the years.

out as bodybuilders. Ever so slightly, they have a pesky habit of holding back on the reins. That's where you come in. We are going to show you how to let go of the reins and do everything possible in order to win.

As mentioned in Chapter 1, it's much easier to withstand the intensity of bodybuiding when you aim to win. Forget about settling for "I'd like to make a good showing" or "I'll be happy to finish in the top five." That negative self-talk just paves the way for accomplishing exactly what you're saying. Plan on winning.

The best way to do this is to start early in your contest preparations. While Goliath is hammering away for sheer size, you are going to sculpt your physique with surgical preciseness. In effect, you will do so many more things correctly that Goliath will end up trashed. That's what this chapter is about: preparing for a contest and trashing the giants you may come up against. Your quality will beat their quantity any time!

PHASE ONE: SIX- TO THREE-MONTH COUNTDOWN

Before we delve into contest preparation, a prevailing myth should be cleared up. It has to do with body weight and the pro bodybuilders. Over the years, many bodybuilding articles have stated that pros stay typically 10 pounds over their contest weight. With very few exceptions, this is utter nonsense. The real figure is closer to 20 pounds, plus or minus 5. If they were truly 10 pounds over their contest weight, they'd look extremely good and no doubt would lose their minds trying to hold to that degree of condition.

Someone who is Shredded or Sliced is in a very suppressed physical state and can easily gain 10 pounds within 48 hours after a show. Frequently, the photos of the pros that appear in the magazines are *with* a 7- to 10-pound increase after their competitions. And they *still* look very good. But that's *not* what they look like during the off-season.

To confirm this contention, simply recall what some of the pro guest posers looked like at your local shows. We're sure you'll agree that many of them were handsomely over the 10-pound mark.

Therefore, you need not even consider bringing your weight to within 10 pounds of a competitive level when your show is still three to six months away. You focus on size at this point. Of course, there should still be some tightness to your physique. We recommend you hover between Hard and Cut during this period of time.

Unless you plan on joining the World Wrestling Federation, the Full House look is not really desirable. This was a popular look during the sixties and seventies, but the nineties are ushering in new levels of peak condition requirements, so keep relatively tight. (See Chapter 2 for specific details.)

During this phase, the main thrust is shape training. Use isolation exercises to start deliberately enhancing the contour of each muscle, while still keeping the basic power movements in your program. Shape training will improve the symmetry of your physique even though you continue to train heavily. Your goal is to give those muscle bellies a more rounded appearance.

To help you in visualizing the type of physical improvement you should be after during this phase, the following list ranks muscles in terms of their cosmetic importance:

- *The "Looker" Muscles*—These are the lateral head of the deltoid, the sweep of the latissimus dorsi muscles, the outside head of the triceps and thigh, the inside of the calf and the degree of narrowness of the waist region. These are the silhouette muscles. When a bodybuilder first steps out on stage, you look at these muscles, especially the side delts and the waistline and calves. They set up the coveted X-look to the body. When the waist is tiny, the shoulders broad, and the calves full, the look is spectacular. If you feel you are deficient in one of these muscles, this is the time to specialize on it, not later on, when lower calorie intake makes muscle acquisition less likely.
- *The "Power" Muscles*—Muscles in this category give the phy-

sique a forceful and athletic look. They are the spinal erectors, front deltoids, rear deltoids, outside and lower biceps, rectus femoris of the thigh, upper pectorals, serratus anterior, intercostals, abdominals, and forearms. They can make your body memorable.

For instance, everyone knows about Gary Strydom's front delts or Samir Bannout's lower biceps, Berry de Mey's middle thigh, Casey Viator's forearms, Franco Columbu's upper pecs. If you would like to give your frame a powerful look, work on these muscle areas. They can make your physique appear strong and visually explosive.

- *The "Balance" Muscles*—They are the traps, glutes, obliques, lower pecs, inner thigh, and biceps peak. When correctly developed, they add a harmony to your structure.

  For example, if the traps are too heavy, they cause the delts to appear narrow, and shoulder width suffers. Thick inner thighs can make the quadriceps above the knee appear thin and poorly developed. Very muscled lower pecs cause the chest to appear droopy. Wide obliques cut into that highly desired X-frame look. A flat biceps takes away from arm size, while an awesomely peaked one makes the triceps appear deficient.

  As you can see, these areas can be easily neglected. If you suspect a weakness in one or more of them, now is the time to seek better balance.

- *The "Busy" Muscles*—This category is composed of the (get out your anatomy book!) brachialis, soleus, tensor fasciae latae, sartorius, tibialis anterior, rhomboids, teres major, infraspinatus, biceps femoris, coracobrachialis, and gracilis. Although everyone's insertions are unique, these muscles are smaller than the others but still add a lot of fine detail to the physique.

  Low body fat really brings out these "busy" muscles big time, and they make you appear much more massive than you actually are. Little 5'2" Mohammed Benaziza (who has won the prestigious Night of the Champions pro competition) is an excellent example of this effect. To really bring out the extra details, experiment with new exercises, and try new tangents of motion, as well as different hand spacings.

Keep these training points in mind during Phase One. If you are not sure about your silhouette, take off your clothes, and cast your shadow on a wall. Stand close to the wall; otherwise you'll end up looking like the Incredible Hulk. Make sure the light is coming from behind you. Then simply take a good look at the symmetry of your outline. What do you need? Be honest with yourself.

Next, stand sideways, and observe your silhouette from that per-

Overall symmetry gives me well-defined "Looker Muscles."

spective. Does your hamstring sweep out below your glutes? Or does it draw a straight line to the back of your knee? Are your glutes well rounded or flat? Does your pectoral region appear full and evenly developed from top to bottom? Is your waist tiny, normal, or humongous? That outline on the wall will never lie, while you might lie to yourself, so be honest.

Phase One Diet

Eating during Phase One is simple and straightforward. Start off by determining how many calories you consume each day. Do this for an entire week. Eat as you normally would, but record each food you eat and the amount consumed. At the end of the week, calculate the average number of calories you consumed in one day.

During this process, weigh yourself every morning, and record your body weight. Assuming your weight is constant, that average caloric intake you calculated is your starting point. In other words, *that* amount of calories keeps you at *that* body weight.

During the sixth and fifth months away from your contest, you are going to add solid body weight to your physique, *provided* your appearance remains relatively the same. You shouldn't put on weight if it means sacrificing your look, however. Instead, strive for a slow, carefully monitored acquisition of additional muscle mass. To accomplish this, you will manipulate your calories.

Start by taking in an additional 500 calories per day for a few days. This will give you an extra 3,500 calories per week on top of your maintenance level of calories. If you gain weight too rapidly, cut down your daily intake by 200 calories until you establish a satisfactory rate of increase. An ideal amount of weight increase would be approximately one pound of weight for every week that goes by, for the next eight weeks.

Although opinions vary greatly on the subject of protein intake, one thing remains clear: you need protein to build muscle. During this portion of Phase One, you can best achieve optimal growth by consuming enough protein. The following equation helps to determine how much you need:

Your Body Weight × 1.2–1.5 = Daily Protein Needs

Therefore, for a 200-pound bodybuilder, the need would be calculated this way:

200 × 1.2–1.5 = 240–300 grams of protein per day

At first, this amount may sound high, but keep this in mind: in every case where spectacular muscle increase was noted in recent

"A balanced physique wins pro shows," says Rich Gaspari, who's won several of them himself. "You should have no weak or strong body parts that stand out from the rest of your physique. Work weak areas like calves at the start of your training session, when your energy reserves are at maximum levels."

France's Francis Benfatto is typical of a new breed of sliced bodybuilder who features less total muscle mass but elegantly balanced physical proportions and shredded muscle. Benfatto placed in the top six in his first try at Mr. Olympia in Chicago in 1990.

years—Richie Gaspari after winning the Universe, Tom Platz before his third-place finish in Mr. Olympia, and Mike Christian after taking his state title—large amounts of protein were noted in their diets. Of course, many other factors contributed as well, but protein figured in these and other cases of significant muscle growth.

Phase One Aerobics

Most bodybuilders associate aerobics with contest training only. This is a mistake. Aerobics are equally important in the off-season. Doing aerobics during Phase One provides several benefits:

- Aerobics improve your recovery time between sets. This allows you to get more out of your leg and back sessions, as well as out of any supersets you might perform.
- Aerobics increase the number and size of your blood vessels. This means that more nutrients and a greater supply of oxygen will reach the muscle tissues.
- Aerobics speed up your metabolism. This benefit is an important one. You can consume more calories and still keep your body weight at a fixed point. This means more growth-promoting calories and a greater chance for muscle growth. It also means that you will burn off greater amounts of body fat.
- Aerobics increase the total volume of blood in your body. More

toxins are removed, and your recovery time increases. Plus, with more blood in your system, you get a much better muscle pump.
- Aerobics prevent muscle wasting. All too often, when it comes time to restrict their calories, bodybuilders reduce them until they get leaner. The drawback from this is that eventually too few are consumed to support the actual muscle itself, so atrophy occurs. Bodybuilders who do this end up looking stringy. Aerobics allow you to keep your caloric intake much higher than if you didn't do them.

The amount of aerobics you should do is 30 to 45 minutes before breakfast every morning. At first, you'll be ashamed of how out of shape you are. That's fine. Within a few days, your aerobic capacity will increase by leaps and bounds. Stick a Walkman on your head, and the time will pass surprisingly quickly. After a couple of weeks, you'll be able to coast at the point where you were originally huffing like wild.

Four months out from the contest, a few things change. Do not add any more body weight. Instead, hold it constant. This will firm up your physique. Next, with that newly found aerobic capacity, start speeding up the tempo of your weight workout. Perform the reps at the same pace, but rest less between sets.

Start cutting down on your simple sugars. Take in more complex carbohydrates instead. Continue working on your weaker body part area, or if you have brought it up to par, select another one to specialize on. Four months out from the show, you should appear big, full, and shapely. You are now ready for the next phase.

PHASE TWO: THREE- TO ONE-MONTH COUNTDOWN

During Phase Two, the most important rule is that the *more slowly* you lose body fat, the *more* muscle you will retain on your physique. We have seen many bodybuilders drop more than seven pounds during a one-week period, and continue to do this for several weeks. This is not dieting. It's a desperation method. It means the bodybuilder waited far too long to get serious.

Starting too late in contest preparation is *the* number one reason why bodybuilders fail to achieve their peak. So during Phase Two, you should lose 1.0 to 1.7 pounds per week. Since you are 12 weeks away from the show, that gives you 12 to 20 pounds to take off. Women bodybuilders and middleweight, lightweight, and bantamweight men would aim toward the lower end of this range. Male light-heavies and heavyweights would be near the upper end of the scale.

Remember, these are general guidelines. There are all kinds of exceptions to the rule when dealing with the huge range of bodybuilding genetics.

During Phase Two, you increase the duration and frequency of aerobic workouts. The recommended amount is one hour before breakfast *and* one hour before bedtime. If weight starts coming off too rapidly, you should eat more. That's right! Under no circumstances should you decrease your aerobics. Taking in more food will prevent the onset of muscle tissue catabolism.

Of course, you don't increase your aerobics immediately up to the suggested level of one hour twice per day. Rather, this should be a gradual process that may take a week or so of getting adjusted. If you increase suddenly, you'll experience a sudden and substantial weight loss. At the time you increase the aerobics, you have to monitor your calories accordingly, so you still strive for that 1.0- to 1.7-pound weight loss.

Typically, many bodybuilders decrease their daily food intake by 200 to 500 calories to achieve the desired weight loss *after* an initial adjustment to the increased aerobics. At this point, you can see changes occur on your body every two or three days. They are subtle ones, but you can notice them.

You'll also notice power decline in certain movements, especially basic exercises, but the drop is not significant. With less fat and water in the joints, the leverage advantage is decreased, so a poundage diminution can be expected under the circumstances.

During the last portion of Phase One, you decreased the length of rest intervals between sets. At the initial portion of Phase Two, you chop down your rest times even more. We are only talking about a few seconds here and there, but the workout intensity increases dramatically as you decrease the *average* length of rest pause following each set.

During this preparatory phase, increase the variety of exercises in your routine. Start training your muscles from all kinds of unusual angles. Use more machines, cables, and dumbbells, and utilize a wide variety of hand spacings on each apparatus in order to produce refinement and quality in your skeletal muscles.

You should still keep power movements in your training schedule, because basic, compound exercises that involve several body parts at once will help you maintain overall muscle mass as you diet. But gravitate away from low-rep workouts, as they emphasize more ligament and tendon strength training and less lean muscle mass building.

Shift to higher-repetition schemes for each set, and perform more isotension within the movements. Squeeze your working muscles intensely at both the top and bottom of every rep whenever applicable. Forget how much weight is on the bar, but *do* make that weight work for you. Concentrate on the feel of the resistance along the full range of motion of every repetition you perform in a workout.

Slowly start to take in a few more fibrous carbs, and correspond-

One of pro bodybuilding's most titled athletes, 42-year-old Robby Robinson is still tough enough to defeat in any competition. He won the first two Night of the Champions competitions and a host of other IFBB Grand Prix events.

Seated presses on a Smith machine have done wonders for Mike Christian's deltoids, which can easily be seen in this photograph. Mike won the overall Nationals and the Heavyweight World Championships prior to turning pro.

ingly eat smaller portions of starchy carbohydrates. Begin taking MCT oils with every meal, too. A medium-chain triglyceride will increase your energy, speed up your metabolism, and lower your body fat. One tablespoon provides more than 100 calories, depending on the brand used. (We recommend CapTri. See page 198.)

Start off by taking one-half tablespoon with each meal for three days. Mix MCTs directly into your food, perhaps using it as part of a salad dressing. Never take MCT on an empty stomach. Gradually increase MCT to one tablespoon per meal for another three days. After that point, stabilize the dosage or increase it, depending on how much more you remove starchy carbs from your diet.

By systematically decreasing your starchy carb intake, you force your body to burn more fat while the MCTs protect hard-earned muscle and maintain consistent energy levels. The key word here is *gradual.* Don't rush it. You are balancing your calorie decrease with an MCT increase. Generally speaking, one tablespoon per meal—up to five or six times per day—is very effective.

Eliminate milk, cottage cheese, yogurt, hard cheeses, all forms of white flour, fruit drinks, fast food, and literally anything else made with sucrose. Eat foods that are close to their natural state. Stay away from highly processed foods of any description.

When you lower your calories, you also lower your intake of vital nutrients. Therefore, take the following supplements to insure against any potential deficiencies that might hold back your progress:

- Vitamin C—5 to 7 grams per day
- Desiccated liver—at least ten 20-grain tabs per day
- Vitamin E—300 to 600 international units per day
- B-complex—a capsule containing at least 200 milligrams of all of the B vitamins
- Digestive enzymes—1 to 3 per meal
- High-potency multiple-vitamin-mineral tablets—at least 2 or 3 per day
- Free-form amino acids—at least 20 throughout the day and 45 minutes before your workout

You should also start tanning at this point. It takes 2½ months to acquire a deep, even tan, providing you have normal skin pigmentation levels. Always use a good sun-screen lotion during exposure, and a moisturizer afterward.

With all of this extra stress, you may notice some overtraining setting in. The symptoms are tenderness in the joints, irritability over small matters, general sluggishness throughout the day, and slow recuperation rates. If this sounds like you, increase your intake of vitamins C and B-complex for a few days, and take a day or two off training. Those energy levels will kick right back in!

PHASE THREE: ONE MONTH TO CONTEST

Everything you did in Phase Two you do more of in Phase Three. To continue losing 1.0 to 1.7 pounds of fat per week, keep decreasing your intake of starchy carbohydrate foods. Bring more fibrous carbs into your diet, and drop down one meal. If you have been eating six meals, for example, switch to eating five per day. Increase your MCT dosage accordingly. Bring your dietary fat levels down very low. If you can afford the expense, increase your consumption of free-form and branched-chain amino acids to 30 per day.

By four weeks out from the show, you should be looking very good. Start practicing your compulsory poses after your workouts. They form the backbone of any successful free-posing routine.

It's also a good time to begin ironing out your free-posing program. Be objective about the poses you select. Make sure they deemphasize your weak areas and highlight your strong points. If it's your first show, it is quite likely you've created a few goomba poses. So make sure you get feedback from an experienced eye when you've finished your routine. You'd be surprised at how many pros could and should pose better, so take all constructive input, and put it to use the next time you're working up a routine.

To avoid sheer boredom, keep changing your mode of aerobic activity. Jogging on soft grass or the beach, fast walking, stationary cycling, outdoor cycling, rowing machines, stair climbing, and avoiding getting eaten by a bear are all excellent choices. Some bodybuilders suggest aerobics classes, but we feel the relentless pounding of the kangaroo-like motions are not conducive to maintaining the extra muscle mass of a bodybuilder.

Don't be overly concerned about your pulse rate when in the midst of an aerobic training session. If you are breathing heavily but could carry on a conversation, yet don't want to, that's about the right pace. Who really wants to yap when they're hungry and sweaty anyway?

At this point, drop all of the basic movements from your weight routine. Replace bench presses with decline dumbbell presses, dumbbell flyes on a slight decline, or dumbbell bench presses with palms facing each other, or try using the Watson bench press bar to increase your range of motion on the exercise. Presses behind the neck or military presses can be changed to Arnold dumbbell presses, overhead dumbbell laterals, lying-side laterals, one-arm cable side laterals, and incline bench lateral raises. Bent-over rows and T-bar rows can be dropped in favor of seated cable rows, close-grip pulldowns, one-arm dumbbell bent rows, or hanging dumbbell rows (achieved through the use of gravity boots and a chinning bar).

Barbell curls can be changed to incline dumbbell curls, concentration curls, low-cable curls (with one or two hands at a time), or hammer curls. Replacing close-grip bench presses or barbell lying triceps extensions could be incline triceps pushdowns, regular pulley pushdowns, incline triceps extensions, dumbbell kickbacks, or close-grip pushups.

Squats can make way for close- or wide-stance Smith machine squats, hack squats, lunges, sissy squats, or leg presses at a variety of angles.

Switching over to another exercise will *not* cause you to lose size. What it does is cause a change in muscle shape and detail, an effect that will benefit you greatly onstage.

Here are some other important points to ponder:

- Drop all aerobics the Tuesday before your show. This helps to enhance the carb-loading effect.
- Your Monday, Tuesday, and Wednesday workouts before the contest should be relatively light, but very quick.
- From Thursday onward, practice your posing. This will help to tighten your skin and bring out greater muscle separation.
- Train your thighs only up to the Monday before the show. Any closer, and you may obscure leg definition.
- Select a posing suit to complement your physique. Those with short legs and a long body will look better with a suit bottom

that sits higher up on the thighs. If you have big glutes, choose a posing suit in a dark color. Women should try to look for a pronounced frontal V-shape for the lower portion of the suit. This adds length to the leg and femininity to the form. Juliette Bergmann (IFBB Pro World Champion) was one of the pioneers of this look.

- Remove excess body hair 10 days before the show. Give periodic touch-ups every few days. This will avoid the inconvenience of any skin irritation that may occur if you do it all at once.
- Stay away from puffy hairdos, as they detract from shoulder-width. This applies more to men than it does to women.
- Begin to apply a coloring agent the Wednesday before the show. Wash off any excess coloration. Two coats per day for four days on a good base tan will be sufficient for even the brightest stage lights.
- Start drinking distilled water from Monday on before your Saturday show. Use it for cooking and brushing your teeth as well. Limit fluid intake starting Thursday. A general guide is four ounces for every meal. Drink about six ounces before you begin to pump up to go onstage.
- Follow a carbohydrate depletion and loading scheme, such as that outlined in Table 18-1.

TABLE 18-1 CARBOHYDRATE DEPLETION CHART

(Grams of Complex Carbohydrates Consumed)

	Slow Metabolism	Fast Metabolism
Sunday	30–70	80–150
Monday	30–70	80–150
Tuesday	30–70	80–150
Wednesday	30–70	140–160 (women) 225 (men)
Thursday	100–300	160–280 (women) 400 (men)
Friday	150–500	220–380 (women) 500 (men)

- On the Friday before the show, cut out MCT and add an equal number of calories in carbohydrates.
- The night before the show, you should look amazing. If you are flat, stay up and continue to carb load. If you are very full, practice your posing, and back off on the carbohydrates.
- If you are holding lots of water, yet feel very hard to the touch, you've spilled over and could look water-filmed the next day. Don't panic, just jump into a sauna for five minutes, or lie out in the sun and pose.
- Back off on your protein intake for Thursday and Friday, since protein won't matter when it comes to the appearance of your physique onstage.

- Take snapshots of yourself to have as a reference point. We've encountered many bodybuilders who would love to show us what they looked like at their show, but who never took any photos. This is kind of a major oversight.

  Art Zeller, famed photographer of the world's greatest body-building stars, tells us Arnold Schwarzenegger still bugs him for slides and wishes he had taken more pictures of himself when in peak condition. Yet back then, he found all of that picture taking a chore. So think ahead. When you are in the best shape of your life, immortalize yourself on film.

That's the countdown from six months down to the day of competition. Key points are:

- Stay tight off-season.
- Do aerobics during that time and shape train.
- Monitor your caloric intake carefully.
- Lose weight slowly.
- Bring greater variety of movement into your workouts.
- Use MCT oils when you need to reduce your caloric intake but don't want to starve your muscles or kill your energy levels.

Then go ahead and get your slingshot ready. You're going after Goliath!

19

NEGRITA JAYDE'S CYCLE CARBING DIET

Dr. Frank Columbu, two-time Mr. Olympia and former training partner of Arnold Schwarzenegger, once said, "If it works, it works, no matter what anybody says." This is true about any winning bodybuilding formula, regardless of where it applies.

When it comes down to contest dieting—for my own particular needs, as well as yours—I've developed a winning formula, which I'll reveal for the first time in this chapter. Using the exact diet outlined in this chapter, I won the Heavyweight and Overall titles at the Canadian Nationals, and my body fat measured in at a minuscule 5 percent, an incredibly low level for a 135-pound female heavyweight competitor.

Extensive tests further revealed that I lost virtually no muscle tissue during my dieting procedure. Starting it at an off-season body weight of 150 pounds (I'm 5'5" tall), I lost 14 pounds of fat and only 1 pound of muscle in reaching 135. And at that body weight, you could have hidden dimes in the cuts in my quadriceps muscles!

Other bodybuilders who have followed the same diet got into the best shape of their lives, too. There were two things they all said about it after competing: they came into a show much bigger and more cut than ever, and they could time their condition with the reliability of a Rolex watch. Mind you, it's not what you'd call the typical precontest diet, but it's effective. In this case, effectiveness is measured by winning.

CYCLE CARBING DIET

My method is called the Cycle Carbing Diet (CCD). It grew out of considerable trial and error while following many of the more standard precontest dietary methods. For example, gradually reducing calories definitely brought in the cuts, but at the same time my muscle roundness checked out.

Drinking water throughout the carbing up process only made me *hold* water and look hilarious, like some puffy wombat from Australia. By following the precise guidelines for sodium depleting and loading, I flushed out *all* that subcutaneous water—four days *after* the show. And while the glycemic index tables imply that rice isn't the best carb loader, I look my best on rice.

Of course, all of these contest prep theories are based on sound scientific evidence and research. Many bodybuilders have used them with excellent results. However, there is a point where standard practice must give way to genetic variation. I had to find a system that worked for me, *consistently*. The low-fat/low-calorie diet, as described in Chapter 18, is effective, but *I* didn't find it a raving success.

Enter the CCD. Taking a closer look at the rather outdated low-carbohydrate dieting technique, I carefully analyzed its weak points. I came up with the following list:

- The low-carb diet creates very low energy levels, making an ordinary training session seem unbearable.
- Weight comes off very slowly on a low-carb regimen. That's because fats have more than twice the amount of calories per gram compared to proteins and carbohydrates.
- Many dieters on a low-carb regimen experienced the "phosphorus jitters." This occurs when the calcium-phosphorus balance is out of whack, because too much phosphorus is consumed in relation to calcium—a common result of consuming a lot of meat (high in phosphorus) and very few dairy products (high in calcium) on a low-carb diet.
- Low-carb diets create phenomenal cravings for carbohydrate-rich foods, leading to the potential of a binge session somewhere along the line.
- Low-carb diets can place the body in a state of ketosis, which results in lost muscle tissue.

With all of these factors against the low-carb diet, it would seem there's not much going for it. But sometimes the obvious answer is easily overlooked. Reasoning further, I wondered what would happen if the carbs were *gently* phased in *and* out during the entire dieting procedure, not just a week before the show.

Using such a procedure would pick up your energy levels, make

The effectiveness of my diet is shown here in the good clarity of my midsection.

the diet more nutritious, remove the cravings for carbs, prevent loss of muscle tissue, *and* give you that full muscle look while dieting. That's something that no other diet gives you. Gradually, through many hours of research and development, the CCD was born.

As soon as I began following the CCD, I noticed an immediate body weight increase for the next competition I entered. I appeared fuller and harder, and the lower half of my physique matched the definition in my upper body for the first time.

To this day, many women bodybuilders diet down into two different conditions—a ripped upper body and smooth legs. The CCD alleviates this tendency in women.

The CCD also makes fat loss very predictable. You can dial in the degree of muscularity desired, because the diet proceeds in a step-by-step, highly controllable fashion. There is no guesswork with the CCD. You will always know what's happening and why it is happening.

That doesn't mean it makes things effortless, however, because it still *is* a diet and will require strong motivation, self-discipline, and consistency. But the CCD won't make you feel beaten to a pulp the way other diets do.

To demonstrate exactly how the CCD works, I'll take you through an entire cycle and explain it in detail. Careful attention will be paid to the various physical states you will encounter. When you know what to expect, you'll also be able to handle it more easily.

CYCLE DAY ONE

The total amount of carbohydrates you consume for Day One is 70 grams. Also, once you've established your maintenance level of calories before this diet, you use that as a reference point and consume half that amount on Day One (but never go below 1200 calories, regardless.) Your carbohydrate intake should consist mostly of fibrous carbs, since selecting only starchy carbs would add up to 70 grams very quickly, and you'd feel ripped off foodwise.

For your workout, avoid going heavy during the first trip through this cycle. Instead, choose medium- to high-rep schemes for your exercises, and try to include supersets and reduced rest intervals to force yourself into using carbohydrates for energy fuel.

If you can, work out in the morning, because you will have more energy then than later in the day. When you eat this way, believe me, you'll notice how much of a difference training early in the day will make on your energy supplies.

Include a very lean cut of beef at some point in your meal plan during Day One. Beef is high in phenylalanine, an amino acid that helps to suppress your appetite. Drink only water, and cook with MCT oil when required. A sample meal plan that fits these criteria appears in Table 19-1.

TABLE 19–1 SAMPLE LOW-CARB, LOW-CAL DIET PLAN

Breakfast	3–7 egg whites	Lunch	150 grams of chicken breast
	25 grams of oatmeal		200 grams of green beans
	100 grams of tomato		1 tablespoon of MCT oil
	100 grams of beef		Bottled water
	1 tablespoon of MCT oil	Midafternoon	100-gram potato
	Bottled water		Bottled water
Midmorning	100 grams of broccoli	Dinner	150 grams of lean beef
	150 grams of cod		200 grams of green beans
	1 tablespoon of MCT oil		1 tablespoon of MCT oil
	Bottled water		Bottled water

The meal plan in Table 19-1 provides 71 grams of carbohydrates, 1,570 calories (based on half of the maintenance figure of 3,000 per day), and 125 grams of protein. Before bed, take 20 grams of arginine powder to increase your natural output of growth hormone and mobilize fat stores. Also take five high-grade amino acid capsules with each meal.

CYCLE DAY TWO

Begin this day by testing yourself on a Ketostix reagent strip. (You can purchase these over the counter at your local pharmacy.) They measure how close you are to a state of ketosis. Remember, if you are short of this state, you *cannot* lose muscle mass.

After testing, you should be in the range marked "trace." If you are not, you ate too many carbohydrates, didn't train hard enough, ate carbs too close to bedtime, or didn't take the amino acid arginine. That's fine, because you simply make the necessary adjustments for Day Two.

If you are past the "trace" range and into the "small" zone, add 10 to 20 grams of carbohydrates to your diet for Day Two. This is a rare occurrence, but it can happen if a bodybuilder works at an extremely laborious physical job during the day.

Keep in mind this important point: you are not going to feel great when you get up in the morning. Reducing your carbohydrate levels can turn the most chipper person into a professional whiner. That's OK, because it's only a temporary condition.

If you are in the "trace" range, eat the same amount of carbs and calories for Day Two. Shuffle the various foods around for the sake of variety, but again include beef during one of the meals.

Once again, your workout should consist of higher reps for all of your movements. Continue to blast through your sets with a minimum amount of rest between them. If you have sufficient top-end energy left to do forced reps, go ahead, but without carbs, you won't be setting any personal records.

At the end of the evening, test yourself again on a Ketostix strip. By this point, you should be somewhere between "trace" and "small," or right into the "small" range. If you are still in the "trace" range, you'll need to drop your calories way down for Day Three. Again, take 20 grams of arginine before bed, and five capsules of free-form and branched-chain aminos with each meal during the day.

CYCLE DAY THREE

The third day is referred to as "the wall." The easiest tasks can seem insurmountable during Day Three. This is your last carb depletion day of the cycle, and also your last workout day. Tomorrow is your day off training.

To make Day Three a success, you must summon forth the inner parts of your self-discipline. Train hard even if the weights you are using strike you as ridiculously light. Without the added leverage that comes with glycogen-loaded cells, basic compound movements such as squats, bench presses, presses behind the neck, rows, and barbell curls all take a nosedive in power-packed performance. This is typical and shouldn't be feared. You want this to happen, because then you know that satisfactory carb depletion is right around the corner.

By the end of the day, you should be firmly into the "small" range on your Ketostix strip, or somewhere between "small" and "medium." Eating as you did during Day Two and training as outlined will basically assure you of that.

The great thing about CCD is that if you are short of the prescribed guidelines, you can make a note of your caloric and carbohydrate intake each day and adjust it for the next depletion cycle. Within two or three trial runs, you will have it down pat.

By simply removing as little as 10 grams of carbs during the next Day Three, you can shift from just "small" to between "small" and "medium" on your ketone test, which is the best range to be in during the end of Day Three. Continue with the five capsules of aminos during each meal throughout the day, and be certain to take the arginine at night before retiring.

CYCLE DAY FOUR

Test yourself with the Ketostix as soon as you get up. You should be in the "medium" range. This is an ideal biochemical environment for carbohydrate loading. Depending on your body weight, sex, metabolic rate, and how far away you are from your competition, a general rule that you can follow is to consume anywhere from 250 to 400 grams of carbs on Day Four. Hypermetabolic types can take in up to 500 grams, while hypometabolic individuals may need only 200 grams during Day Four.

Honest effort brings honest results, and Lee Labrada shows how it's done with a set of reverse-grip pulley pushdowns for the long head of the triceps.

The majority of your carbs should be starchy ones, but I find that pasta smooths me out and seems to create more water retention than any other complex carb. So I stick with rice, potatoes, oatmeal, yams, and peas. If you're not sure of your own requirements, try eating the same carb sources I do for a starting point. Then after a few runs through this carb-loading day, you'll know which carbohydrate foods give you the best results in your own case.

You can consume up to 500 calories above your maintenance level, but make sure your food is evenly spaced throughout the day. This is also *the* day that you can eat some of those goodies you've been eyeing—like nonfat yogurt or that scoop of low-cal sherbet. It's OK to eat them in moderation. They'll break the diet's monotony and will not harm your appearance in any way. Just don't go wild on them. It's still a diet.

Some bodybuilders prefer to pass altogether on this opportunity to consume junk food, feeling that it weakens their sense of self-discipline once they go back on the real diet. You should know yourself well enough when it gets to this point; act according to what you know is best for you.

A typical meal plan for Day Four is shown in Table 19-2. That meal plan provides about 3,200 calories, 330 grams of carbs, and 190 grams of protein. It is approximately 200 calories over the established maintenance figure.

TABLE 19-2 SAMPLE MEAL PLAN FOR DAY FOUR

Breakfast	6 egg whites 50 grams of oatmeal ½ cantaloupe 100 grams of beef 1 tablespoon of MCT oil Mineral water	Midafternoon	170 grams of strawberry yogurt 100-gram potato 150 grams of chicken breast 1 tablespoon of MCT oil Mineral water
Midmorning	1 banana 100-gram potato 1 cup of orange juice 1 tablespoon of MCT oil Mineral water	Dinner	100 grams of lean beef 50 grams of rice 200 grams of broccoli 1 tablespoon of MCT oil Mineral water
Lunch	50 grams of rice 150 grams of chicken breast 200 grams of green beans 1 tablespoon of MCT oil Mineral water	Late evening	50 grams of oatmeal 1 banana 150 grams of chicken breast 1 tablespoon of MCT oil Mineral water

If you're behind schedule and need to lose weight in a hurry, you should omit the late-evening meal altogether. As a general rule, however, eat no less than 400 to 700 calories beneath your caloric maintenance amount.

On Day Four, your body will absorb the extra nutrients like a sponge, and you will feel yourself fill up with glycogen. So don't

TABLE 19-3 OVERVIEW OF SIX-DAY DIETARY CYCLE

Category	Day One	Day Two	Day Three	Day Four	Day Five	Day Six
Carb intake	Low carbs	Low carbs	Low carbs	High carbs	High carbs	High carbs
Calories	50% total	50% total	50% total	100% + total	100% + total	100% + total
Training	High reps, supersets	Higher reps, training	Higher reps, training	Off	Usual-style training	Usual-style training
Ketones	"Trace" range	"Small" range	"Small–medium" range	"Medium" range	"Normal" range	"Normal" range
Arginine?	Yes	Yes	Yes	No	No	Yes
Beef?	Yes	Yes	Yes	No	No	No
Fibrous or starchy carbs?	Fibrous	Fibrous	Fibrous	Starchy	Starchy	Starchy
Junk food?	No	No	No	Tasty treat day	No	No
Aerobics	Yes	Yes	Yes	Optional	Optional	Optional

skimp on the loading of carbs by a single iota. Enjoy it! Since it's a rest day, relax and let those carbs ooze back into your depleted muscles.

It's not necessary to take the arginine before bed during Day Four.

CYCLE DAY FIVE

Day Five is a mirror image of Day Four, except that the opportunity for a dietary fling has passed. This is your day back from a training layoff, so you must brace yourself for what's in store. The true extent of your carb depletion reveals itself during Day Five. Even though you've consumed plenty of starchy carbs and your calories were above the maintenance levels, you will still feel quite feeble in the gym.

The reason? Carbohydrates need time to kick in. You might notice a good pump in a trained muscle, but the fullness is transitory. Those carbs won't actually kick in until the later part of Day Six.

Day Five is an excellent time to find out which carbohydrate foods seem to load you better than others. Signs of a fully carbo-loaded state are:

- It feels easy to pose the muscles.
- Veins start to appear more prominently near the skin's surface.
- Your muscles feel very hard to the touch.
- Slight action causes them to pump fully.
- All the muscle groups appear rounder and more fully contoured.

As with Day Four, you don't need to take the arginine before bed.

CYCLE DAY SIX

Somewhere during Day Six, those loading signs will become very apparent. Your strength returns as well, and your mood is completely back to normal. During this time, you'll feel as though you are not even on a diet. In fact, many bodybuilders find this day a motivational one. Their enthusiasm usually peaks, and they're eager to start dieting again. At the end of the day, you start back on the arginine. The following day, you repeat the dietary cycle.

Table 19-3 gives you the generalized overview of my dietary principles. The following pointers will help to highlight the more specific aspects of the Cycle Carbing Diet:

- Expect to lose five to seven pounds during the depletion phase. More than this means you were holding an above-average amount of water.
- Once you carb up and reach a fully loaded state, you get back *almost* all of those five to seven pounds, but you *look better*. In

One of the best teenage competitors ever, Shawn Ray has grown up to be one of the best, regardless of age. He's placed as high as third in the Mr. Olympia and has won IFBB Pro Grand Prix titles. His legs have come up dramatically in recent years, lifting him into the top three in the 1990 Mr. Olympia show in Chicago.

Mike Quinn, a former overall U.S. Champion, is the self-styled bad boy of bodybuilding. His upper-body development is among the best in the sport, but comparatively weak legs have kept him from winning any pro titles.

the process of cycling through the carbs, the typical figure you lose is about 1–1½ pounds of body fat per six-day cycle.

- The CCD will not allow you to hit a weight loss plateau. You can take your physique to the exact level you desire. The only stipulation is that you give yourself enough time to cycle your body weight down to the level you desire.
- Smaller bodybuilders will notice they load toward the top of Day Five. Larger ones will load near the top of Day Six.
- It is far better to cut back slightly on your loading days if you desire further weight loss than it is to reduce your carb intake to a lower level on the depletion days.
- Adding aerobics during the depletion phase will markedly accelerate the process of carb depletion.
- Aerobics may be added during the carb-loading point of the cycle, but only at night and not for longer than a total of 30 minutes. This will help to rid the body of excess fluids but will not tax the carb stores and negate the loading itself.
- As the contest approaches, it's generally recognized that a 300- to 500-calorie drop below caloric maintenance values during loading will delay the process of loading. Expect this if you want to lose more weight.
- You will look your best on the third day of loading (Day Six). Oddly enough, many bodybuilders report "cleaner" cuts—but without muscle fullness—before they start to carb load. This in part is due to a loosened skin texture, which can help to highlight the grooves and separation of certain muscles.
- After you pass through one cycle, you'll find your greatest strength is on the *first* day of depletion. This is due to maximal glycogen storage at that point.
- If you feel you are still not fully carbed up by the end of Day Six, try taking one more day to carb up. It is far better to do this than to begin a depletion phase when not fully loaded with carbs. Then during your next cycle, make the necessary changes to be carb-loaded by Day Six.
- The beauty of the CCD is that when you are depleting, your basal metabolic rate won't start to slow down significantly until the third day. When that happens, the addition of carbs during Day Four speeds it up markedly, making it possible to gain muscle weight while simultaneously burning fat. Also, the inertia of the enhanced metabolism *continues* into the first couple of days of depletion. So you burn fat at a slightly elevated level rather than simply reduce your calories systematically week after week.
- Tests were performed on several bodybuilders to see how their thyroids were functioning after contest dieting. The tests revealed that the CCD maintained the efficiency of the thyroids of bodybuilders who used that dietary approach. Conversely, after gradual and progressive caloric restriction, the thyroids of the

Phil Hill (left) and Robby Robinson duke it out at the posedown of a recent IFBB Pro Grand Prix event. Both men have been big winners on the pro circuit.

same bodybuilders needed time to reestablish their former normal levels of operation. In essence, the CCD method does not slow down your thyroid, because you're depleting calories and carbs for such a short period of time. It's the long duration of low-calorie dieting that can slow down the thyroid, thus necessitating plenty of time to get it back up to normal function.

- Drink extra fluids (particularly pure water) during the depletion phase of the CCD. This helps to flush out toxins and mobilizes fat stores.
- The use of L-carnitine during the low-carb period also will help in fat removal.
- Keep a record of which complex carbs loaded you best. These will form the principal loaders for your final carb-down and carb-up for competition.
- It will take three runs through the CCD before you master it. When that happens, you can predict to the *meal* when cosmetic enhancement starts to occur during the loading phase.
- Remember: The entire effectiveness of the CCD can be ruined the minute you take in *too many* carbs during the depletion phase. This delays the body's chemical eagerness to "accept" the carbs, and in turn delays when you can start loading. Never give in to the Monty Hall in your mind! Forget the deals; there are none. It's results that count onstage at a competition! Stick to the diet, and you'll be impressed with the way you look. So will the judges and your fellow competitors. The CCD can make you look wicked!

INDEX